# Christianity and Science

# Christianity and Science

John Weaver

scm press

Published in 2010 by SCM Press
Editorial office
13–17 Long Lane,
London, EC1A 9PN, UK

SCM Press is an imprint of Hymns Ancient and Modern Ltd
(a registered charity)
St Mary's Works, St Mary's Plain,
Norwich, NR3 3BH, UK
www.scm-canterburypress.co.uk

British Library Cataloguing in Publication data

A catalogue record for this book is available
from the British Library

978 0 334 04113 9

Typeset by Regent Typesetting, London
Printed and bound by
CPI Antony Rowe, Chippenham, Wiltshire

# Contents

For Elizabeth, Richard and Joanna

# Preface

Throughout this book I draw on my studies of both geology and theology. I began my studies at University College of Wales, Swansea, with a PhD in structural geology following my initial degree. After seven years as a lecturer and subsequently senior lecturer in geology at the now University of Derby I went to Oxford to read theology.

This text draws on my two previous books,[1] in which I began to explore the relationships between modern scientific discoveries and the doctrine of creation. I have also incorporated my more recent examinations of environmental issues,[2] and the current debate over evolution.[3] Material from *In the Beginning God* is used with the permission of the series editor, Paul Fiddes.

All biblical references quoted in the text are taken from the New International Version.

This book follows the pattern of lecture courses I have taught at Oxford and Cardiff Universities during 1997–2010 on Christianity and science in dialogue.

Beginning with explorations of how we understand science and interpret the Bible, the text moves on to discuss five key areas in which science and theology are engaged in a search for understanding: cosmology and the origin of the universe; the natural world and the evolution of life; the mind-brain and the nature of personhood; the genetic modification and manipulation of plant, animal and human life; and the environmental crisis that faces the whole world. The book concludes with a chapter that explores how our understanding of God and God's activity in the world has developed and been shaped by the dialogue we have been exploring. This includes a discussion of suffering and 'natural evil'.

I wish to express my thanks to Professor Paul Fiddes, Professor Keith Ward and Professor John Hedley Brooke for all the encouragement they have given to me over the years. It was Paul Fiddes who first encouraged me to apply my scientific background in an exploration of the interaction of science and faith in understanding the doctrine of creation. Keith Ward introduced me to the work of the John Templeton Foundation, from whom I received an award in 1998, and John Brooke further encouraged me in my thinking about the dialogue between science and Christianity through the Ian Ramsay Centre in Oxford. I also wish to express my thanks to my colleagues at the South Wales Baptist College, especially Simon Woodman, for their advice and support.

Finally I want to thank my wife Sheila for carefully reading every word of the text through its various editions, making helpful suggestions about expression and understanding, and being my patient support throughout the writing process.

## Notes

1 Some of the material in this book first appeared in my two previous texts on the subject: John Weaver, 1994, *In the Beginning God: Modern Science and the Christian Doctrine of Creation*, Macon: Smyth & Helwys, Oxford: Regent's Park College; and John Weaver, 1999, *Earthshaping Earthkeeping: A Doctrine of Creation*, London: SPCK/Lynx.

2 John Weaver and Margot Hodson (eds), 2007, *The Place of Environmental Theology: A Guide for Seminaries, Colleges and Universities*, Oxford: Whitley Publications, Prague: IBTS; and John Weaver, 'Co-Redeemers: A Theological Basis for Creation Care', in *Perspectives in Religious Studies*, vol. 36, No. 2, National Association of Baptist Professors of Religion, Georgia: Mercer Press, 2009.

3 John Weaver, 2009, 'The Challenge of Evolutionary Theory for the 21st Century Church', in *Faith & Thought*, No. 46, April, Lancaster: The Victoria Institute.

# Introduction

## Setting the scene

In his novel *Angels and Demons*,[1] Dan Brown has several philosophical passages where his characters explore the nature of God, science and belief. Near the beginning of the book, the hero Robert Langdon has a discussion with the daughter of murdered CERN project physicist Leonardo Vetra, Vittoria, who is also a CERN project physicist. Langdon asks Vittoria: 'As a scientist and the daughter of a Catholic priest, what do *you* think of religion?' Her answer indicates a belief in the universal nature of faiths, which all proclaim that life has meaning. The conversation continues with Langdon asking:

> 'Do you believe in God?'
>
> Vittoria was silent for a long time. 'Science tells me God must exist. My mind tells me I will never understand God. And my heart tells me I am not meant to.'
>
> *How's that for concise*, he thought. 'So you believe God is fact, but we will never understand Him.'
>
> '*Her*,' she said with a smile. 'Your Native Americans had it right.'
>
> Langdon chuckled. 'Mother Earth.'
>
> '*Gaea*. The planet is an organism. All of us are cells with different purposes. And yet we are intertwined. Serving each other. Serving the whole.'[2]

Near the end of the book, with the Vatican under threat of total destruction, the Camerlingo, the late Pope's chamberlain and financial secretary (the highest officer in the papal household), addresses the world through television discussing the so-called victory of science over faith. He expresses the view that science's victory has come at a price for every human being. Science is now the God that humankind worships. Science has sought to explain everything and has filled human beings with scepticism, reducing the wonders of nature to mathematical equations and accidental occurrences. As the speech draws to a climax, we hear more of Brown's philosophy through the Camerlingo's speech:[3]

Who is this God science? Who is the God who offers his people power but no moral framework to tell you how to use that power? What kind of God gives a child *fire* but does not warn the child of its dangers? The language of science comes with no signposts about good and bad. Science textbooks tell us how to create a nuclear reaction, and yet they contain no chapter asking if it is a good or a bad idea.

As the speech draws to its conclusion, the Camerlingo says:

Whether or not you believe in God . . . You must believe this. When we as a species abandon our trust in the power greater than us, we abandon our sense of accountability. Faith . . . *all* faiths . . . are admonitions that there is something we cannot understand, something to which we are account-able . . . With faith we are accountable to each other, to ourselves, and to a higher truth. Religion is flawed, but only because *man* is flawed. If the outside world could see this church as I do . . . looking beyond the ritual of these walls . . . they would see a modern miracle . . . a brotherhood [Roman Catholic cardinals and priests] of imperfect, simple souls want-ing only to be a voice of compassion in a world spinning out of control.

For an author castigated by the Roman Catholic Church over his later book *The Da Vinci Code*,[4] this is a remarkable defence of the Church. It also provides a summary of my own reasons for the need of a dialogue between science and Christianity.

How do we view the world in which we live? We open our laptop, switch it on, and the programs run, and the screen offers templates and shortcuts that enable us to produce all manner of documents. We log on to the inter-net and information about almost everything imaginable is immediately downloadable in micro seconds from all around the world.

A visit to the dentist or the doctor includes hi-tech equipment to diagnose and offer remedial treatment for most simple problems. At the garage our car's performance and exhaust emissions are analysed by computer; and at the supermarket our loyalty cards inform the company of our regular buy-ing habits so that they can send us adverts and money-off coupons for goods they know we want to buy. To say nothing of mobile phones and in-car GPS systems that tell us *and* others where we are at any given moment in time.

Science and technology have an impact on every aspect of our lives.

Karen Armstrong, writing in the *Guardian* on 12 July 2009,[5] takes a look at our modern world where belief is understood as assent to rational truth. She noted that ancient peoples understood the world through both *logos* (reason or science) and *mythos* (dealing with emotion and experience). In times of crisis or sickness, when people needed to make sense of life, they recited a symbolic story of the origin of the cosmos. Thus the Genesis myth, a gentle polemic against Babylonian religion, was balm to the bruised spirits of the Israelites who had been defeated and deported by the armies of Nebuchadnezzar during the sixth century BCE. Nobody was required to 'believe' it; like most peoples, the Israelites had a number of other mutually exclusive creation stories, and as late as the sixteenth century Jews thought nothing of making up a new creation myth that bore no relation to Genesis but spoke more directly to their tragic circumstances at that time.

Here is the key question: 'Is the Christian message of a benevolent creator, an intentional universe and a life that has meaning still defensible?' The seventeenth-century Roman Catholic Church saw reason in the shape of science opposing faith as represented by the Church. From its viewpoint the scientific discoveries of Copernicus, Galileo and Kepler undermined the philosophical system of Aristotle, on which Church doctrine was positioned. The nineteenth-century Protestant Church saw reason in the shape of science opposing faith as expressed in the Bible. At this time a growing scientific academy felt oppressed by a largely Protestant Church, and this led to the anti-clericalism of Victorian England.

We have seen the emergence of two opposing authorities in the last two hundred years: scientific truth and biblical truth. These in our postmodern world have led to conflict. We find an insular, self-centred view that the only truth is my truth. This position is held by some who study Scripture, but is also prevalent in Western culture at large. Michael Pfundner and Ernest Lucas encourage both scientists and theologians to read the philosophy of science, which raises questions about presumptions and methodology, while also revealing the danger of removing the theological framework on which all modern science is based.[6]

We find this confirmed in the words of Francis Collins, head of the Human Genome Project, one of the world's leading scientists, working at the cutting edge of the study of DNA, the code of life. He begins his book *The Language of God*, with an account of the announcement of the completion of the hereditary code of life on 26 June 2000. At the celebratory announcement US President Bill Clinton said: 'Today we are learning the language in which God created life. We are gaining ever more awe for the complexity, the beauty, and the wonder of God's most divine and sacred gift.' Francis Collins comments:

Was I, a rigorously trained scientist, taken aback at such a blatantly religious reference by the leader of the free world at a moment such as this? Was I tempted to scowl or look at the floor in embarrassment? No, not at all. In fact I had worked closely with the President's speechwriter in the frantic days just prior to this announcement, and had strongly endorsed the inclusion of this paragraph. When it came time for me to add a few words of my own, I echoed this sentiment: 'It's a happy day for the world. It is humbling for me, and awe-inspiring, to realize that we have caught the first glimpse of our own instruction book, previously known only to God.'[7]

## Where science and faith meet

Take a look at the news media any day and see the range of national and international issues, in which science and technology are having an impact on daily life, and the ethical and moral principles on which society is based. It is here that we see the value of a dialogue between Christianity and science. The following are examples of issues where science and faith meet.

### Environmental crisis and world poverty

Changing weather patterns resulted in decimated crops in several of the world's poorest countries in 2009, leaving millions in need of food aid and humanitarian workers warning about the dangerous effects of climate change.[8] For example, Oxfam reported that farmers in Nepal produced only half their usual crop, and the humanitarian news service IRIN reported that livestock were dying of malnutrition in Yemen. Meanwhile, heavy rains caused flooding and soil erosion in a number of African countries. These were the result of extended atypical weather events of drought, rain or untimely combinations of both, in places where subsistence farmers have long depended on predictability.

Nepal's farmers are suffering the effects of a changing climate. More than 3 million people, about 10 per cent of the population, needed food aid in 2009, and this figure is set to climb over the coming years. The lack of food production has had a severe impact on Nepali families, not only reducing the amount available to eat, but also diminishing their ability to buy surpluses at market, as costs increase and incomes decrease.

The massive glaciers of the Himalayan mountain range are also rapidly changing and could even be at risk of disappearing by mid-century if global emissions of carbon dioxide and other pollutants are not reduced, according to the world's climate scientists. The people of Nepal and its Asian neighbours downstream are extremely dependent on the rivers running off those glaciers to irrigate croplands and provide drinking water. There is a massive threat to food production as China and India, the world's leading producers of wheat and rice, see significant decreases in their ability to produce those crops.

In addition to exacerbating food shortages, ice melt in Antarctica and Greenland could force hundreds of millions of people worldwide to seek refuge on higher ground. At the Earth's poles, snow is melting, sea ice is breaking up, and temperatures are rising, all at faster rates than elsewhere on the planet, raising the likelihood of severe sea-level rise. Some refugees would remain within their own countries, while many others would flee to foreign countries, but both groups would impose heightened burdens on the local communities and national governments forced to support them as they build new lives from scratch.

Aid workers, who are active in scores of countries worldwide, emphasize that poorer communities tend to be the least able to cope with weather-related disasters and the other effects of climate change, and ironically and unfairly are also, by and large, the least responsible for causing climate change. Nepal, for example, is one of the world's poorest countries and extremely vulnerable to climate change, yet it emits only 0.025 per cent of the world's greenhouse gases. The United States, by comparison, is responsible for about 20 per cent of the world's greenhouse gas emissions, though only making up about 5 per cent of the world's population.

There is a growing awareness of the vital importance of addressing the global climate change crisis. The film *The Age of Stupid*,[9] launched in 2009, follows the lives of six people: an Indian businessman, a Nigerian medical student/fisherwoman, a Shell employee in the United States, an Iraqi refugee family, a British wind farm developer, and an 81-year-old French mountain guide, each of whom is living with or trying to mitigate the effects of climate change. It has been described as the first successful dramatization of climate change to reach the big screen; it is a powerful, well-researched and emotional film. The former president of the global environmental organization Friends of the Earth, Tony Juniper, hoped that the film would spur political action.

These issues will be explored in depth in Chapter 6.

### Designer babies

The BBC reported in March 2009 that a US clinic had sparked controversy by offering would-be parents the chance to select traits like the eye and hair colour of their offspring.[10] The Los Angeles Fertility Institutes run by Dr Jeff Steinberg, a pioneer of IVF in the 1970s, expects a trait-selected baby to be born next year. His clinic also offers sex selection. UK fertility experts are angered that the service will distract attention from how the same technology can protect against inherited disease.

The science is based on a laboratory technique called pre-implantation genetic diagnosis (PGD). It involves testing a cell taken from a very early embryo before it is put into the mother's womb. An embryo is selected that is free from defective genes or in this case an embryo with the desired physical traits such as blonde hair and blue eyes, to continue the pregnancy and discard any others. The LA clinic allowed couples to use its services for both medical and cosmetic reasons.

For example, a couple might want to have a baby with a darker complexion to help guard against a skin cancer if they already had a child who had developed a melanoma. But others might just want a boy with blonde hair. The clinic was offering this cosmetic selection to patients already having genetic screening for abnormal chromosome conditions in their embryos.

But pro-life campaigners see this as the inevitable slippery slope of a fertility process that results in many more embryos being created than can be implanted. Dr Gillian Lockwood, a UK fertility expert and member of the Royal College of Obstetricians and Gynaecologists' ethics committee, questioned whether it was morally right to be using the science in this way:

> If it gets to the point where we can decide which gene or combination of genes are responsible for blue eyes or blonde hair, what are you going to do with all those other embryos that turn out like me to be ginger with green eyes?

She warned against turning babies into 'commodities' that you buy off the shelf.

In the UK, sex selection is banned, and choices are currently permitted only in relationship to the baby's health. Italian fertility law does not permit the creation of surplus embryos or selective testing.

We will explore the issues surrounding genetic engineering and stem cell technology in Chapter 5.

### Natural disasters

If God is all-powerful, all-loving, all-knowing and ever ready to intervene, we have some difficult questions. How can God be both good and almighty when disasters occur? The L'Aquila earthquake took place on 6 April 2009.[11] It measured 6.3 on the Richter scale and hit central Italy at 01:32 GMT, causing thousands of people to lose their homes and more than 250 deaths. It was felt across the whole of Italy, but most strongly in central Italy. According to the US Geological Survey, the earthquake struck at a depth of 10 kilometres (6.2 miles), with an epicentre approximately 95 kilometres (60 miles) north-east of Rome, close to L'Aquila. The city has experienced major earthquakes in the past, but nothing on this scale since 1703.

Most of the damage was experienced in and around the city of L'Aquila, which includes one of the oldest centres of learning in Europe, the University of L'Aquila. More than 4000 buildings in the city collapsed. Enzo Boschi, the chairman of Italy's National Institute for Geophysics and Vulcanology, stated that the damage was extensive because the buildings were not designed to withstand earthquakes.

Italy is a well-known complex earthquake zone. It doesn't have the relative simplicity of a major plate boundary such as the West Coast of California where two large plates are sliding against each other along the San Andreas Fault. The collision of Africa and Europe, which produced the Alps and the Apennines some 40 million years ago, has left a highly fractured area with a lot of micro-plates moving around, which creates a lot of different types of fault movement, producing earthquakes. One major fault line runs north–south along the Apennine Mountain Range, and another more minor east–west fault line runs across the centre of the country. These produce frequent small earthquakes.

We understand the geology of the Earth's crust and are able to recognize where earthquakes are most likely to occur, and explain how and why they happen. But our failure to be able to predict when and precisely where along a major fracture system they may occur leads to the risk of suffering and death.

This leads us to recognize that there are important theological and moral questions in the light of deaths as a result of natural disasters. The moral questions will include the location of human habitation and industry in places susceptible to natural disaster, and the theological questions will revolve around the nature of God, who is the creator of a world in which such disasters occur.

These are conversations that will be developed further in Chapter 7.

## Methodology

It can be suggested that religion deals with mystery.[12] Science, on the other hand, is about seeking to understand the workings of the material world. It seems impossible that science will ever be able to completely explain all mystery. If we get worried about science conflicting with our faith beliefs, Philip Meyer suggests that we might try the following exercise. Draw a circle and place all those things – events, experiences and so on – that we can verify by scientific reason and experiment within that circle. The infinite area that lies beyond the circle represents the unknown, the mystery.

As we continuously carry out research in science and technology, we expand our knowledge and understanding of the world, and the circle increases in size, but as the circumference of the circle, the boundary between the known and the unknown, increases, we recognize that there is even more mystery beyond what is known to us. Every scientific discovery raises new questions. The mystery, being infinite, is never diminished. As Meyer says, infinity minus one is still infinity.

Faith traditions help us to organize our thoughts about the mystery. Without the framework that faith perspectives give there is a tendency for mystery to overwhelm us, and it becomes difficult to make sense of the universe in a way that integrates our own personal experience into the vastness of space and time. To quote some evangelistic booklets – it is making sense of the 'Big Questions': Who am I? Where am I? What am I? Where is the Universe? Is there a God?

Science is a way of thinking that holds all material knowledge as tentative. Scientists accept a theory because it works and because it can become part of a coherent structure of thought that helps us make sense of the physical world. But scientists are always ready to revise their conclusions if a more appropriate theory is developed. Scientific propositions are framed in a way that can be tested, that is, falsified (proved to be wrong). Faith-based propositions, on the other hand, are not falsifiable (cannot be proved to be right or wrong). Believing, then, is a matter of choice – a step of faith.

Thus it is perfectly possible to believe that the Earth is 6000 years old by citing a timescale for history based on Genesis, although science through radiometric dating will suggest that the oldest rocks on the planet are some 3800 million years old. At this point the creationists, who calculate their dates from a literal interpretation of the Bible, have no problem telling the geologists that when God created the world, God made the rocks that old. But such an argument, as we will discover, raises profound questions about methodology, interpretation and, more importantly, the nature of God.

Science looks for theories that give the simplest answer to the facts that are discovered: for example, the Copernican theory of the solar system, developed by Galileo, which placed the Sun at its centre. Religious and scientific belief up until this time held to the Aristotelian view that the Earth was at the centre, with the Sun, the stars and planets revolving around it. With no fixed reference point, it is perfectly possible to believe that the Earth is the centre of the solar system, except that such a view complicates all efforts to predict eclipses and the movements of the planets. Pre-seventeenth-century astronomers referred to the planets as 'wandering stars' and tried to describe their motion against the background of stars and galaxies with a system of loops within loops that they called 'epicycles'. But with improvements in the instruments used to study the stars and planets they needed more complicated epicycles to explain what they saw.

Copernicus' conceptual revolution of the Sun at the centre gave a simpler explanation and led to further scientific insights and discoveries. Scientific knowledge is cumulative. One theory opens the door to another. Expressing belief without verification through our experience of reality presents difficulties in verification, but also in term of further development of ideas. We will need continually to enter into a dialogue between our life, experience, belief and reality.

## Cheap tricks and other dangers

We are constantly faced with the demand for instant analysis and catchy headlines, which result in a popular science, designed not so much to inform as to sell newspapers or increase the viewing audience. We have to differentiate between real science and what I like to call *Reader's Digest* or tabloid science. One example involved the important cosmological discovery in April 1992 by NASA's COBE (Cosmic Background Explorer) satellite of ripples in the background radiation at the farthest extent of the universe. The newspapers, TV and radio leapt upon the story with headlines such as 'The secret of the universe – found' and 'God is redundant'. When John

Humphrys interviewed the project director George Smoot on Radio 4's *Today* programme, and confronted him with the headlines of God's redundancy, the scientist calmly told him that the discovery was a further pointer to purpose in the origin of the universe and of human life. The ripples supported the Big Bang hypothesis of the universe's origin, and were seen as the seeds from which the galaxies might have been formed. Their discovery produced a great sense of relief for many cosmologists, confirming their theory of an expanding universe. But the headline 'God is redundant' is far more exciting, and will sell far more newspapers than talk of confirming scientific theories about the initial physical conditions of the universe.

This should make us alert to the articles we read in the media. *Guardian* journalist Nick Davies[13] gives the example of the 'Millennium Bug', which proved to be an erroneous conclusion drawn by a computer operative in Canada, but which became a worldwide news story that cost governments billions of dollars: 'This is Flat Earth news. A story appears to be true. It is widely accepted as true. It becomes a heresy to suggest that it is not true – even if it is riddled with falsehood, distortion and propaganda.'[14] Nick Davies maintains that there is a need to check the sources: for example, the 'Millennium Bug' was the passing thought of a Canadian technology consultant in May 1993, which by 1998 became a media storm. But computer specialists were, from the beginning, pointing out that it would only affect very few computers. But all the media joined in the sensational story, and no one in the computer industry knew what the extent of the problem might be. Davies comments that most of the media sources – 'the vested commercial and political interests, the know-nothings, the religious and the mad – knew even less'.[15] When you ask how such stories can take centre stage, Davies states that 'Ignorance is the root of media failure. Most of the time, most journalists do not know what they are talking about. Their stories may be right, or they may be wrong: they don't know.'[16] So we need to take greater care and have more discretion when we access media accounts of scientific and technological discoveries.

Modern scientific discoveries are providing us with many answers to the nature of life, the universe and everything, but the problem of the question of ultimate meaning remains.[17] We will need to recognize at the outset that there is a limit as to how far science can ever take us in our understanding of the world in which we live. The former NASA astrophysicist Robert Jastrow was probably correct in his assessment:

For the scientist who has lived by his faith in the power of reason, the story ends like a bad dream. He has scaled the mountains of ignorance; he is about to conquer the highest peak; and as he pulls himself over the final rock, he is greeted by a band of theologians who have been sitting there for centuries.[18]

## *Boundary questions*

Nancey Murphy, in her book *Reconciling Theology and Science*, has produced a model that seeks to explain a hierarchy of sciences. The hierarchical model has a long history – the higher sciences permit a study of more complex organizations or systems of the entities at the next level down, as shown in Figure 1.

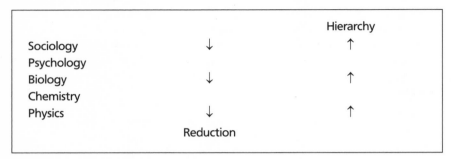

Figure 1

In contrast is the opposite direction of explanation – the reductionist approach of the logical positivists, which originated with a group of scientists and philosophers in the 1920s and 1930s (the Vienna Circle).

> The positivists were interested in a more radical unification of the sciences than mere hierarchical ordering. They wanted to show that each science could be reduced to the one below – that is, that entities at a given level could be entirely explained in terms of the operation of its parts, the entities at the next level down.[19]

While this has clear advantages for the conduct of scientific research it runs into problems, for example in the area of human freedom. Are we really free, or controlled by physics of our subatomic parts?

We discover that there are questions that are answered at the level we are considering; questions that can only be answered by reference to a lower level; and also questions that can only be answered at a higher level – boundary questions. Some of the most fundamental boundary questions can be answered by theology. For example, there are questions of meaning and purpose, unless of course it is all meaningless. Steven Weinberg (Professor of Theoretical Physics at the University of Austin, Texas, and a Nobel Prize winner with Abdus Salam on the symmetry of forces in the early universe), declared in his book *The First Three Minutes* that 'the more the universe seems comprehensible, the more it also seems pointless'.[20]

Weinberg believes that doing science gives human beings some sense of grace in the midst of the tragedy of being trapped in a hostile world. From his perspective it would appear that doing science gives point to living, but the discoveries thus made present existence as pointless. Such a state of affairs would seem to be a recipe for suicide. Murphy's model sees theology as the overarching explanation of the ultimate boundary questions, as shown in Figure 2.

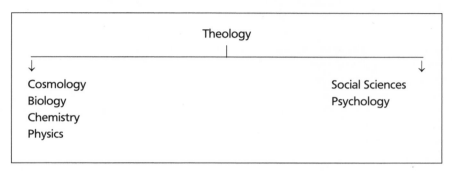

Figure 2

### Fact and theory; truth and certainty

We might question whether it is possible to bring together the fields of science and theology. Are they too disparate? And do they not speak different languages and use different methodology? If we believe that God is the creator of the whole of life, the universe and everything, then we must see God's involvement in the domain of scientific research, and not merely confine God-talk to the church and seminary. Lesslie Newbigin rightly attacked the division between the public world of scientific facts and the private world of beliefs and values.[21] UK Prime Minister Gordon Brown expressed this view in an interview given in August 2009, when he said:

> In Britain we are not a secular state as France is, or some other countries. It's true that the role of official institutions changes from time to time, but I would submit that the values that all of us think important – if you held a survey around the country of what people thought was important, what it is they really believed in, these would come back to Judeo-Christian values, and the values that underpin all the faiths that diverse groups in our society feel part of.

Asked if he thought it would be better if Christianity were 'privatized', he replied:

I think it's impossible because when we talk about faith, we are talking about what people believe in, we are talking about the values that under-pin what they do, we are talking about the convictions that they have about how you can make for a better society.[22]

Scientists have their own beliefs, doubts, questions and certainties; and the world of public decision-making clearly needs the values, ethics, morality and perspective that an understanding of the Christian faith might bring to it.

It is the scientist who is now posing the questions to which theology does have meaningful answers. Modern cosmologists are posing questions about the beginning and end of the universe, about the place of *Homo sapiens* within it, and the reasons for apparent design and purpose within the evolution of the cosmos. On Christmas Eve 1968, as the first astronauts orbited the Moon, Frank Borman read the opening verses of Genesis 1, and the entire world was able to hear something of his beliefs. Yet at this juncture we need to stress a point that will be made many times in this book, that God's existence is not proved by scientific discovery. For example, some years before Borman, the first man in space, the Russian astronaut Yuri Gagarin, declared that he did not find God in the heavens.

The modern popularity of science is evidenced by the plethora of books dealing with human life and the universe, beginning in the late 1980s and early 1990s with such books as Stephen Hawking's *Brief History of Time*, Paul Davies' *God and the New Physics* and *The Mind of God*, Roger Penrose's *The Emperor's New Mind*, Richard Dawkins' *The Selfish Gene* and *The Blind Watchmaker*, and Stephen Gould's *Wonderful Life*, and continuing in the twenty-first century with such books as Jerry Coyne's *Why Evolution is True*, Francis Collins' *The Language of God*, and Paul Davies' *The Goldilocks Enigma*.[23] The interest in these books reflects the modern concern with questions of origins, purpose and meaning to life. The growth of the Green Movement and New Age religion can also be seen as part of this search, with the central concerns for the environment of the planet and the use of resources, together with monistic beliefs in a world soul, and the interconnectedness of human life with the whole of the cosmos, with books like Robert White's *Creation in Crisis: Christian Perspectives on Sustainability*, George Monbiot's *Heat: How can we Stop the Planet Burning?*, and John Houghton's *Global Warming: the Complete Briefing*.[24]

Albert Einstein was right to state that religion without science is blind, and that science without religion is lame,[25] but the deciding factor will be the way in which these two areas are brought together. Science is presenting an ever clearer picture of the universe of which we are a part. We are understanding more and more of the complex patterns and structures of the galaxies, of human life and of the subatomic particles that compose all things. Cosmologists speak of the discovery of design and pose questions about purpose. There is a growing weight of evidence to suggest that human life could only have developed on this planet through a unique set of parameters that were established at the birth of the universe itself, which again suggests purpose, but with the additional possibility of humankind being at the centre of that purpose. The fragile conditions that enabled life to develop are now seen to be adversely affected by human activity, leading to the pollution of the environment, the exhaustion of natural resources and the destruction of the protective ozone layer. These are all aspects of the dialogue between science and theology that we shall explore in the following chapters.

### The perspective of science

Scientific research over the last couple of centuries has seen a cone of expansion, which grows ever larger. Stephen Hawking remarked: 'A lot of (Nobel) prizes have been awarded for showing that the universe is not as simple as we might have thought.'[26]

Scientific studies take place for a number of reasons:

1 there is basic human curiosity
2 there are the benefits that come from use of the earth's resources and from technological advances, and
3 there is the search for meaning and truth about the world in which we live.

Science is involved in a rational exploration of the universe; it is a search for understanding of the nature and patterns of the physical world. Science is only effective because it describes things the way they are. The discovery of the physical laws, such as gravity, that govern the universe is part of objective reality; those laws are objective truth and not the invention or imagining of some scientist. The whole field of science is one of discovery and not construction; there is an honesty and integrity in the search for meaning. Scientific results are frequently cross-checked and validated or questioned when other workers repeat the same experiments.

But there are, of course, the spectacles, even blinkers, of a scientific worldview, which will include various presuppositions and theories. This will mean that all facts are, to a greater or lesser extent, interpreted facts. There will be both the personal commitment of the scientists in their search for truth and the personal judgement of the individual researcher. This may mean the eliminating of background information that is not relevant to the particular work, but that later research may prove to be of vital importance. Objective observation has been questioned: for example, Michael Polanyi[27] has emphasized the part played by personal judgement in scientific research. We have to recognize that scientific experiment or observation can be both fact-laden and theory-laden; the theory may often be in the mind of the observer before they conduct the experiment; and for any collection of data there may be more than one possible solution. Yet for all this the one goal that drives scientific investigations is the desire for knowledge, to understand better the way the world is.

Science has a number of things to say to theology:

1 Physics does not allow us to build metaphysical models.
2 Science will not allow us to go beyond our understanding.
3 The history of the universe is pointing to a God who does not work by magic, but who has been patiently at work, over a long period of time, in an evolving universe. There is a picture of the outworking of divine love here, which we will have to consider in some detail. Science reveals an interplay of chance and necessity within the evolution of the universe, which points us towards another aspect of divine love, namely freedom.
4 Science presents us with a universe that has a beginning and that will have a definite end, in which carbon-based life will be extinguished.
6 Lastly, it is the human mind that is able to observe, investigate and understand the world that we experience. Scientific research has demonstrated that the mind does not function like a computer. It may be possible to reduce everything else to subatomic particles, acting under the laws of physics, but there are aspects of the mind, namely those of personhood, which do not compute. Once more we are pointed towards the possibility of God.

## Theological understanding of the world

Theology, like science, is a search for truth in our understanding of the reality of the universe; it also is a search to understand the way the world is. Theology has its factual information, but this is of a different quality to that of science. Theology depends on what is sometimes referred to as 'the Anglican Triad' of Scripture, tradition and the reasoning of the community of faith.

Scripture is the revelation of God in the history of Israel and in the experience of the first Christians. The documents that make up the Bible are themselves interpretations of events; they represent the inspiration of God, and have been sifted and tested in the light of the experience of the community of faith. Tradition takes that interpretation and testing a stage further, as the community of faith, in the light of continuing experience, has developed both interpretation of Scripture and the formulation of doctrine. Finally, in every age, the community of faith must apply critical reason, in the light of their own experience of the world and God, to Scripture, doctrine and their interpretation. All of this is seen by Christians as the work of the Holy Spirit, the presence of God, bringing enlightenment to the whole of life within the world, both material and spiritual. But, whereas science can repeat experiments, to recreate experiences, Christian experience is personal and contains within it a uniqueness. Such a uniqueness is exemplified in the incarnation, crucifixion and resurrection of Christ.

John Polkinghorne[28] is right to point to Christian mystical experience as one of the strongest indicators of the validity of the claim that religion is in touch with reality. Experiences of conversion, inspiration, guidance and healing, while not being universal experiences, nevertheless do have a universal character. Like scientific research, Christian experience of God and understanding of God's self-revelation are constantly examined within the community of faith, where experiences are shared.

Theology takes a further step of interpretation than science; it takes our ability to understand the rational universe and sees in this a deeper rationality at the heart of the cosmos, which includes human life. It was this step that led Anselm and Aquinas to attempt proofs for the existence of God. Theology sees creation as an expression of the purposes of God. The account of creation in Genesis 1 presents us with a picture of order and purpose brought about by the command and activity of God. Conscious human life is seen as the crown of God's creation, and entering into the care and control of the world. Creation is seen as the act of God's free will, it is contingent (it need not have been the way it is), and is the expression of love. The laws of nature are seen as signs of God's faithfulness and reflect God's character. Human free will and the role of chance within physical and biological processes are expressions of God's self-denying love. Polkinghorne is right to comment: 'The world created by the God of love and faithfulness may be expected to be characterized both by the openness of chance and the regularity of necessity.'[29]

What science has observed is a universe in which chance and necessity both play a part; in the evolution of life there are animals and plants that mutate and survive and those that do not, but there is a guiding mechanism that leads to the possibility of human beings; and in physics there is uncertainty in the behaviour of the smallest particles and unpredictability in some systems (known as chaotic), but overall they operate within the framework of dependable physical laws. In this the theologian sees the faithfulness of God, God's planning and God's self-limiting love, that allows a universe with free will.

Theology, in the experience of the people of God in the Old Testament, the New Testament and the Church of Jesus Christ, points to the providential activity of God in the universe, as well as in human life. The regularities of nature, in the laws of physics, the motion of the Sun and planets, the processes at work in the Earth's crustal layers, the weather systems and climate, are all demonstrations of God's providential ordering and care. The Bible points us to see God as the source of order, and to see God intimately involved with creation. The supremely exciting contribution that theology makes is the insight that God makes himself known in Jesus Christ. The

Genesis account of creation shows us that God has put relationship at the heart of the universe. Human beings are created in the image of God, to care for creation, and to worship their creator. God is seen to be in dynamic relationship with creation. This comes into clear focus in Jesus Christ, where the divine takes human flesh and shares our life. The social sciences have recognized a human longing for ultimate reality; this longing finds its rest in the Christ of the gospel, and the resurrection of Christ is the ground, fore-taste and guarantee of life beyond death. Here is the disclosure of ultimate reality and purpose for humankind.

Yet theology is not without its difficulties. Theology seeks to make sense of the universe, but in this is confronted by suffering and evil. We are forced to face questions such as, 'Does a creation that includes a holocaust or the 2004 Boxing Day tsunami demonstrate the work of a loving God?' Suffer-ing presents us with a mystery, but Christianity meets this mystery at the profoundest level in the cross of Christ. It is here that God is involved in the suffering of the world.

Theology addresses science in a number of places:

1 First of all, while science deals with the minutiae of particles or the mega theories of the universe, theology attempts to pull the whole of human experience – physical, mental, emotional and spiritual – together, produc-ing a holistic view of the universe in which we exist.
2 Second, theology is able to bring answers to the questions that science is posing. Theology hears the questions raised by the fine-tuning of the uni-verse and the anthropic principle, and sees within these the hand of God described at the beginning of Scripture.
3 Last, theology is able to speak of nothing lying outside the will of God, and is able to bring together the purpose of the universe, the meaning of life, and the question of what lies beyond death, or beyond the end of the universe's life. Theology brings together those issues that affect both science and itself. Because the theological view of the world is a total all-embracing view, Polkinghorne is right to conclude that there must be a consonance between science and theology.[30]

### Bringing science and theology together

Both theology and science are seeking to make sense of the world that they experience, and their methodologies are not totally different. In each case the search for a rational understanding is motivated by belief and a desire for truth. As such there must be a common ground for dialogue. Science is able to investigate the universe because human beings have a measure of transcendence over the world, and theology is able to bring a greater degree of understanding because it recognizes the transcendence of God, who reveals God's purposes to humankind.

Understanding the world in which we live is an undertaking that unites science and theology, and the search for truth will not succeed without a commitment to belief and a readiness for testing, confirmation and correction. However, we need to recognize that it is at the philosophical level, rather than the technological level, that such dialogue might take place. It is at the philosophical level that science and theology meet. As we noted earlier, Michael Pfundner and Ernest Lucas encourage both scientists and theologians to read the philosophy of science, which raises questions about presumptions and methodology, while also revealing the danger of removing the theological framework on which all modern science is based.[31]

## Defining the issues

### *Models and paradigms*

In his Gifford Lectures, Ian Barbour helpfully draws parallels between the methods and models of science and theology.[32] Science begins with observation and experimental data and produces concepts and theories, as in Figure 3.

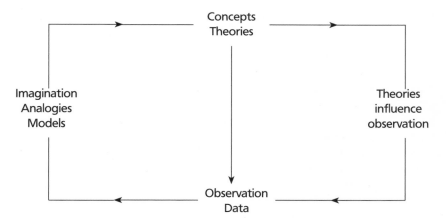

Figure 3

Any theory or model is part of a network of theories and concepts that makes up the store of scientific knowledge and tradition. There is therefore no theory-free observation or experiment. The form of questions we ask will to a certain extent determine the answers we receive, as any national opinion pollster knows. We need to recognize that our preconceptions may determine our questions, and as a result our conclusions are always incomplete, tentative and subject to revision. For example, early geologists would not have sought to link the occurrence of earthquakes and volcanoes, with fold mountain belts or deep-sea trenches, because they had no concept of plate tectonics and the movement of continents. So we see that there is an interconnection between models, concepts, theories and observation and experiment.

The picture in theology is similar, with beliefs replacing theories, and data coming in the form of religious experiences, ritual and the traditions of the faith (see Figure 4).

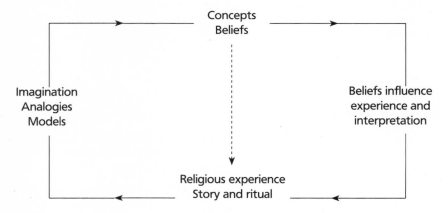

Figure 4

Like scientific observations, there are no uninterpreted experiences. The Christian experiences of conversion, God's presence, guidance, courage, peace, healing, moral obligation, or recognition of the universe as the ordering of God, will be put down to psychological feelings and needs, wishful thinking, coincidence and irrational faith by those who do not hold such religious belief. For this reason religious experiences need to be checked against the accepted beliefs of the community of faith over the past centuries and in the present.

Both science and theology use models to present meaning and to evoke understanding. Science collects data and builds a model which may form the basis of a theory. To take an example from what used to be my own professional area, geologists collect the data of earthquake epicentres, fracture patterns, oceanic topography, subsurface structures, distribution of volcanoes, igneous and metamorphic rocks, together with fossils and evidence of past climates contained in sedimentary rocks, and then produce a plate tectonics model of the Earth's crust (see Figure 5). The model (in this case a patchwork of six 'plates') displays what cannot be observed directly and is therefore usually regarded with what has been called a 'critical realism'; there is some caution about how far, how adequately and in what ways it describes the phenomenon it is portraying (as with the model of light travel-

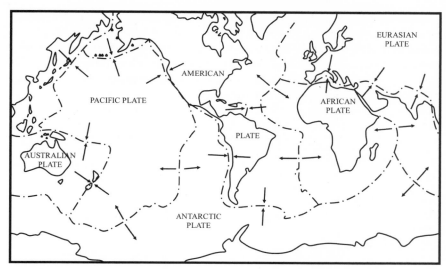

Figure 5

ling in waves or particles), but it is still believed to represent what is really there. It helps understanding, promotes the development of theories, and can be confirmed or modified by further information arising within the scientific community.

In a similar way, theology presents models of God, which are largely derived from the images and metaphors contained in biblical accounts of people's experience of their relationship with God and God's unveiling of Godself to them. For example, we develop the model of God as Father, which has its main basis in the unique experience of sonship by Jesus Christ who in turn taught his disciples to address God as 'Father'; this model is tested through our own personal experiences, and those of the community of faith through the ages. The model of 'Father' may, of course, be difficult to use for those who have had an experience of human fathers that was destructive or dominating, and so it is critical that all models of God should be received and understood in the context of the whole community of faith and not individualistically. The community preserves the witness to God's revelation of Godself which redefines all human concepts of relationship; in this case, the way that Jesus revealed the Fatherhood of God challenges all human ideas of patriarchy. We must also note that there are passages that indicate the Motherhood of God, for example Isaiah 66.13, Hosea 11.1–4, and Matthew 23.37. Religious models thus help our understanding, but also have the additional function of evoking a response from people. In this sense, they have an important role in evangelism.

In commenting upon Barbour's two diagrams (or 'models'), I have been indicating my appreciation for their illuminating quality. However, my aim in this book is to work towards an integration of a scientific and theological view of the world, and so I venture to include a third diagram, Figure 6, which is indebted to the other two, but which attempts to express the interactions between the approaches of science and theology to the world. This is the first of several diagrams that will explore the integration of theological and scientific world-views in one perspective.

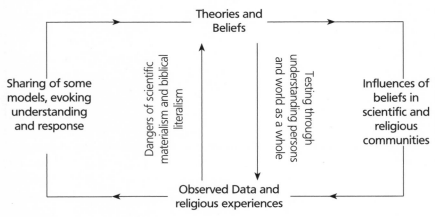

Figure 6

## *Conceptual revolutions*

New questions and perspectives may be revolutionary. Paul Thagard, in his book *Conceptual Revolutions*[33] considers the way in which new truths are assimilated. So, for example, the move from separate creation to evolution represents a conceptual revolution. Taxonomy redefined human beings as one of the groups of creatures created by God, but evolution suggested that human beings had evolved from lower orders of animals (see Figure 7).

Alongside the conceptual revolutions in the history of science, recent disasters have led to a questioning of the unchecked optimism and reliability associated with scientific and technological advancement. Theology has also had its problems in recent times, with the publicity given to scholarly arguments concerning the divinity of Christ, the trustworthiness of Scripture and the traditions of the Church, and the lack of a clear response to ethical and moral issues.

There is therefore a clear need for dialogue between the Christian faith and the scientific fields. In our age, science has found a new humility through failure, blunder and the recognition of a universe that is not infinite, but which has a beginning and an end. Western theologians and the Western Church have also begun to recognize that there are serious questions being

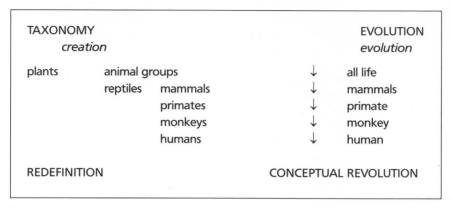

Figure 7

asked of it by cosmology, medical science, Christians in the developing world, and by ordinary people outside the Church who, although wanting something in which to believe, are no longer content unquestioningly to accept the propositions of the Christian faith. While science is seen as objective, public and factual, and theology as subjective, personal and related to feelings, there is a recognition that human beings have a psychosomatic unity that requires a holistic world-view.

### Scientific materialism, biblical literalism and technological pragmatism

In spite of comparisons between science and theology, there have been, and still are, conflicts between these two fundamental sources of human knowledge about the world. The conflict is at its most acute between the scientific materialist and the biblical literalist, and these ways of thinking are represented on the 'integrated model' (see Figure 6) by the upward vertical arrow. Both derive from an attempt to make direct inductive arguments, from either religious experience or observed data, without being sensitive to the part played by models, imagination and analogies. From the scientific side, science is seen as the only source of reliable, factual knowledge, while religion is seen to be subjective, emotional, traditional (that is, old-fashioned) and superstitious. From the side of biblical literalism, science is seen as deceived and deceiving, and centred upon sinful human beings, while uncritical biblical study provides the only sure truth. Biblical literalism confronted Galileo, Newton, Lyell and Darwin, and has continued as a force in the Church, first in the United Kingdom, and more recently in the United States of America through 'creation science'. The lack of understanding of what science is actually saying leads many Christians to fall back on a dogmatic presentation of the Bible, and to have a total disengagement with the discoveries of modern science. Scientists, likewise, with an inadequate understanding of why the Bible was written and of what it is actually saying, may dismiss the claims of theology and operate as if the material world were the sum total of reality.

Both of these attitudes are the result of a failure to fully understand what the other is saying. For a dialogue to take place there is a need to overcome some of the extreme positions that are held. Those who hold such positions tend to present arguments that reveal a failure to come to grips with the limitations of science in giving a complete explanation of the world we experience, or human limitations in solving the world's problems through technology, or a failure to understand the context and genre of biblical material.

Scientific materialism is a basic distrust in the reliability or reasonable nature of Scripture, church tradition and Christian belief. This leads to an attitude that accepts uncritically every new suggestion made by science and seeks in some way to accommodate this into belief. This view will assume that science is right; where it contradicts religious belief, it is always that belief that must be altered. Richard Dawkins, for example, in his book *The God Delusion*, completely rejects any supernatural agency. As he draws his argument to an end he states:

> As a scientist, I am hostile to fundamentalist religion because it actively debauches the scientific enterprise. It teaches us not to change our minds, and not to want to know exciting things that are available to be known. It subverts science and saps the intellect.[34]

Peter Atkins, Professor of Chemistry at Oxford, says, 'It is not possible to be intellectually honest or to be a true scientist and believe in gods.' He maintains that religious belief is 'outmoded and ridiculous'. Belief in gods is a 'worn out but once useful crutch in mankind's journey towards truth'. 'We consider the time has come for that crutch to be abandoned.' 'To say that "God made the world" is simply a more or less sophisticated way of saying that we don't understand how the universe originated. A god, in so far as it is anything, is an admission of ignorance.'[35]

Biblical literalism is a basic mistrust in science and scientists, whether they are Christians or have no beliefs at all, based on a dogmatic attitude towards Scripture, which accepts every verse in a literal and uncritical way. Ken Ham, who is the President of Answers in Genesis USA,[36] emphasizes the authority of the Bible and how compromise, by denying a literal interpretation of Genesis, has opened the door to many social problems. Genesis is accepted as being literally true, the Earth and all life created by God in six days about 10,000 years ago.

An Australian geologist took fundamentalist Christians to court for teaching creationism (a literal interpretation of Genesis 1—9). Professor Ian

Plimer of the School of Earth Sciences at the University of Melbourne accused creationists of selling 'misleading and deceptive' materials.[37] Creationism teaches that life on earth is the result of God's creative action, and not the result of 'blind' scientific processes. Creationism does not attempt to explain how God did this. Its exponents suggest that God used processes that are no longer operating anywhere in the natural universe. They refer to this as Special Creation, which cannot be explored by scientific investigation.

We are dealing with cases of bad theology and bad science here. I would maintain that these are 'safe' positions to take, involving no mental struggles or heart searching – as long as you are able to hold your ground. But I believe that real theology must be worked out in the grey and uncertain areas of dialogue and interaction between science and theology. This will mean taking science seriously, seeking to understand what science is revealing and the questions and implications of its findings for the Christian faith. It will also mean taking Scripture and the doctrines of the Church seriously; it will mean listening to critical scholarship and philosophical debate and drawing deeper understanding from seeking to address the questions and issues raised by such works.

Technological pragmatism has led and is still leading human beings to mistreat the planet and individual lives. Ecology has brought to light the unforeseen effects that human interference with natural processes often has; and this is why we can no longer plead inadvertence as the excuse for technological excess. Ruth Conway notes that 'we are part of a world frantically pushing at technological frontiers . . . we are also part of a world whose technologies are threatening the very basis of life'.[38] She believes that our human-centred culture is in the grip of a technological power that is out of control.[39]

Without a moral perspective, two attitudes can arise in the scientific arena:

1 Technological pragmatism, seen as an aspect of management. 'The ethical questions are not faced explicitly; the solution to a problem consists in finding an appropriate technique to control or eliminate it.'[40] This view is anthropocentric.
2 Evolutionary humanism, where the theory of evolution is the overriding ontological principle. Humans as the most complex product of the process are able to control and determine the development of the planet.

Jerry Mander states that reverence for the Earth is an 'idea that is subversive to Western society and the entire technological direction of the past century'.[41]

Ruth Conway is more critical when she concludes that

it is by listening to those on the underside of technological advance that fundamental perspectives will be shifted and worldviews transformed. It is the experience of those who shoulder the burdens, not those who reap the profits, which provide the crucial criteria for a technology that respects the integrity of creation.[42]

## The scope of this text

The patterns of the physical world are exciting; there is a wonder and order that is both beautiful and exciting; and scientists are often heard to use words like 'wonder' and 'awe' when considering their researches and results. One of the greatest surprises that these patterns and results are showing is that the present state of the universe has depended on a 'fine-tuning' of the initial conditions that brought it into existence. This is what is generally known as the 'anthropic principle'. It is being suggested that a universe that has the evolution of conscious human life must have been planned with that end result in mind. In other words, science is discovering purpose in the world, and suggests the possibility of a 'Mind' or purposeful 'Designer' behind the universe.

However, Carl Sagan concludes his introduction to Stephen Hawking's *A Brief History of Time* with these words:

> This is also a book about God . . . or perhaps about the absence of God. The word God fills these pages. Hawking embarks on a quest to answer Einstein's famous question about whether God had any choice in creating the universe. Hawking is attempting, as he explicitly states, to understand the mind of God. And this makes all the more unexpected the conclusion of that effort, at least so far: a universe with no edge in space, no beginning or end in time, and nothing for a creator to do.[43]

The purpose of this book is quite opposite from Hawking's here. It is to present a dialogue between science and theology in which the role of the creator becomes increasingly clear in God's transcendence, immanence and self-limiting love. Modern science has revived the old design argument of natural theology (Thomas Aquinas), and has given it new teeth. It presents us with an understanding of the universe that includes a beginning and an end. It also demonstrates a universe that has a 'fine-tuning' which is suggestive of purpose. From these two features is developed the anthropic principle, which proposes that the conditions for human life are written into the very fabric of the universe.

For the moment we are left with much that is unknowable. At one level we can discuss a rational, mathematical universe, and yet this is not a complete answer. There is something more than mathematical about emotions, judgements, music and art. We cannot have a mathematical theory of everything because some things would be therefore excluded on the grounds that they were not scientific. We can compress the complexities of inanimate objects such as planets and stars into an idealized equation, but we cannot do the same thing with the complexities of human personality. John Barrow concludes his search for 'Theories of Everything' by noting that science is most at home attacking problems that require technique rather than insight. But, he says, there are prospective features to the universe such as beauty, simplicity and truth that cannot be encompassed by laws and rules, and so no non-poetic account of reality can be complete. His final conclusion is that

> There is no formula that can deliver all truth, all harmony, all simplicity. No Theory of Everything can ever provide total insight. For, to see through everything, would leave us seeing nothing at all.[44]

From a Christian perspective I want to maintain that belief in a personal God has advantages over a theory as a final explanation. In encounter with God we know what is ultimately real, but we know God precisely as mystery. It is because God is known, not because God is unknown, that we affirm that we cannot know God fully.

## Key texts

Ian Barbour, 1990, 'Models and Paradigms', in *Religion in an Age of Science*, Gifford Lectures 1989–1991, vol. 1, London: Harper & Row, pp. 31–65.
Michael Pfundner and Ernest Lucas, 2008, *Think God, Think Science: Conversations on Life, the Universe, and Faith*, Milton Keynes: Paternoster.
Paul Thagard, 1992, *Conceptual Revolutions*, Princeton: Princeton University Press.

## Further Reading

Francis Collins, 2007, *The Language of God: A Scientist Presents Evidence for Belief*, London, New York: Simon & Schuster/Pocket Books.
Richard Dawkins, 2007, *The God Delusion*, London: Transworld.
John Houghton, 2007, *The Search For God. Can Science Help?* Cheltenham: John Ray Initiative.
Alister McGrath, 2004, *The Science of God*, London: T&T Clark.
Nancey Murphy, *Reconciling Theology and Science*, Ontario: Pandora Press, 1997.
Keith Ward, 2008, *Why There Almost Certainly Is a God*, Oxford: Lion.
Keith Ward, 2008, *The Big Questions in Science and Religion*, Pennsylvania: Templeton Foundation Press.
Robert Winston, 2005, *The Story of God*, London: Bantam Press.

## Notes

1 Dan Brown, 2001, *Angels and Demons*, London: Corgi Books, also explored in the film of the same name: *Angels & Demons*, 2009, Sony Pictures Studios: California, starring Tom Hanks, Ayelet Zurer and Ewan McGregor.

2 Brown, *Angels*, pp. 133–4.

3 Brown, *Angels*, pp. 418–25.

4 Dan Brown, 2004, *The Da Vinci Code*, London: Corgi Books.

5 'Metaphysical mistake'. http://www.guardian.co.uk/commentisfree/belief/2009/jul/12/religion-christianity-belief-science

6 Michael Pfundner and Ernest Lucas, 2008, *Think God, Think Science: Conversations on Life, the Universe, and Faith*, Milton Keynes: Paternoster.

7 Francis Collins, 2007, *The Language of God: A Scientist Presents Evidence for Belief*, London, New York: Simon & Schuster/Pocket Books, pp. 1–3.

8 http://us.oneworld.net/issues/environment/-/article/366419-climate-changes-creating-hunger-ahead-summit

9 *The Age of Stupid*, 2009, produced in UK, Cert (UK): 12A, runtime: 90 mins, directed by Franny Armstrong, and starring Pete Postlethwaite.

10 http://news.bbc.co.uk/1/hi/health/7918296.stm

11 http://blogs.physicstoday.org/newspicks/2009/04/2009-laquila-earthquake.html

12 See Philip Meyer, 'There is always the mystery. Why faith and science will remain worlds apart', http://blogs.usatoday.com/oped/2008/02/there-is-always.html

13 Nick Davies, 2008, *Flat Earth News,* London: Chatto & Windus.

14 Davies, *Flat Earth*, p. 12.

15 Davies, *Flat Earth*, p. 27.

16 Davies, *Flat Earth*, p. 28.

17 To consider the philosophical question of the meaning of the universe we might consider the powerful computer named 'Deep Thought', created by Douglas Adams in *The Hitch Hiker's Guide to the Galaxy* (London: Pan Books, 1979, p. 135). Adams describes how two computer programmers ask the computer for the answer to life, the universe and everything. Seventy-five thousand generations later, another two programmers stand in front of the computer, expectant to hear 'the answer to the great question of life' . . .

'Good morning,' said Deep Thought at last.

'Er . . . Good-morning, O Deep Thought,' said Loonquawl nervously, 'do you have . . . er, that is . . . '

'An answer for you?' interrupted Deep Thought majestically. 'Yes, I have.'

'To Everything? To the great Question of Life, the Universe and Everything?'

'Yes' . . .

'Though I don't think,' added Deep Thought, 'that you're going to like it.'

'Tell us!'

'All right,' said Deep Thought. 'The Answer to the Great Question . . .

. . . Of Life, the Universe and Everything . . .

'Is . . . '

'Yes . . . ???'

'Forty-two,' said Deep Thought, with infinite majesty and calm.

'Forty-two!' yelled Loonquawl. 'Is that all you've got to show for seven and a half million years' work?'

'I checked it very thoroughly,' said the computer, 'and that quite definitely is the answer. I think the problem, to be quite honest with you, is that you've never actually known what the question is' . . . '

18 R. D. Jastrow, *Reader's Digest*, October 1980, p. 57, quoted in D. Wilkinson, 1993, *God, the Big Bang and Stephen Hawking*, Tunbridge Wells: Monarch, p. 71.

19 Nancey Murphy, 1997, *Reconciling Theology and Science: A Radical Reformation Perspective*, Kitchener: Pandora Press, Scottdale: Herald Press, p. 13.

20 Steven Weinberg, 1979, *The First Three Minutes*, London: André Deutsch, p. 149.

21 Lesslie Newbigin, 1983, *The Other Side of 1984: Questions for the Churches*, Geneva: WCC.

22 http://www.telegraph.co.uk/news/newstopics/politics/gordon-brown/5988706/Gordon-Brown-insists-Britain-is-still-Christian-country.html

23 Stephen Hawking, 1988, *A Brief History of Time*, London and New York: Bantam Press; Paul Davies, 1983, *God and the New Physics*, London: Dent; Paul Davies, 1992, *The Mind of God*, New York and London: Simon & Schuster; Roger Penrose, 1989, *The Emperor's New Mind*, Oxford: Oxford University Press; Richard Dawkins, 1986, *The Blind Watchmaker*, London: Longmans; Richard Dawkins, 1989, *The Selfish Gene*, Oxford: Oxford University Press; Stephen Jay Gould, 1990, *Wonderful Life: The Burgess Shale and the Nature of History*, London: Hutchinson Radius; Jerry A. Coyne, 2009, *Why Evolution is True*, Oxford: Oxford University Press; Francis Collins, 2007, *The Language of God: A Scientist Presents Evidence for Belief*, London, New York: Simon & Schuster/Pocket Books; Paul Davies, 2007, *The Goldilocks Enigma: Why is the Universe Just Right for Life?* London: Penguin Books.

24 Robert S. White (ed.) 2009, *Creation in Crisis: Christian Perspectives on Sustainability*, London: SPCK; George Monbiot, 2007, *Heat: How Can We Stop the Planet Burning*, London: Penguin; John Houghton, 2009, *Global Warming: The Complete Briefing*, Cambridge: Cambridge University Press.

25 In Albert Einstein, 1941, *Science, Philosophy and Religion: A Symposium*.

26 Stephen Hawking, 1988, *A Brief History of Time*, London & New York: Bantam Press, p. 78.

27 Michael Polanyi, 1958, *Personal Knowledge*, London: Routledge & Kegan Paul.

28 John Polkinghorne, 1988, *One World: The Interaction of Science and Theology*, London: SPCK, p. 29.

29 John Polkinghorne, 1988, *Science and Creation*, London: SPCK, p. 52.

30 Polkinghorne, *Science*, pp. 1–2.

31 Pfundner and Lucas, *Think God*.

32 Ian Barbour, 1990, 'Models and Paradigms', in *Religion in an Age of Science*, Gifford Lectures 1989–1991, vol. 1, London: Harper & Row, pp. 31–65.

33 Paul Thagard, 1992, *Conceptual Revolutions*, Princeton: Princeton University Press.

34 Richard Dawkins, 2007, *The God Delusion*, London: Transworld, p. 321.

35 Peter Atkins, speaking at the annual festival of the British Association for the Advancement of Science, as reported in the *Electronic Telegraph*, issue 476, Wednesday 11 September 1996.

36 See www.answersingenesis.org.

37 Paul Vallely, 'Creative Tension: Evolution still on Trial', *Independent*, 8 April 1997.

38 Ruth Conway, 1999, *Choices at the Heart of Technology: A Christian Perspective*, Harrisburg PA: Trinity Press, p. 2.

39 Conway, *Choices*, p. 4.

40 R. P. Moss, 'Environment', in David Atkinson and David Field (eds), 1995, *New Dictionary of Christian Ethics and Pastoral Theology*, Leicester: InterVarsity Press, p. 349.

41 Jerry Mander, 'In the Absence of the Sacred', in Richard Foltz (ed.), 2003, *Worldviews, Religion, and the Environment: A Global Anthology*, Belmont: Wadsworth/Thomson Learning, p. 65.

42 Conway, *Choices*, p. 34.

43 Carl Sagan, 'Introduction', in Stephen Hawking, 1988, *A Brief History of Time*, London and New York: Bantam Press, p. x.

44 John Barrow, 1990, *Theories of Everything*, Oxford: Oxford University Press, p. 210.

# 1

## The Bible and Science[1]

### Introduction

An exploration of the dialogue between Christianity and science cannot ignore some of the lively debates that exist, especially in the United States, concerning the place of the Bible. Recent US court rulings over the teaching of creationism and intelligent design[2] alongside or in place of Darwinian evolutionary theory have served to highlight the debate. A fundamentalist or literalist reading of the Bible maintains that the text should be interpreted in a literal way with the result that creation of the universe takes place in six days and that all elements both inanimate and animate are separate creations of God. It is such an interpretation that results in the conflict between some Christian groups and the majority of the scientific community. In contrast are the views of the scientific materialist or scientific atheist, who asserts that the discoveries of science are the sum available total of knowable truth about the earth and the universe, and that each level of existence is explained by the level below it – reductionism. Religious believers are at best seen to be superstitious and irrelevant, and at worst irrational and dangerous for the progress of humanity. We will develop this discussion in Chapters 3 and 7.

To adopt a literalist or fundamentalist position is to make an assumption that all passages in the Bible have the same literary form. A cursory examination of the following passages demonstrates some of the differences that exist: 2 Kings 21.19—22.7; Jonah 4.1–11; Isaiah 40.1–8; 43.1–7; Amos 5.18—6.7; Psalm 103.1–5; Psalm 51.1–12; Psalm 8; Leviticus 19.2a–18; Proverbs 13.1–12; and Song of Songs 4.1–15. We ask how we would describe the material in each passage, and what sort of material we are reading: history, story, prophet of good news, prophet of judgement, hymn of praise, prayer of confession, prayer of adoration, laws, wise sayings, or love poem?

We will also want to ask questions about the purpose behind the passage: to whom is the passage addressed, and what is the context; when, where, to whom, from whom, and with what purpose and meaning? We need to recognize that the Old Testament has a context in space and time. Israel was an emerging nation, fairly small in size, in the midst of a cauldron of political upheaval and struggles for power and control. Israel's neighbours included the empires of Egypt, Canaan, Assyria, Babylonia and Persia. Likewise, the New Testament, largely set in the context of the small country of Palestine, part of the expanding Roman Empire, under Roman occupation, and influenced by both Greek and Roman culture.

## How did we get here?

### *A late twentieth-century development*

I grew up in the 1960s in a Baptist church in Cardiff, where my father was a deacon and Bible teacher, while following his 'day job' as head of biology in a large grammar school. He helped me to understand the variety and evolution of the natural world. My own passion was for geology, and at university my two professors were Christians. Frank Harold Trevor Rhodes was the author of the seminal *The Evolution of Life*, published by Penguin Books in 1962, and the late Dick Owen, who supervised my PhD, was a beloved Methodist lay preacher and a most knowledgeable speaker on the geology of the South Wales Coalfield. As I grew up and studied as a Christian in South Wales, biology, geology, evolution and church sat happily together. So, as I explore this subject, I ask: what has changed?

In 1960, John Whitcomb and Henry Morris published *The Genesis Flood*,[3] which posited a literal reading of Genesis 1—11, six-day creation and Noah's Flood. This seems to have been foundational to creationism and the Creation Science Movement, and to the subsequent rejection of such a position by reductionist science. When we try to look at the Old Testament systematically we run into the problem of imposing a system on material which cannot be handled in that way. We are dealing with writings that cover over 1000 years of change in the history of a people.

### *The Bible and science through the Christian centuries*

The Bible essentially explains why things exist rather than how they came into being. We are presented with a revelation of God who is transcendent – God who brought creation into being; God who is immanent – God involved with creation; and God who is personal – God who enters into relationship with human beings. We are encouraged to discover the God who has created and is creating, who is the beginning and the future of all life. Sam Berry observes that

> the Genesis account of creation is of a progress from nothing (or more strictly, God only) through geological and biological change to humankind. Nowhere in the Bible are we told the mechanisms God used to carry out his work; indeed it is only by faith that we know that God is involved (Hebrews 11.3).[4]

One key aspect of any dialogue is our interpretation of the early chapters of Genesis. It is important to hear the views of early Christian theologians such as Origen, Jerome, Gregory of Nyssa, Ambrose, Augustine, and many Jewish scholars of the time, who all saw the accounts of creation as allegory and symbolism. When we appreciate their views we are led to recognize that the creation stories are theology rather than history. The six days of Genesis 1, for example, are literal 24-hour days, because we are presented with the focus on Sabbath worship (on the seventh day) of the God who has faithfully and lovingly ordered creation, and has declared it to be good. Michael Roberts observes that a strict six-day creation and a 4004 BCE beginning were never 'the dominant view and was the official position of no church in Europe or America (until the late twentieth century). The chaos-restitution interpretation [a long period of chaos during which the long geological time span of earth's history occurs] promulgated first by Hugo Grotius (1583–1645) . . . opened the door for the churches' acceptance of geological time.'[5]

When Israel proclaimed its creation faith, recorded in Genesis 1.1—2.3, she was in the darkest period of her history, in exile in Babylonia. The removal of the leadership of Judah to Babylon at the beginning of the sixth century BCE was a body blow to the nationhood and religious life of Israel. The Exile is a watershed in Israelite history. It is in this context that the writers of Genesis 1 began to reflect upon the faith of Israel. This priestly writer, or group of writers, reflected upon the traditions of their faith, the writings that the religious community had preserved and brought with them into exile, and upon the history of God's dealings with his people. To this they added their experience of the world, and the religious views held by their Babylonian captors. The writers took all these experiences and, through their faith in Yahweh, a newly edited version of the Scriptures took shape. The very first belief that they wanted to express was that the covenant God of Israel was the God of all creation. Through Genesis 1—11 creation is linked with the history of Israel as God's chosen people, beginning with Abraham. The God of the covenant, the sustainer and redeemer of Israel is the creator of the universe.[6]

Genesis 1 is different in literary form from the rest of Genesis and indeed of the Old Testament; it is neither exhortation, parable, prophecy, song, nor a list of the contents of the store cupboard of creation. Indeed, the first 11 chapters of Genesis tell the story of the primal history of the world. It begins with creation, in primordial time and space. After this the universal history becomes focused into the history of God's chosen people, through Abraham and his descendants. It is an expression of Israel's living awareness of her dependency on nature and God's faithful will, even in times of darkness and despair. Christians find this exemplified in the incarnation and resurrection of Christ, whom the apostle John describes as co-creator with God (John 1.1–3). God's relationship to creation is a personal covenant of gracious love.

We can conclude that a literal interpretation of Genesis 1—11 does not do justice to the text and misses out on the depth of God's truth that it contains.

## The current debates

The challenges presented by the current scientific understanding of the origin of the universe and the evolution of life on planet Earth are not so much in the questions themselves as in the reaction and perceived implications of these theories for science and for the Christian faith. At their worst they provide scope for conflict, but at their best for a constructive dialogue, which provides an opportunity for a Christian apologetic.

We find that there are scientists who believe that everything in this world can only be explained by science, and Christians who believe that the only way to understand the origin of this world and its life is through a literal reading of Genesis 1—3. Both of these extreme positions suggest that the Big Bang origin of the universe and the theory of evolution lead to atheism, and both emphasize that the literal interpretation of Scripture is at the crux of the argument. This is bad science and bad theology. On the one hand life is reduced to nothing but atoms and molecules, where there is no room for meaning or for human freedom, and on the other hand, a biblical interpretation that fails to recognize the context and genre of the text – giving a one-size-fits-all approach to the reading and understanding of Scripture.

There is a false dichotomy in the more extreme views that posit nature in opposition to God. This is far removed from the ways in which both scientists and theologians of the seventeenth and eighteenth centuries viewed the world. They saw the discoveries of science as revealing the ways in which God worked in the world. For example, Darwin's theory of evolution put God back into the world as an active participant, rather than the machine minder of Sir Isaac Newton, who was outside creation. It was therefore no surprise that Christian scholars Charles Kingsley, Frederick Temple, Aubrey Moore and John Henry Newman in the UK, and Benjamin Warfield, James Orr and Asa Gray in the USA, welcomed Darwin's ideas. In fact, Darwin himself, and also his keenest advocate Thomas Henry Huxley, both left room for God in their assessment of the origin of the world.

Current church leaders have a similar approach. Rowan Williams, the Archbishop of Canterbury, interviewed by the *Guardian* in March 2006 about teaching creationism in schools, said:

> I think creationism is, in a sense, a kind of category mistake, as if the Bible were a theory like other theories. Whatever the biblical account of creation is, it's not a theory alongside theories. It's not as if the writer of Genesis . . . sat down and said well, how am I going to explain all this . . . 'In the beginning God created the heavens and the earth . . .'[7]

## Reason, revelation and truth

### The nature of the biblical texts

R. E. Clements makes an important point when he states that it is 'no longer sufficient for us to view the biblical writings as expressive of single interpretations, which may then subsequently have been added to. Already a complex history of meaning lies contained in the traditions which underlie the text of scripture.'[8] For example, the Matthean understanding of Isaiah 7.14 (Matt. 1.23) or Paul's use of the promise to Abram (Gen. 12.1–3; 15.1–6), in his account of justification by faith (Rom. 4; Gal. 3), indicate that we do not have monochrome readings of Scripture: the texts are subjected to a continuous process of interpretation and re-interpretation.[9]

We must enter into the Jewish and Christian communities of faith who are concerned with the Scriptures as theology – the word and revelation of God. It is important that we understand both the New and Old Testament Scriptures in the context of the communities of faith that wrote them down and preserved them. The Old Testament does not present faith in the form of a creed or of theological treatises, but rather is a collection of ancient literature and history, written in a variety of forms and for a variety of purposes. The Scriptures do not set out to prove the existence of God, but rather are records of the experience that people had of the reality of God in their lives.

A number of dimensions to faith in the Old Covenant community have been identified by Clements. There is a literary dimension of faith – we have a collection of writings that function as a religious work when read in a religious context, where the meaning may be grasped and responded to by the faith community.[10]

There is a historical dimension of faith – there is evidence through the various narratives of a growing understanding of the transcendent and universal nature of God, particularly seen in the exilic and post-exilic writings. The theological reflection that God is not confined to Jerusalem and its Temple becomes a vital factor in the faith of an exiled people.

There is also a cultic dimension of faith, expressed in the Old Testament language of 'holiness', 'uncleanness', 'acceptable' and 'unacceptable gifts', but not through images of God. Clements is right to point out that 'the fact that the God of Israel had no image which could be set in a sanctuary and viewed as the representation of his person was clearly one factor of significance here',[11] as it helped Israel to withstand the shock of exile and to develop a more reflective spiritual attitude to worship, which had a knowledge of God beyond the cult.

The intellectual dimension of faith presents a different world-view from ours. It is more ideological and symbolic than our rational thought world. But while a mythological thought world would define the answers that the

Old Testament provides to our questions, an awareness of the personal and moral nature of God has moved biblical thinking away from the magical.

### Interpretation of the Bible

The main approach to Old Testament study has tended to be literary and historical, which is to be expected given that we are dealing with ancient documents, but the danger is that other possible ways of listening to the texts are neglected. There is also a tendency by modern Christians to neglect the Old Testament, which leads to a separation of what is being used within worship, for example the psalms and what is being understood theologically.

The problem of the historical approach is that it tends to place historicity at the top of the agenda, with the result that a negative evaluation of the historicity, of for example the patriarchal narratives, implies a negative response to the important theological views that are being expressed. We should take careful note of the ways in which the New Testament interprets and uses the Old Testament, for example the reworking and reinterpreting of the prophetic literature within the New Testament community of faith.

While it is ancient literature, it is also human literature, preserved and interpreted by people like us. As Clements helpfully reminds us, 'the Old Testament is clearly and unmistakably a product of belief in God's electing will [of Israel]'.[12] We need to understand the ways in which the Jewish interpreters of the Hebrew Bible have carried out their task. For example, a number of methods of understanding and interpreting the Hebrew Scriptures can be recognized, with the last mentioned being considered as the highest level of understanding:

| | |
|---|---|
| *Pshat* | simple meaning of the text |
| *Remez* | a hint, allusion |
| *Darash* | make a homily or sermon |
| *Sod* | symbolic, secret, beyond logic, mystical.[13] |

### The framing of the creation story

Let's consider the background to the story of creation as we find it in the opening chapters of Genesis. The Jews find themselves in exile in Babylon: 'By the rivers of Babylon we sat and wept when we remembered Zion' (Ps. 137.1). When Israel proclaimed its creation faith, recorded in Genesis 1.1—2.3, she was in the darkest period of her history, in exile in Babylonia. The removal of the leadership of Judah to Babylon at the beginning of the sixth century BCE was a body blow to the nationhood and religious life of Israel. The Exile is a watershed in Israelite history. In the space of 23 years we move from the restored national pride, extended boundaries of the state, and exclusive worship of Yahweh under Josiah (640–609 BCE), to the invasion and conquest of Israel by the Babylonian army under Nebuchadnezzar, and the subsequent destruction of Jerusalem with its Temple in 587 BCE, and the deportations to Babylon in 597, 587, and 582 BCE. That this did not mark the end of the story is of itself a surprise, but that this was a time when Israel's faith was reworked and strengthened is truly amazing.

The cream of the nation's political, intellectual and religious leadership had been deported to Babylon. The total for the three deportations amounted to about 4600,[14] but if these were all adult males then the figure was probably nearer 12,000 to 15,000 people, which would have represented something like 5 per cent of the population of Judah. But these, suggests Bright, would shape Israel's future, 'both giving to her faith its new direction and providing the impulse for the ultimate restoration of the Jewish community in Palestine'.[15]

Rex Mason helpfully presents the major question for the exilic community as: 'Since Yahwism before the exile had been so much the official religion of the Davidic nation state, how was it to be defined and understood now?'[16] They were stateless, the covenants with Abraham and David appeared to be in tatters and, even more fundamental, Yahweh had deserted them. But it was her faith in Yahweh that had called Israel into being. Could this faith prevent her total annihilation, even now? This was a theological emergency, the cult had been dealt a mortal blow. The status of Israel's God is thrown into question, for in a time when it was believed that each nation had a god, Israel's God had apparently fallen to the power of the gods of Babylonia. There would probably have been a wholesale loss of faith on the part of the people: a theological explanation was urgently required.

In his book *Hopeful Imagination*, Walter Brueggemann[17] presents a view of the pivotal nature of the exile: it is the end of the known world and marks its 'relinquishment', and the 'reception' of a new world given by God through his prophets Jeremiah, Ezekiel and Deutero-Isaiah. Israel must let go of the old world of king and Temple, which God has removed, and look for the new world that he is preparing for them.[18] Bright suggests that their community was based on Sabbath observance, a test of their obedience to the covenant,[19] and a sign instituted with creation.[20]

We now begin to see the context for the creation story of Genesis 1. It forms the opening pages of Israel's redefinition of her faith in Yahweh, when all seemed to be lost. As such it is a brave affirmation in the face of a great weight of contrary evidence. Their account of creation, in which God is the one and only creator of all that exists, presents a polemic against the Egyptian, Canaanite and, especially, Babylonian accounts of creation.

So we can let the Jews in Babylon tell the story of creation.[21]

The people of Israel had been in exile in Babylonia for a number of years, and their situation was depressing in every way. They were aliens in a foreign land, with a different culture, different religion, and different climate and environment from their own. On top of this they were prisoners with an existence that was not far from slavery. The understanding of their captors was that the gods of Babylon were victorious over the God of Israel, and they were often tempted into believing this version of the truth. One community was living in mud-brick houses alongside the irrigation channel, called the River Chebar, in an inhospitable climate and land. They had been granted permission by their overlords to establish their homes, and they had sought to bring a degree of order and meaning to their existence. The local inhabitants made fun of their plight and derided their religion. Spiritually they were depressed. Their Temple in Jerusalem, the place where they had believed that God dwelt in a special way, was over a thousand kilometres away, and worse still, it was in ruins. Their view was that they were far away from God, and that their very condition demonstrated God's impotence. Ezekiel and Isaiah of Babylon declared that God was not confined to the land of Israel and the Temple in Jerusalem, but was with them in Babylon, and God was ready to forgive them and bring about a new Exodus.

It is in this context that the writers of Genesis 1 began to reflect upon the faith of Israel. This priestly writer, or group of writers, reflected upon the traditions of their faith, the writings that the religious community had preserved and brought with them into exile, and upon the history of God's dealings with the people; they thought about the story of God's relationship with them over the years, from the Patriarchs to Egypt, from the Exodus to David, and from Solomon's Temple to the Exile. To this they added their experience of the world, and the religious views held by their Babylonian captors. The writers took all these experiences, and, through their faith in Yahweh, a newly edited version of the Scriptures took shape. The very first belief that they wanted to express was that the covenant God of Israel was the God of all creation. Out of their experience they opened their major work with what we now know as Genesis 1:

> In the beginning God created the heavens and the earth . . . And God said . . . And God said . . . God saw all that he had made, and it was very good.

Throughout Genesis 1—11 creation is linked with the history of Israel as God's chosen people, beginning with Abraham; the God of the covenant, the sustainer and redeemer of Israel is the creator of the universe.

Although there are certainly points of contact between Genesis 1—11 and the Babylonian creation epic, there is a profound difference between the struggles of Marduk with Tiamat and the Genesis 1 narrative. It may not be fair to try to make comparisons as we would not be comparing like with like. Gordon Wenham notes, for example, that *Enuma elish* is concerned to glorify the god Marduk; the creative acts simply illustrating his power.[22] The Priestly writers were also probably familiar with the Egyptian accounts of creation, but the significance of Genesis 1 is the way in which they use other accounts; and it is illuminating to see how these other accounts of creation were modified.

Thus Claus Westermann[23] states that while the Priestly writer (P) follows the example of presenting creation in a succession of generations – important in Egyptian, Sumerian and Babylonian accounts – P has no genealogy of the gods. P rejects the struggle motif and the births of the gods, and instead presents creation as God's act of making, and as the decree of God's word; these writers are monotheists. Wenham[24] concludes from this that Genesis 1 is a deliberate statement of the Hebrew view of creation over against rival views, and that it is a 'polemical repudiation of such myths'. Rival cosmologies are attacked in a number of areas: God created all that is out of nothing,[25] in contrast to the idea of matter existing eternally alongside the gods; the dragons that rival the gods in Canaanite mythology are now seen to be merely the creation of God;[26] the struggle of the gods to divide the waters is replaced by a simple divine decree;[27] the Genesis account avoids naming the Sun, Moon and stars, which were part of Babylonian astrology. The heavenly bodies are created by God, they are not objects of worship, as they were in other Near Eastern cultures. The Sun and Moon are for signs and seasons. Mason helpfully suggests that as with the signs of Sabbath, in Genesis 2, and rainbow, in Genesis 9, these can also be seen as signs of God's relationship, his covenant, with Israel and with all creation.[28] Throughout all this God simply creates, rather than employing mysterious incantations.

In addition there is the place of human beings; in Babylonian tradition they were an afterthought – they have a walk-on part as servants of the gods – but in Genesis they are seen as the climax of creation. This and the other features mentioned above represent a deliberate rejection of other cosmologies. Their faith is strengthened by these reflections.

The stories from the past reminded those in exile of what God had done in the nation's history, that even in times of suffering and rebellion God had not deserted them. The God of salvation was the God of creation, and was also the God of new beginnings. It is to this hope that the prophets look. In their redefinition of the faith they have recognized that Yahweh is not confined to Israel: the creator God of Israel's covenant is the God of the universe and the nations. Thus Deutero-Isaiah speaks about God guiding the course of history.[29]

After the death of Nebuchadnezzar in 562 BCE life became more unsettled in Babylonia, and was probably more difficult for the exiles as well. After a number of brief reigns, Nabonidus came to the throne in 556 BCE. He neglected both the worship of Marduk and also the city of Babylon that housed Marduk's temple, leaving his son Belshazzar as his representative in the capital. He was overthrown in a bloodless invasion in 539 BCE by Cyrus of Persia. Cyrus allowed freedom of worship for all the peoples of his empire, and he encouraged displaced people groups to return home. With the rise of Cyrus events took on more global proportions and might be seen as being beyond little nations with their own deities. Israel's faith would need to be of universal proportions if it was to make sense of the events of history.

Deutero-Isaiah speaks into this situation[30] and looks towards a new exodus.[31] Yahweh, not Marduk, is the creator of the universe[32] and Yahweh is sovereign Lord of history[33] and Cyrus is Yahweh's instrument in history. Yahweh is the redeeming God of Israel, who can be trusted.[34] This message of salvation applies not only to the exiles,[35] but also to all the nations,[36] to the ends of the earth,[37] the beasts,[38] heaven, earth, mountains and trees.[39] God is creator and Lord of history;[40] God is doing a new thing;[41] God is proclaiming a new covenant, like that with Noah,[42] like that with David,[43] and redemption through a new exodus.[44] There is, as in the Priestly writers' work, a polemic against the foreign nations and their gods,[45] and the ever-present connection between God's word and events. God predicts the fall of Babylon,[46] which demonstrates Yahweh's superiority over the Babylonian god Marduk.

It is here in the Exile that the Jewish faith develops its fullest expression of the uniqueness of God. Clements points to the prohibition of images as the feature that most clearly expresses their monotheism.[47] An image could be thought to convey a degree of access and therefore control over a god. Yahweh is seen to possess freedom and transcendence that would be compromised by such an image. It is interesting to note that in Daniel 3 (set in this historical context), when the three Jewish exiles refuse to bow down to the golden image built by Nebuchadnezzar and in consequence find themselves placed in the 'fiery furnace', they sing a psalm in praise of the God of creation.[48]

### Redefining Israel's faith

A creation story presupposes that time began at some point in the past and has continued up until the present. The creation story in Genesis shows the connection between the beginning and what follows. The story gives structure to time. It is precisely by the way in which the story creates a context and makes a connection between events from beginning to end that events take on meaning, says Ellen van Wolde.[49] She is right to conclude that such stories form part of reality, for

> with images expressed in language, and with words which sometimes stand at the very edge of what can still be said or understood, people try to understand something of another reality. For them it is a matter not just of belief, but also of a kind of sense of life.[50]

The first 11 chapters of Genesis tell the story of the primal history of the world. It begins with creation, in primordial time and space. After this the universal history becomes focused into the history of God's chosen people, through Abraham and his descendants.

Stanley Jaki believes that Genesis 1 is conspicuously void of mythical elements:

> the unusually systematic character of Genesis 1 should suggest that it contains a literary device to make very explicit the message about the total dependence of all on God. Written as Genesis 1 was in such a way as to instruct and enlighten the uneducated, that device had to be such as to be instinctively grasped by them.[51]

The Priestly (P) and the Yahwist (J) documents, parts of which make up Genesis 1.1—2.3 (P) and 2.4—3.24 (J), are expressing a faith in God's acts of salvation that come through God's election, or God's free choice to relate Godself to people. The faith that is central to these passages is a faith in the God who made a covenant with Abraham, though this God is of course the creator of the world. G. von Rad[52] says that Israel looked back in faith from her own election, to the creation of the world, and Westermann[53] sees creation faith as the spiritual high point of Israel's understanding of her calling. But Brevard Childs finds that Genesis depicts a wider relationship that God establishes with creatures; he believes that von Rad's subordination of universal history to the particular salvation history of Israel runs into serious literary and theological problems, and concludes that 'the canonical role of Genesis 1—11 testifies to the priority of creation. The divine relation to the world stems from God's initial creative purpose for the universe, not for Israel alone.'[54]

Nevertheless, von Rad's conclusion that the Genesis account is not myth or saga but priestly doctrine is attractive. It is ancient, sacred knowledge, which has been preserved and reformed, expanded and reflected upon with the experiences of faith. It is both cosmological and theological knowledge; it is theological reflection upon what faith is able to declare objectively. Von Rad is right to note that it is only in Genesis 1 that we find direct theological statements about creation; he describes this as moving in the realm of 'theological definitions'.[55] It is a profound passage on beginnings and identity, and as such compares with the opening verses of the Gospels of Mark (1.1) and John (1.1–5).

We can therefore maintain that Genesis 1 presents us with an account of creation which is not only of theological importance, but which is also perceptive of the observable world in which it was written. It would seem to make sense that if the world, at least in part, reveals the nature of God, then a biblical account of creation, inspired by God, would not only tell us about theological truths but also something of the observable world.

Genesis 1 is the dramatic opening chapter to both the Jewish and Christian Scriptures. It introduces the creator and the creatures, and sets the scene for the relationship of human beings and God. Genesis 1 is unique, but may still be compared with other passages that reflect the mystery of God's creativity, such as Psalms 8 and 148 or Job 38. It goes beyond these passages in the scope and comprehensiveness of its vision, says Wenham,[56] and in its present form it is a careful literary composition that introduces the narratives that follow. The writer does not primarily attempt or want to explain creation; rather he desires to evoke a wonder in creation that will lead to worship, a proper relation between human beings and their creator.

It is possible to see Genesis 1 as an exilic/post-exilic dynamic world-view, which reveals all that the Creator wishes us to know. It should not be dragged out in support of fundamentalist arguments nor should there be a constant seeking to show how each new scientific discovery supports or denies its truth. It is not that form of literature. Jaki concludes:

> Although that majestic chapter could have lost its credibility through the endless series of interpretations given to it as age followed age, it has retained a unique appeal through the ages in proof of its intrinsic soundness. This alone should commend its superhuman quality and origin.[57]

We have discovered, as Brueggemann declares, that creation is not careless, casual nor accidental, it is God's intention (see Eph. 1.9–10) that creation embodies an obedient unity. God creates by speaking in ways that finally will be heard. 'His word has the authority of suffering compassion.' We see in the early chapters the troubled relation of creator/creation and God's enduring resolve to have creation on God's own terms. As we move into the history of the special people of Israel, 'still to be settled is the way in which the world will come to terms with the purposes of God, willingly assenting to be God's good creation'. Because this remains unresolved and the relationship unsettled, the message is one of promise.[58]

## Myths

At this point we might pause and reflect on the exilic faith we have been discussing. We have recognized that the Genesis account of creation plays an important part in the redefinition of the faith of Israel, as she comes to terms with defeat, destruction, deportation and exile. This owes much to the influence of the creation myths of the ancient Near East, which leads us to ask at this point, what sort of account of creation is Genesis 1? If Genesis 1 is not to be taken literally, does it therefore fall into the realm of myths and legends? Ancient stories about creation were all channels of meaning, to help societies cope with their experiences of the world in which they were born, lived and died. They were not essentially accounts of the observable 'scientific' features of the earth and sky, but rather they were vehicles of the hopes, aspirations and even fears of people. Cosmologist John Barrow comments:

> The primitive belief in order and in the sequence of cause and effect displayed by myths is consistent with the belief that it is necessary to have some reason for the existence of everything – a reason that pays due respect for the natural forces that hold life and death in their hands.[59]

Van Wolde makes a similar point at the beginning of her exploration of creation stories:

> Without a story about the beginning, human beings face chaos, and their origin seems to be an abyss. In order to provide a foundation or existence, the beginning was filled with meaning. Moreover, every culture attaches a meaning to the beginning, often in the form of stories. These are not stories in the sense of tales, but realities in which people live. These are stories which give people roots.[60]

Such stories, unlike science, are not necessarily factual, but rather, and more importantly, give meaning to the facts. Barrow points out that whereas the world of experience and observation is bewilderingly plural and complex, most myths represent a primitive and simple causation for the world. They portray the victory of light over dark, the cracking of some cosmic egg, the story of two world parents, or the defeat of monsters by gods.

If Genesis 1 falls into this category then a final reflection on the function of myths from Bruce Masse et al. may prove helpful. Myths are semi-historical stories believed to be true by the cultures in which they are told – they combine realism with supernatural mythic elements. They are to be considered as truthful – they are accounts of

> major events that typically happened in the remote past of that culture, when the world was different to today . . . The concepts of world view and science are intimately related, and it may be said that myth is the science of cultures which do not verify 'truth' about nature by experiment.[61]

Mythology provides information about past events that can be remembered in a non-literate culture. One instructive example comes from the tribes of the Andaman Islands, who survived the tsunami of 26 December 2004. They had a myth about a 'wave that eats people' brought about by the angry spirits of their ancestors. To avoid its clutches they had to run for high ground if the sea suddenly receded.[62]

The world in which the Bible took shape was full of stories about creation. One of the first questions that even the most primitive society probably would ask is 'How did this world come about?' It is probable that all people groups question the origin and meaning of life, and we find that many of them have developed their own stories of creation. For example, according to a Chinese account of creation there was a huge egg called Chaos.[63] Inside the egg there slept a god called Pan Ku, who held a hammer in his right hand and a chisel in his left (the first geologist no doubt!). Pan Ku lived for 18,000 years and grew 9 kilometres in height each day (60 million kilometres in total). Then he died – a very tall person! After his death, his body formed the earth, his head the mountains, his breath the winds, his voice the thunder, his bones the rocks, his teeth the precious stones, his blood the seas, his hair the trees, his sweat the rain, and the insects on his body were human beings. At this point the emperor of the world sent time and light into being. He achieved this by standing on the highest mountain with the sun in his left hand and the moon in his right.

Another early tradition on origins arose in India around 2000 BCE and was codified in the Rig Veda (*c.* 1200 BCE). According to this tradition, in the beginning there was the One, who breathed by its own energy. Then desire entered the One and Thought was created. From that came light, and then all the rest. According to the Greek writer Hesiod (*c.* 750 BCE), the beginning of the world is chaos, together with the divine beings of Gaia, Tartarus and Eros. Next is the birth of the Titans, followed by various disputes and the birth of the gods. The twelve major gods make their home on Mount Olympus, from where this pantheon rules the world.

Geologist Cesare Emiliani comments on Genesis 1 that 'as one can see, the Jews make the world very simply, in six days and in (almost) logical order. The story makes rather good sense.'[64] But then goes on to reflect upon the Greek creation story that 'one must admit that this story is much more interesting than that chronicled in the Bible. At the end of creation, the Jews still had the same old god, but the Greeks had 12 major gods to choose from, plus a vast number of minor ones'.[65] We might consider the apostle Paul's reflection upon this in his meeting with the philosophers at Athens, recorded in Acts 17. He questions whether they think that the creator of the universe lives in a temple built by human beings? Whether they think that God needs their gifts of money and food to sustain God's life, because God created everything and gave life to every living thing. Paul quotes their own Greek poets, who knew this truth: 'in him we move and have our being' and 'we are his offspring'. If they are God's creation, it is a waste of their time to make gods of silver, gold, wood or stone to worship. How ignorant can you be, says Paul.

## The biblical material

### The Near Eastern background

We find that the Genesis accounts of creation, and the other passages in the Old Testament that are concerned with creation, are not unique. There are many accounts of creation from other peoples, but in particular parallels are found with stories of creation and flood in Babylonian, Canaanite and Egyptian mythology. Recognition of such parallels might lead us to ask whether Genesis presents us with a similar picture of creation or whether it represents something different. I maintain that the Bible presents us with accounts of creation which are both of theological importance and are perceptive of the observable world in which they are written. But first we will need to consider their relationships with creation stories preserved by Israel's neighbours.[66]

There is clearly a common stock of mythical material in the ancient Near East, although known in different forms. John Bright rightly points out that it is logical to assume that the traditions which lie behind the creation narratives in Genesis were brought from Mesopotamia by migrating groups in the first half of the second millennium. He supports this with the evidence that a fragment of *The Epic of Gilgamesh* was found in fourteenth-century Megiddo.[67] We can also see that the stories of the Garden of Eden (Gen. 2—3) and Tower of Babel (Gen. 11) have a clear Mesopotamian background. Wenham suggests that Genesis 1—11 comes from a different pre-literary tradition than the patriarchal narratives of Genesis 12—50. The early chapters use and modify stories well diffused throughout the ancient world (Sumerian flood story and Babylonian parallels with the flood story), whereas the patriarchal stories with their focus on the origins of the nations were probably passed down through the Israelite tribes.[68]

Genesis shares much of the thinking of the ancient world of the Near East but presents an alternative world-view, challenging assumptions about the nature of God, the world and humankind. As we noted earlier, Genesis appears to be a polemic against many of the perceived notions of the gods and the world, and as such does have much in common with ancient thought. While there are aspects in common with, for example, *The Epic of Atrahasis* and *The Epic of Gilgamesh*, the writers of the opening chapters of Genesis need not have read these, as they would have been part of the philosophical culture of their world. There is common agreement that there is an invisible supernatural world, that god(s) were personal and could communicate, that human beings are both physical and spiritual, and are in the image of God. Yet, the polemical thrust is clear throughout the creation narratives and beyond, for example, in the accounts of creation, human beings have a central place, rather than being an afterthought – created to supply the gods with food; the flood is the result of sin and not of noisy human neighbours leading the gods to send a flood; Babel is not the centre of Babylonian civilization and the gate to heaven, it is folly. As Wenham concludes, the originality of the writers' message was in affirming the unity of God in the face of polytheism, God's justice rather than God's caprice, God's power as opposed to God's impotence, God's concern for human beings rather than God's exploitation. Whereas Mesopotamia clung to the wisdom of primeval human beings, Genesis records their sinful disobedience, all of which, for the biblical authors, are the central themes.[69]

We know that Israel was influenced by the pagan religions of the nations around them. We can take examples from Josiah's clean-up operation as recorded in 2 Kings 23.1–25. The Canaanite fertility cults of Baal and Ashtarte, the astral cults of Assyria and Babylon, worship of the sun, moon and stars of heaven, were all in evidence. These all involved a cost of allegiance, but none more extreme than the sacrifice of children to Molech. As the period of settlement in Canaan wore on, the cult of Yahweh had become one among many, and not always the principal one. This helps us to understand the ways in which the biblical writers deal with questions of creation and origins.

### Old Testament understanding of the creator and creation

The account in Genesis 1, in its historical context, is unique. God, earth and sky are put in relationship; God created sky and earth; God faces chaos, speaks, divides, forms, orders, distributes, populates, blesses and verifies that it is good. As Pedro Trigo concludes, 'only God and creation, God and the divine deed exist'.[70] This leads David Atkinson to state: 'one can imagine what a rock of stability this chapter would have provided for the people of God when faced with the lure of pagan myths around them'.[71] This would certainly apply to Jewish exiles in Babylon, as we discussed earlier.

This concept of God, from the beginning, is opposed to the myths of the surrounding peoples. The Old Testament shows unmistakable knowledge of the story of conflict between God and the dark waters of chaos, together with the monsters that live within it; some speak of unruly waters threatening to bring chaos;[72] and others speak of monsters emerging from the depths to challenge God's power.[73]

In Genesis 1—3 we find God to be the author of the whole world. The creation of human beings may be seen as the focal point of Genesis 1, but not its conclusion, for, of all the days of creation, it is the day that God ceased to work that is blessed and sanctified.

In the polemic against the myths and religious concepts of the ancient Near East we see that God created the whole universe out of nothing – a rejection of matter pre-existing the gods; the sea monsters and the astral bodies are created – they are not rival deities; human beings are not servants of the gods – they are God's representatives on earth; and finally the seventh day is not a day of ill omen – it is a day of blessing and sanctification. Wenham recognizes four features that can be emphasized: (a) God is without peer or competitor; (b) God is more than creator, God is law-giver – light and dark, land and sea, night and day; (c) the world reflects its creator – the perfection of God's will; (d) we see the true nature of human beings – in the image of God, in relationship with God, and able to subdue the earth.[74]

When we consider the biblical accounts, we recognize clear differences. These are first and foremost in the view of God, for whereas Israel's covenant-God makes God known in personal and moral action, and can therefore be experienced as spiritual personality independent of nature, the Babylonian and Canaanite conceptions of God remain rooted in nature myths where natural forces are personified, the gods emerging along with the rest of matter. Events are cyclical, with the stars determining events. Although Israel shared a cyclical pattern with regard to seasons, New Year and enthronement, she also conceived a purposeful process in time, with creation as the beginning of her purposeful history. The Old Testament, like the New Testament, presents us with the freedom and sovereignty of God with regard to the world, but at the same time the intimate connection between the world and God.

Unlike the gods of other ancient Near Eastern stories, Yahweh is not identified with nature; Yahweh is above it and beyond it, yet at the same time is directly involved in the work of creation.[75] Westermann states that the link with existing traditions is important, unless the Yahwist (J) and Priestly (P) writers simply wished to state that Israel's saviour was the creator of the world. The creation stories look back to the tradition that is received and forward to the history of Israel as the people of God. The primeval story links Israel with the history of the nations. In the transition from Genesis 11 to 12 we see that the primeval story is the prologue to the history of God acting with Israel.[76] The stories as told by J and P are adapted to convey what they wanted to communicate to the people of their time. The primeval story is linked to the nation's history, which frees creation from the realm of myth and gives it the resemblance of history. This is made clear in Deutero-Isaiah and Job 38—41, where in distress or despair the people look to the creator, and in their creator find the God who saves.

In similar vein, Weiser says that the psalms go back to an early date in Israel's history and were a part of the celebration of the covenant. Whereas the other Near Eastern religions performed a myth that was the destiny of the god, 'the heart of the Old Testament hymn is the self-revelation of Yahweh in his theophany'.[77] For the people of Israel, unlike their neighbours, the hymns of praise are a part of their salvation history, which was their living experience. The praise of Yahweh as creator is related to the people's experience of God's saving deeds. Creation as the work of the creator was seen through their experience of the covenant: the God of

Abraham, Isaac and Jacob was also the creator of heaven and earth. The theme of creation is tied up with salvation history; Yahweh is Lord of history. Borrowing from the creation myths of other religions links nature with history, demythologized or historicized and used in a metaphorical sense depicting Yahweh's victory over the powers of chaos. Day warns that while the images of the myths were demythologized and historicized for some, those who practised a syncretistic form of Yahwism, equating Yahweh with Ba'al[78] and worshipping the host of heaven,[79] would have seen the divine conflict with the dragon and the sea as living. For the others, Israelite monotheism would have transformed the myth out of all recognition.[80]

The important question that will underlie our reflection is: what sort of God do we believe in? There are a variety of myths in ancient cultures, some of which are nature-denying and some of which emphasize its importance in the scheme of things. When we look at the Genesis accounts of creation we need to recognize the land in which Israel grew, where there was a need of constant toil in the digging of irrigation ditches, planting vineyards, and rotating crops and pasture, to keep the wilderness or chaos in check. Israel grew up among peoples who saw the divine revealed in nature, in the rhythms of the natural world, especially fertility and sexuality. Any trust placed in the Canaanite gods by the Israelites was attacked by the prophets of Yahweh. Israel's God was revealed in concrete historic events, the God who liberates, the God of the exodus, though also the faithful God of the seasons. Through liberation they were brought to a land of promise, where they celebrated the covenant and the Passover. They assumed the reality and activity of God, who had revealed God to Abraham and Moses, and who is the Lord and sole creator of the universe.

Yahweh is Israel's God and is not identified with the gods of other nations. Yahweh is superior to the gods of Egypt,[81] and, in exile, over those of Babylon.[82] There is a strong polemic against the Astral religion of other nations. Trigo helpfully draws attention to the central position of the disproportionately long section in Genesis 1 dealing with the sun, moon and stars, those regulators of time.[83] This may indicate the tremendous force of the belief to which the Genesis account is opposed, and the danger these astral religious beliefs posed to the faith of Israel. There was a malign influence in worshipping the astral powers which influenced all of life. An agricultural people depended, after all, on the cycles of Sun, Moon and seasons, which coincided with the appearance and disappearance of stars. Israel herself saw the Sun, Moon and stars for 'signs and seasons' for the great festivals in her calendar, when God graciously met with the people to renew them. But Trigo is correct in emphasizing that

> the text of Genesis demythologizes everything it possibly can. First it detaches the heavenly bodies from light, relegating them to a more modest, derived function. Second it omits their names, referring to them generic-

ally as luminaries. Third, it deprives them of any influence on human destiny. Their role is to light the earth and distinguish day from night.[84]

It is God who made them, yet the feature that expresses the uniqueness of Yahweh most clearly is the prohibition of images. An image could be thought to convey a degree of access and therefore control over the god. Yahweh is seen to possess freedom and transcendence that would be compromised by such an image. It is in the exilic age that the sharpest polemic against images is found, in which the reasons become theological – Isaiah 40.18–20 and 44.9–20. You cannot make a god; God is the creator of all things.

We have recognized the development of the biblical accounts of, and reflections upon, creation in the context of the mythical stories of origins found in the ancient Near East. We have noted the purpose of those myths in establishing order, stability, worship and monarchy for Israel's neighbours. However, it has become increasingly clear that Israel's own stories of creation are polemical, and have a propaganda role in establishing Yahweh as the one true God of world history and world creation. In demythologizing the stories of their neighbours, Israel historicized creation and linked it with their tradition, their development as the people of God, from Abraham onwards.

### The developing pictures of God in the Old Testament

'Our faith is a present experience; but it has biblical roots,' says Pedro Trigo[85] as he begins a dialogue with Genesis 1, which he rightly states 'was composed at a moment of great need, and of national prostration and disenchantment. It represents the victory of a robust faith then – one which could communicate serenity and hope.' But it is also important for our own understanding of faith that we consider creation, for, as Brueggemann says, 'It is the same God who calls the world and who calls the special community (church). Both creations, world and community of faith, spring "fresh from the word"; both have been evoked by the speech of this God.'[86] Genesis has this same interest, shown in the broad division: 1—11 the world; 12—50 a special people. The twin focus is the call and promise of God.

We have already noted that the biblical accounts of creation belong in the context of the mythical stories of beginnings found in other ancient Near Eastern religions. A myth's function is to give justification to that which is essential for human life and society. In an examination of the Ugaritic stories and of *Enuma elish* we recognize that the primary function of the myth is to maintain the stability of the present state; this is a common feature of the circle of stories about creation or beginnings of the world and of human beings. Such stories are not intellectual enquiries into the origin of the universe, but rather seek to answer the question of existence itself.

Some ancient myths have a creation without divinity, others, like those of the ancient Near East, have a creator god. When Israel spoke of God as creator they shared this belief in common with their neighbours. But the difference comes in the uniqueness of Israel's creator God, and in God's covenantal relationship with creation. The Flood is a story of salvation which presumes the punishment of humanity by means of a flood. The discovery of the Gilgamesh epic shows that the biblical story stands in a well-established tradition, which predates it by a thousand years or more. The presupposition in the flood stories is that the creator god(s) can also make the decision to destroy. This leads Westermann to comment:

> the complementarity and almost equal distribution in cultures of creation and flood stories means that human consciousness of its own and of the world's state goes hand in hand with a consciousness that there may be a total destruction which transcends both the death of the individual and the annihilation of the cosmos.[87]

The salvation by God and the subsequent covenant with Noah and the whole of creation, which is grounded in the flood story, becomes an important event for the Old Testament religious community.

The creation stories in Genesis 1—3 look back to the tradition that is received and forward to the history of Israel as the people of God. The primeval story links Israel with the history of the nations. In the transition from Genesis 11 to 12, we see that the primeval story is the prologue to the history of God acting with Israel.

Brueggemann notes that there are three ways in which human and non-human creation are treated: undifferentiated, both the same before God, as in Genesis 9.9–10; human beings superior to non-human creation, as in Genesis 1.25–30 and 2.15; and anthropocentric, totally human-centred with no mention of non-human creation, as in Genesis 11.1–9. He maintains:

> The theologians who work in a distinctively Israelite way in Gen. 1—11 want to affirm at the same time (a) that the ultimate meaning of creation is to be found in the heart and purpose of the creator (cf. 6.5–7; 8.21) and (b) that the world has been positively valued by God for itself. It must (therefore) be valued by the creatures to whom it has been provisionally entrusted (1.31).[88]

We can describe this view of creation as covenantal and affirm that the creator has a purpose and a will for creation, which includes freedom and love; and that creation has freedom to respond to the creator in various ways, which we find to include a mixture of faithful obedience and rebellious self-assertion. These points will become important as we speak about both the environment in Chapter 6 and suffering in Chapter 7.

We see in the early chapters the troubled relation of creator with creation and God's enduring resolve to have creation in God's purposes. Yet even when we move into the history of the special people of Israel, this remains unresolved and the relationship unsettled, and so the message is one of promise.

Job 38—41 presents an insight into the Wisdom writers' understanding of the creator and of creation. From the beginning God creates the sky, sea, light and darkness, the stars and the weather. Job is invited to marvel at the wonder, pattern and purpose of creation. All life has its place in God's ordering and care. Job must find himself within the whole of creation.[89] Human beings belong, enjoying the creator's handiwork. Divine wisdom is greater than human understanding, and at the end Job realizes his lack of understanding and has nothing left to say. Atkinson concludes that there is a difference between the God of the philosophers and the God who makes himself known. Job's friends' understanding of God was a belief in the workings of natural causes, the logic of reward and punishment, a sterile faith in a God who was far removed, El Shaddai, rather than Yahweh of the covenant. God is known as revealed through Jesus Christ, who is the covenant God of creation, Abraham, Isaac, Jacob, Moses, and of the New Covenant in Christ.[90] He maintains that wisdom, power and justice describe the God in whose hands all the mystery of this world is held, including suffering. This God is not merely the end of a philosophical or logical argument – God's ways and thoughts are higher than ours (Isa. 55.9). Atkinson rightly notes that we live in a culture that needs rational answers and in a church culture that wants certainties. 'The book of Job, instead, brings us face to face with the living God, and invites us to live in his light with all our logical gaps, untidy edges and struggling faith.'[91]

### New Testament perspectives on creation and the creator

The Jews of the New Testament period shared the beliefs in creation that we have been discussing so far in this chapter. The passages that speak of creation assume such faith; there is no sense in which the existence of God as creator has to be proved, that part of the creed is taken as read. Thus we see in the great chapter about faith in the Epistle to the Hebrews (11.1–3), the writer begins with their faith in the universe created at God's command. We see, for example, in Jesus' parables an understanding of the ordering of creation, of the seasons and of plant growth. The apostle Paul demonstrates the same understanding when he compares the growth of the Church with the growth of plants in 1 Corinthians 3.5–7. In debate with the educated elite of Athens, recorded in Acts 17.24f., and in his letter to the church at Rome (Romans 1.20), Paul points to nature as a witness to the creator God.

**Luke 12.13–21.** Following on from our observations on God's words for Job, the man in Luke's story was a fool because he mixed up working for a living with the meaning of life and creation. There is a need to recognize that the land is God's. Margot Käßmann says that it is

> when a person or a people starts to forget these connections between justice and ecology, the consequences can be tragic. Many rich people, like Luke's successful farmer, begin to lose their sense of reality. For Luke sin is related to exalting oneself; and salvation is not so much moral improvement as the liberating insight that it is God's grace and being part of the community that will save us.[92]

We can apply this parable to starvation in one part of the world, while in another they are destroying food mountains or embarking on obesity-busting diets. We recognize a clear understanding of the stewardship of creation by human beings, who demonstrate the nature of the creator God. We will consider these issues when we look at genetic engineering in Chapter 5 and the environment in Chapter 6.

**John 1.1–3.** John, like the Old Testament writers, contextualizes his message into a community where there were Greek and Jewish influences and, in similar fashion, proclaims about creation from his community's experience of God, in Christ. He thus interprets the creation of the universe by the Word of God.

Gordon Kaufman presents his own interpretation of John 1.1–2 as 'In the beginning was creativity, and the creativity was with God and the creativity was God.'[93] His view of God as 'creativity itself' demonstrated throughout the cosmos is attractive. Such a God is always creative and is 'the ultimate source and ground of all our human realities, values and meanings . . .'[94]

Renthy Keitzar recognizes both an evangelistic thrust – Jesus the same as the creator, who gives eternal life to believers, we become restored, a new creation – and an ecological relevance – the world is created by God and is subject to the control of Jesus.[95] God sends his son to the world because he loves it (John 3.16).

It is possible for us to understand that in the incarnation God expresses the truth and nature of the creator and God's desires for creation.

**Romans 8.18–23 and Colossians 1.15–20.** In Christ there is a new creation, but as ever in the New Testament, there is a now but not yet aspect. There are the first fruits of the Spirit, but still creation groans as it waits for God's human creatures to reach their perfect humanity. To believe in Christ in this world is to believe against reality – Christ is risen, but we live in a world of suffering, pain and destruction. It is hope, because now we see salvation for all creation only appearing in outline. But this cannot be a hope with no implications, human beings must act in hope: the Spirit gives us the possibility to be what we are to become – the children of God.

This same theme is in focus in Colossians 1.15–20. Note verses 19–20:

> For God was pleased to have all his fullness dwell in him, and through him to reconcile to himself all things, whether things on earth or things in heaven, by making peace through his blood, shed on the cross.

The whole of creation is brought back into relationship with God through the cross. This takes place as human beings find their restored relationship with the Creator, through the cross. God is deeply and passionately involved in his world; God is no absentee landlord, but indwelling, accompanying, incarnate and present as Holy Spirit. There are important implications for the relationship of human beings both to the Creator and to his creation, and we will address these issues more carefully in Chapter 6.

## Conclusion

The comprehensive statements about creation belong to later texts: Deutero-Isaiah, the Priestly writers and some psalms, which are difficult to date. This does not mean that Israel before the sixth century BCE did not worship God as creator – the environment of Canaan was saturated with creation myths, and pre-exilic psalms, for example Psalms 19 and 104, demonstrate a belief in God as creator. However, it was probably in this later period that Israel was able to fit creation theologically into her tradition, recognizing the theological connection between creation and her salvation history.

While in Deutero-Isaiah creation is subordinate to salvation,[96] each reference to creation reinforces confidence in Yahweh's power and readiness to save. This soteriological understanding of creation is not confined to Deutero-Isaiah; for example Psalm 89, celebrating the covenant with David, also includes a section dealing with creation, seen as God's saving acts (verses 5–18). Von Rad believes that this soteriological understanding of creation lies behind the creation stories of J and P, which in turn move on to Abraham and the covenant. This expansion of the credo broadened its theological basis, but this was only possible because creation was regarded as a saving work of Yahweh.[97] Elsewhere von Rad notes the use of the struggle motif between God and chaos, which parallels the Babylonian mythology. This leads him to suggest that 'it is the poets and prophets who unconcernedly and casually make use of these obviously more popular ideas'.[98] Day would, as we have already noted, suggest that these 'popular ideas' were more likely Canaanite in origin.[99]

When we consider the Wisdom literature we find creation, as God's activity, being presented as a basis for faith, as we recognized in our discussion of Job 38—41 above. But this does not necessarily represent a later aspect of theological reflection, as a similar message can be found in Psalm 19.1–6 and Psalm 104.

Throughout our examination of the biblical material we have noted not only the importance of relationship – God with creation; God with human beings; and human beings with God, with each other, and with creation – but also the culmination of this relationship in worship. The climax of creation is worship (Gen. 2.1–3). It is clear that the days of Genesis 1 are the six days of the week, a theological framework to emphasize the place of the seventh day, the Sabbath, in which the recognition and worship of the creator continues without ceasing, for the seventh day does not come to an end. The climax of the Flood story is also worship (Gen. 8.20–22), and the psalms celebrate creation through worship. As we consider the discoveries of science and the scientific accounts of creation, in the following chapters, we will discover aspects of praise, awe and wonder, as well as the familiar feature of a broken creation, namely human self-centredness. This will lead us forward into renewed discussion of the nature of God's covenant with creation and humanity.

## Key texts

David Atkinson, 1990, *The Message of Genesis 1—11*, Leicester: InterVarsity Press.
Gordon J. Wenham, 1987, *Genesis 1—15*, Waco: Word Books.

## Further reading

M. Kölbl-Ebert (ed.), 2009, *Geology and Religion: A History of Harmony and Hostility*, Geological Society of London, special publication no. 310.
Ernest Lucas, 2005, *Can we believe in Genesis Today?* Leicester: InterVarsity Press.
L. Piccardi and W. B. Masse (eds), 2007, *Myth and Geology*, Geological Society of London, special publication no. 273.
Ellen van Wolde, 1996, *Stories of the Beginning: Genesis 1—11 and Other Creation Stories*, London: SCM Press.
G. von Rad, 1961, *Genesis*, London: SCM Press.
G. von Rad, 1975, *Old Testament Theology, Volume One*, London: SCM Press.
Claus Westermann, 1984, *Genesis 1—11*, London: SPCK.

## Notes

1 A major proportion of this chapter was first produced in my earlier work *Earthshaping Earthkeeping: A Doctrine of Creation*, London: Lynx/SPCK, 1999, chs 1–3.

2 It is helpful to posit the following definitions of creationism and intelligent design. Creationism and creation science propose that the Earth and the universe were created by God in six days about 6000 years ago in accordance with the record in Genesis 1. William A. Dembski, in *The Design Revolution: Answering the Toughest Questions about Intelligent Design* (Downers Grove IL: InterVarsity Press, 2004), states that intelligent design 'starts with the data of nature and from there argues that an intelligent cause is responsible for the specified complexity in nature'. He is concerned that modern theology, mistakenly, has a theodicy and theology of nature that rules out intervention. Intelligent design is defined as design that is due to an actual intelligence, but the attributes of that intelligence are open. Such design is in contrast to Richard Dawkins' view in *The Blind Watchmaker* (London: Longmans, 1986) that biology deals with complicated life forms that have the appearance of purposeful design.

3 John C. Whitcomb and Henry M. Morris, 1960, *The Genesis Flood: The Biblical Record and its Scientific Implications*, Phillipsburg NJ: Presbyterian and Reformed Publishing.

4 R. J. Berry, 1996, *God and the Biologist*, Leicester: InterVarsity Press/Apollos, p. 6.

5 Michael B. Roberts, 'Genesis Chapter 1 and geological time from Hugo Grotius and Marin Mersenne to William Conybeare and Thomas Chalmers (1620–1825)', in L. Piccardi and W. B. Masse (eds), 2007, *Myth and Geology*, Geological Society of London, special publication no. 273, p. 48.

6 Weaver, *Earthshaping Earthkeeping*, ch. 1.

7 BBC, 'Creationism and intelligent design', http://www.bbc.co.uk/religion/religions/christianity/beliefs/creationism_print.html

8 R. E. Clements, 1978, *Old Testament Theology: A Fresh Approach*, London: Marshall, Morgan & Scott, p. 14.

9 Clements, *Old Testament Theology*, p. 12.

10 Clements, *Old Testament Theology*, p. 27.

11 Clements, *Old Testament Theology*, p. 43.

12 Clements, *Old Testament Theology*, p. 190.

13 See further E. Schürer, 1979, *The History of the Jewish People in the Age of Jesus Christ*, Edinburgh: T&T Clark, vol. 2, pp. 314–80.

14 Jeremiah 52.28–30.

15 John Bright, 1972, *History of Israel*, London: SCM Press, p. 345.

16 Rex Mason, 1997, *Propaganda and Subversion in the Old Testament*, London: SPCK, p. 52.

17 Walter Brueggemann, 1992, *Hopeful Imagination: Prophetic Voices in Exile*, London: SCM Press, p. 4.

18 Isaiah 43.18–19.

19 Isaiah 56.1–8; 58.13–14.

20 Genesis 2.2–3; Bright, *A History of Israel*, p. 349.

21 See Weaver, *Earthshaping Earthkeeping*, pp. 4–5.

22 Gordon J. Wenham, 1987, *Genesis 1–15*, Waco: Word Books, p. 8.

23 Claus Westermann, 1984, *Genesis 1–11*, London: SPCK, p. 81.

24 Wenham, *Genesis 1–15*, p. 9.

25 Others have noted that the Hebrew of Genesis 1.1–2 is ambiguous and could be interpreted as meaning that God acted in shaping and ordering a pre-existent

chaos. Yet this would not undermine Wenham's and my own view that Genesis 1 bears witness to the sole, supreme power of the one God, and is thus a rejection of much ancient mythology.

26 Genesis 1.21.

27 Genesis 1.6–10.

28 Mason, *Propaganda and Subversion*, pp. 54–5.

29 See Isaiah 40—45.

30 Isaiah 44.28—45.4.

31 Isaiah 43.14–21.

32 Isaiah 40.28.

33 Isaiah 45.11–13, 18; 48.12–16.

34 Isaiah 40.27–31; 51.1–16.

35 Isaiah 41.16; 51.11; 52.9; 54.1; 55.1.

36 Isaiah 42.11–12.

37 Isaiah 42.10.

38 Isaiah 43.20.

39 Isaiah 44.23; 49.13; 55.12.

40 Isaiah 40.21–28; 44.24–28.

41 Isaiah 43.19.

42 Isaiah 54.9; see also 43.2.

43 Isaiah 55.3b–5.

44 Isaiah 43.14–21.

45 Isaiah 41.1–5, 21–29; 43.8–15; 44.6–20; 45.20–25.

46 Isaiah 46.1–2.

47 Clements, *Old Testament Theology*, p. 75.

48 Daniel 3.59–90, Septuagint reading; see also Psalm 148. When faced with the choice of worshipping the gold image or death by burning, Shadrach, Meshach and Abednego say to Nebuchadnezzar: 'If we are thrown into the blazing furnace, the God we serve is able to save us from it, and he will rescue us from your hand, O king. But even if he does not, we want you to know, O king, that we will not serve your gods or worship the image of gold you have set up' (Dan. 3.17–18). Their song of praise, sung within the furnace, proclaims that every part of creation praises Yahweh. This song follows the pattern of the creation Psalm 148. See also the comments of Ernest Lucas, 2002, *Daniel*, Leicester: InterVarsity Press/Apollos, pp. 81–97.

49 Ellen van Wolde, 1996, *Stories of the Beginning: Genesis 1—11 and Other Creation Stories*, London: SCM Press, p. 177.

50 van Wolde, *Stories of the Beginning*, p. 178.

51 Stanley L. Jaki, 1992, *Genesis 1 through the Ages*, London: Thomas More Press, p. 28.

52 G. von Rad, 1961, *Genesis*, London: SCM Press.

53 Westermann, *Genesis*.

54 B. S. Childs, 1979, *Introduction to the Old Testament*, London: SCM Press, pp. 154–5.

55 G. von Rad, 1975, *Old Testament Theology, Volume One*, London: SCM Press, p. 140.

56 Wenham, *Genesis*, p. 10.

57 Jaki, *Genesis*, p. 301.

58 Walter Brueggemann, 1982, *Genesis*, Atlanta: John Knox Press, pp. 18–19.

59 J. D. Barrow, 1990, *Theories of Everything*, Oxford: Oxford University Press, p. 9.

60 Van Wolde, *Stories of the Beginning*, p. 1.

61 W. Bruce Masse, E. W. Barber, L. Piccardi and P. T. Barber, 'Exploring the Nature of Myth and its Role in Science', in Piccardi and Masse, *Myth*, p. 10.

62 Masse et al. in Piccardi and Masse, *Myth*, p. 18.

63 See W. E. Soothill, 1913, *The Three Religions of China*, London: Oxford University Press, pp. 154–5.

64 Cesare Emiliani, 1995, *Planet Earth: Cosmology, Geology, and the Evolution of Life and Environment*, Cambridge: Cambridge University Press, p. 2.

65 Emiliani, *Planet Earth*, p. 3.

66 For a full discussion of the parallels and contrasts between Genesis 1—11 and the mythological accounts of creation and flood in Ugaritic and Babylonian texts, see Weaver, *Earthshaping Earthkeeping*, pp. 12–26, and John Day, 1985, *God's Conflict with the Dragon and the Sea: Echoes of a Canaanite Myth in the Old Testament*, Cambridge: Cambridge University Press; and S. Dalley, 1989, *Myths from Mesopotamia*, Oxford: Oxford University Press.

67 Bright, *A History of Israel*, p. 88.

68 Wenham, *Genesis*, pp. xxxvii–xxxviii.

69 Wenham, *Genesis*, p. 1.

70 Pedro Trigo, 1992, *Creation and History*, Tunbridge Wells: Burns & Oates, p. 93.

71 David Atkinson, 1990, *The Message of Genesis 1—11*, Leicester: InterVarsity Press, p. 16.

72 Psalms 18.15; 29.3–4, 10–11; 77.16–18; 93.3–4; 104.6–9.

73 Psalms 74.12–17; 89.9–13; and Isaiah 27.1; 51.9–11; Job 7.12.

74 For a fuller discussion of these points, see Wenham, *Genesis*, pp. 37–8.

75 Psalm 24.1.

76 Westermann, *Genesis*, pp. 64–5.

77 Artur Weiser, 1962, *The Psalms*, London: SCM Press, p. 55.

78 See Hosea 2.16.

79 See Zephaniah 1.5.

80 Day, *God's Conflict*, p. 189.

81 Exodus 7.10–12, 22; 8.7 etc.

82 Isaiah 40.12–14, 18–28; 41.21–24.

83 Genesis 1.14–19; Trigo, *Creation*, pp. 102–3.

84 Trigo, *Creation*, p. 103.

85 Trigo, *Creation*, p. 88.

86 Brueggemann, *Genesis*, p. 1.

87 Westermann, *Genesis*, p. 52.

88 Brueggemann, *Genesis*, pp. 12–13.

89 David Atkinson, 1991, *The Message of Job*, Leicester: InterVarsity Press, p. 152, notes that in Job 38 and 39 very little of creation is in human control and a great deal of God's creation is secret and not open to human power and human competence. This might create a great deal of fear, but God's power is demonstrated through an examination of two frightening creatures: the beast and the dragon, Behemoth and Leviathan, of the pagan myths. These are fearful mysteries that Job is

powerless to control. Yet even the most monstrous and frightening are under God's control.

90 Atkinson, *The Message of Job*, p. 161.

91 Atkinson, *The Message of Job*, p. 155.

92 Margot Käßmann, 'Covenant, Praise and Justice in Creation: Five Bible Studies', in David Hallman (ed.), 1994, *Ecotheology: Voices from South and North*, Geneva: WCC and Maryknoll NY: Orbis Books, p. 44.

93 Gordon D. Kaufman, 2004, *In the beginning ... Creativity*, Minneapolis: Fortress Press, p. ix.

94 Kaufman, *In the Beginning*, p. 103.

95 Renthy Keitzar, 'Creation and Restoration: Three Biblical Reflections', in Hallam, *Ecotheology*, p. 61.

96 Isaiah 42.5; 43.1–3; 44.24b–28.

97 Von Rad, *Old Testament*, pp. 138–9.

98 Von Rad, *Old Testament*, p. 151.

99 Day, *God's Conflict*, p. 61.

# 2

## Cosmology and the Structure of the Universe

### Overview

How would the 'wise men' of Matthew's account of the gospel tell their story? They spent much time in the study of the stars, no doubt seeking to understand the universe and their existence within it. Their view of the universe would have been similar to that of Aristotle or maybe Aristarchus. A 'new star appeared' – a comet? a nebula? – whatever it was, it led them to Jerusalem and King Herod, and from there to Bethlehem and a very different king. T. S. Eliot wrote:

> A cold coming we had of it
> . . . were we led all that way for
> Birth or Death? . . .
> We returned to our places, these Kingdoms,
> But no longer at ease here, in the old dispensation,
> With an alien people clutching their gods.[1]

Was it now different? They had followed a star and found a king. The wise men of Jerusalem had quoted a Jewish prophecy about the Messiah of Yahweh, proclaimed in Micah 5.2, and 'their star' had led to a baby or toddler in Bethlehem. Is Eliot right? Could they no longer go back to their myths of creation, maybe of Apsu, Ea, Qingu and Marduk, or of Aten, or even their science? And what of the modern stargazer? Stephen Hawking, seeking the 'mind of God',[2] or Paul Davies wondering if we are truly meant to be here:

> What is man that we might be party to such a privilege? I cannot believe that our existence in this universe is a mere quirk of fate, an accident of history, an incidental blip in the great cosmic drama. Our involvement is too intimate . . . We are truly meant to be here.[3]

Can they still go back to their agnosticism, or their cosmological equations and remain unchanged?

57

## Greek science and the medieval picture of the universe

If the Magi were to tell their story, as wise men who studied the stars, they would speak out of the scientific understanding of their age: Egyptian, Babylonian and Greek. The Egyptian view of the universe was dominated by the flood cycle of the Nile, which was essential for their livelihood. They noted that the level of the Nile began to rise with the heliacal appearance of Sirus, the brightest star in the sky in the morning twilight above the eastern horizon. Sothis, as they called it, became the divine star responsible for the Nile's rising and was identified with the goddess of agriculture and fertility. This cultural environment in Egypt did not lead to a flowering of astronomy.

In Babylonia the stars had been observed as far back as Sargon of Akkad, in the early fourth millennium BCE. The major constellations, made known to the Greeks and Romans by Aratus and Eudoxus in the fourth and third centuries BCE, had probably been known for over 2500 years. It was from the Babylonians that the Greeks derived their first notions of astronomy. The Greeks were, as far as is known, the first people to make detailed observations of the size and structure of the universe. Notable among their scientists were:

- Thales, who forecast an eclipse of the Sun in 585 BCE, and improved the art of navigation by the stars
- Anaximander (c. 610–540 BCE), a student of Thales, claimed the Earth was free in space, and that the Sun, Moon and stars went under the Earth to reappear
- Pythagoras (c. 582–507 BCE) claimed the Earth was a sphere (after seeing the curved shadow of the Earth on the Moon during eclipses), which moved with the Sun and other heavenly bodies in circles about a central point
- Aristotle, who held to a geocentric model
- Aristarchus, who was the first to propose a heliocentric universe
- Hipparchus and Ptolemy, who held to a geocentric system, and produced star charts that lasted for over a thousand years.

Aristotle (384–322 BCE) presented the argument for change and causation, identifying the Prime Mover as the origin of the universe. Aristotle conceived of a universe with a spherical stationary Earth at the centre, surrounded by a spherical heaven, on which rotate spherical stars.

Aristarchus (310–230 BCE) suggested that the Sun and the stars remained in fixed positions, while the Earth moved around the Sun in a circular orbit. His work was largely ignored by his contemporaries, but was known to Copernicus, who some 1700 years later revived the heliocentric model.

Hipparchus (second century BCE) produced a star catalogue of some 850 stars. He sought to measure the distances between the Earth and the Moon and Sun, and made careful measurements of the seasons of the year. Ptolemy (second century CE) built on Hipparchus' star catalogue, and described the solar system in his great work, known by its Arabian name, *Almagest* (*c.* 140 CE). Ptolemy's cosmology explained how sundials work, and enabled the calculation of eclipses. However, the planets had to follow eccentric paths, they had no uniform circular motion, to maintain the Earth at the centre of Ptolemy's universe. In Ptolemy's classification the Earth is unique and the planets are wandering stars; the Moon and Sun are planets; and the rest of the stars are fixed. This model fitted with the Aristotelian physics of his time.

Our knowledge of the solar system has grown more in the last 30 years than in the previous 2000 years. When Newton said, 'If I have seen further, it is because I have stood on the shoulders of giants',[4] he could have been speaking for almost all who have followed in his footsteps during the Enlightenment. George Smoot expresses something of the excitement felt by science when writing in 1993 he says:

> As we approach the end of the millennium, cosmology is experiencing a wonderful period of creativity, a golden age in which new observations and new theories are extending our understanding – and awe – of the universe in astonishing ways.[5]

Modern science is building on a long history of discovery. The coming together in the 1970s of studies of the very large (astronomy) and the very small (particle physics) has provided the possibility of answering ultimate questions. Cosmology claims to be able to look back to $10^{-43}$ seconds after what is believed was the Big Bang origin of the universe. But at the moment of creation, the universe probably existed under very different conditions and operated according to different laws than it does today. Smoot concludes that 'reality in cosmology sometimes evades our comprehension'.[6]

It is the scientist who is now posing the questions to which only philosophy or theology has any meaningful answers. Modern cosmologists are posing questions about the beginning and end of the universe, about the place of *Homo sapiens* within it, and the reasons for apparent design and purpose within the evolution of the cosmos.

### Revolutions in science

By 1520 a literal interpretation of Genesis 1 was becoming very difficult. The appearance of the Sun on the fourth day was a real problem when it was understood that light came from the Sun. The appearance of animal and plant life was also causing difficulty. By 1650 a new view of the cosmos was appearing. Jaki rightly recognized that all of a sudden Genesis 1 becomes of no concern for those who take the newly born science for their guide about matters physical. This is not to say that their dicta would thereby become reliable about the origin of the world. But from now on there opens up a gap between Genesis 1 and the genesis of the universe as suggested by science . . . [7]

Paul Thagard observes that 'Scientific knowledge often grows slowly with gradual additions of new laws and concepts. But sometimes science undergoes dramatic conceptual changes when whole systems of concepts and laws are replaced by new ones.'[8]

In 1970, Thomas Kuhn noted that the development of scientific knowledge included revolutions, which he described as 'paradigm shifts'.[9] For Thagard, a conceptual change is revolutionary if it involves the replacement of a whole system of concepts and rules by a new system. If knowledge of science were neatly accumulative, fact piling on top of fact, there would be no need to speak of revolutions, but he recognizes seven historical cases that can be called revolutionary:

1 Copernicus' Sun-centred solar system replacing the Earth-centred system of Ptolemy
2 Newtonian mechanics replacing the cosmology of Descartes
3 Lavoisier's oxygen theory, which replaced the phlogiston theory of Stahl
4 Darwin's theory of evolution by natural selection, which replaced the divine creation of species
5 Einstein's theory of relativity, which replaced and absorbed Newtonian physics
6 quantum theory, which replaced and absorbed Newtonian physics
7 the Plate tectonics theory that indicated the Earth's dynamic crust, and established the existence of continental drift.[10]

Conceptual revolutions require a mechanism that can lead people to abandon an old conceptual system and adopt a new one. This does not take place in a slow evolutionary way, but revolutionary thinking and discoveries require a new set of explanatory hypotheses. These revolutionary changes in thinking did not immediately, nor always in the long term, lead to an abandonment of belief in the Creator-God. Scientists in the late seventeenth century such as Robert Boyle (1627–91) and John Ray (1627–1705) envisaged scientific enquiry as a form of worship. 'The image of nature as temple, the scientist as priest, was explicit in Boyle . . . God's craftsmanship in creation could be celebrated by the skilled anatomist.'[11] Boyle spoke of 'pregnant hints' revealed to him from a greater chemist than he.

Natural philosophers of the seventeenth century would insist that a doctrine of creation gave coherence to scientific endeavour in as much as it provided a model of an ordered universe, which was the creation of a rational god. Johannes Kepler (1571–1630) could speak of thinking God's thoughts after him, and René Descartes (1596–1650) could speak of discovering the laws that God had put into nature. In John Ray's *The Wisdom of God Manifested in the Works of Creation* there is a wonder and praise for nature. Ray saw the conceptual revolution of the Copernican system as the elegance one might expect from a divine architect. The process of choosing the simpler theory in science as correct led Michael Faraday in the nineteenth century to 'a God who had ensured that the book of his works would be as simple to comprehend as the book of his words'.[12]

### Copernicus, Galileo, Kepler

Polish priest Nicolaus Copernicus (1473–1543) began to study the movements of the planets in 1513. He suggested that the Sun and not the Earth was the centre of our solar system, and set out his heliocentric theory in 1543, shortly before his death. Copernicus knew of the work of others such as Aristarchus and Heracleides (fourth century BCE pupil of Plato), who suggested that the Earth was not stationary but rotated about its own axis, and that Mercury and Venus revolved about the Sun like satellites.

Copernicus was followed by the Italian Catholic philosopher Galilei Galileo (1564–1642), who developed a telescope with a magnification of 32, capable of observing the planets. Galileo adopted the Copernican heliocentric theory, observing the mountainous regions of the Moon, the stars of the Milky Way, the satellites of Jupiter, the phases of Venus, and Sun spots. However, Galileo's publications brought him into conflict with the Catholic Church. Galileo's writings, especially in the area of dynamics, which derived in large part from his studies of ballistics, paved the way for Newton.

Yet before Newton, German astronomer Johannes Kepler (1571–1630), established the law of elliptical orbits of the planets and formulated important truths that applied to gravity, in particular recognizing that the tides on Earth could be ascribed to lunar attraction.

### Newton

Sir Isaac Newton (1642–1727), an English mathematician and physicist, probably contributed more to scientific understanding than any other man or woman, before or since. His laws of motion and gravity made sense of the planetary observations of Kepler, and represent the second of Thagard's conceptual revolutions. Newton's recognition of gravity in 1666 (apples fall off trees, according to the apocryphal story) laid the foundations of a scientific world-view that has dominated Western society for 300 years. Newton presented his three laws of motion in 1687 in his magnum opus *Philosophiae naturalis principia mathematica*. Through Newton's work we have the picture of a dynamic universe, which is never at rest. Newton assumed an equal distribution of stars in an infinite universe. With the stars at an equal distance from each other the gravitational pull is equalized, although the situation envisaged would remain unstable.

For Newton, God was not at the centre of the natural process, but outside, holding the whole dynamic system within a timeless and motionless framework. Newton thought of the universe as the rational design of God, with its infinite size related to the all-embracing Spirit of God. For Newton, God was the transcendent creator, the controlling force outside the universe, keeping the boundaries, but such a God could not be on the inside as one of its participants. Newton's work both affirmed God and at the same time limited what God could be and do. The possibility of miracles, revelation, the incarnation or any intervention by God was not possible within a universe governed by natural laws.

Copernicus, Galileo and Newton together had overturned the entire Aristotelian system. But the move away from a cosy Earth-centred universe was not very comforting. Blaise Pascal, the French mathematician (1623–62), expressed the sentiments of many, says Smoot, when he wrote, 'The eternal silence of those infinite spaces strikes me with terror.'[13]

### Relativity and an expanding universe

The author of the third conceptual revolution in science, Albert Einstein (1879–1955), had a number of predecessors, including in the 1840s: Faraday, who developed the field theory for magnetic forces; Young, who proposed the wave theory for light; William Thomson, Lord Kelvin, in the field of thermodynamics; James Clerk Maxwell, who in 1861 developed the mathematical theory of electro-magnetic fields and assumed electromagnetic radiation; J. J. Thompson, who in 1897 discovered electrons; and Ernest Rutherford, who in 1911 recognized the atomic nucleus with electrons in orbit.

Max Planck (1858–1947), a German physicist, proposed the quantum theory in 1900, which stated that energy is emitted in packets called photons or quanta. He introduced this theory to explain the distribution of energy across the range of frequencies radiated by hot objects. He showed that the amount of energy in each quantum increased as the wavelength of the radiation became shorter. His theory marks the divide between the classical physics of Newton, Kelvin and Maxwell, and the modern physics of Einstein.

Einstein established the important principle that the speed of light was always the same, no matter how you measured it. This was the basis of his Special Theory of Relativity. In 1915, Einstein presented his General Theory of Relativity, which demonstrated that gravity is a field like a magnetic field, and is described in the concept of a space–time continuum. This is the combination of 3D space with the fourth dimension of time. Einstein predicted that light bends under the gravitational pull of large astral bodies. One recent commentator on this theory has helpfully likened space–time to a rubber sheet stretched flat. If a heavy object such as a golf ball were to be placed on it the sheet would change shape; there would be a downward curvature in the sheet.[14] This is the way that gravity affects space–time.

Einstein believed in a changeless, uncreated cosmos, with matter evenly distributed. In itself, however, the General Theory of Relativity actually required an expanding universe, as in a static universe the gravitational force would be self-destructive, causing the whole system to collapse in on itself. Einstein therefore introduced a cosmic constant to counteract the gravitational force.

His theory of relativity undermined the Newtonian view of a universe working like a machine, composed of individual parts. Einstein's universe is an interacting whole of space and time. God, for Einstein, was manifested in the laws of nature: impersonal, sublime, beautiful, indifferent to human beings, but still important to them.[15] Einstein affirmed the religious sense of wonder and mystery when looking at creation, but could not accept the idea of a personal God. God was the great unknown and unknowable. Human beings were part of the mystery; he said, 'The most incomprehensible thing about the universe is that it is comprehensible.'[16]

The scientific revolutions of the Enlightenment period have required substantial changes in concepts such as force, gravity, mass, planet, wave and particle. In the twentieth century, the relativity and quantum theories showed the inapplicability of Newtonian theory to objects that are very massive, very small or fast moving. The revolutions produced by these theories were more cumulative than other scientific revolutions, but they still involved considerable conceptual change and rejection of previously held views. In all four revolutions in physics, the replacing theory had greater explanatory coherence than the one it replaced.[17]

Einstein's theory of general relativity implied an expanding universe. But, says Smoot, Einstein was not happy with a beginning at a single point, which made it impossible to know what happened before. He therefore proposed a cosmic constant to counteract gravitational attraction, thus leaving us with a static cosmos. His equations, however, predicted a dynamic universe, but for once he didn't trust them.[18]

Edwin Hubble in 1924 from studies of the Andromeda Nebula was able to calculate that its distance from Earth put it outside our galaxy. Astronomers were then able to recognize nebulae as separate galaxies. The picture of a cosy universe no larger than our galaxy could no longer be held. Hubble also built on Vesto Melvin Slipher's observations, which had uncovered the first evidence of an expanding universe.

In 1912, Slipher noted that there was a shift towards the red end of the spectrum in the light received from galaxies. One possibility was that this indicated that they were moving away from us. Hubble built on the red shift in light coming from distant galaxies and produced 'Hubble's Law' – there is a direct correlation between the distance to a galaxy and its red shift. The evidence was clear, the universe was expanding. He calculated that galaxies were moving away from the Earth at up to 25,000 miles/sec. On this basis the universe had a beginning, which Hubble calculated to be about 2000 million years Before the Present (BP). Einstein recognized the truth of this and said in 1930 that his disbelief of his own equations was his 'greatest blunder'.[19]

In spite of this evidence, Fred Hoyle, Thomas Gold and Herman Bondi continued to present the idea of a steady state universe in the late 1940s and early 1950s. They conceived of the continuous generation of matter which guaranteed a homogeneous universe in space and time. They argued that this theory was compelling, for it is only in such a universe that the laws of physics are constant. It removed the problem of a Big Bang beginning where the laws of physics would not apply, and also it had the advantage that it did not have to contemplate the question of 'before' creation. Hoyle included as one of his reasons for accepting this hypothesis that it did not require a god, and was furthest away from the account of creation in Genesis 1. Although we might observe that, the hypothesis of continuous creation does not contradict the concept of an ever-caring creator.

Confirmation for the view of an expanding universe came through the field of radio astronomy in 1963 when quasars were identified moving away at 150,000 miles/sec. As a result of these findings the age of the universe increased to some 10,000 million years BP. The steady state theory of Gold and Bondi was again questioned through the discovery, by Arno Penzias and Robert Wilson in 1964, of background heat radiation in the universe. This background radiation in the universe was seen to be the relic of the Big Bang fireball which marked the beginning to this expanding universe. This thermal radiation has a temperature of $2.7°$ Absolute or $-270.3°$ Celsius, which, although very cold, is the left-over 'heat' of the Big Bang itself.[20]

Further confirmation came in 1977 through research carried out by the U-2 spy plane. It carried a differential microwave radiometer high up in the atmosphere, from where it monitored cosmic background radiation in space. This was shown to be remarkably smooth – the apparently homogenous afterglow of the Big Bang.

So we can suggest that the universe has a biography – a beginning, and an end yet to be written. Our solar system is part of this story. It formed from a rotating disc of dust and gas of a solar nebula. There were planetesimals (from a few metres to the size of Mars) from which the planets accreted. It appears that planets have different compositions because they gathered together different populations of planetesimals. Stuart Ross Taylor notes the unique nature of the Earth–Moon system:

> The evidence appears decisive that the Moon formed towards the end of the period of planetary accretion through the collision of a Mars-sized impactor with the Earth, and that the material forming the Moon came

not from the terrestrial mantle, but from the metal-poor silicate mantle of the impactor. Such an event would have removed any pre-existing atmosphere, and melted the terrestrial mantle, with consequences for mantle crystallization and evolution which have yet to be worked out in detail.[21]

There are many unusual features about the solar system. It is probably unique, and other planetary systems must be expected to differ substantially from our own. When it formed, the universe was already some 10,000 million years old. Countless stars had formed and died since that event (Big Bang) and had enriched the interstellar medium in the heavier elements. Only hydrogen, helium and a little lithium and beryllium were produced in the Big Bang; the heavier elements, from which the Earth was constructed and which comprise 2 per cent of the solar system, were formed in nuclear reactions in stellar interiors and supernovae.[22] Our solar system lies in one arm of the spiral galaxy of the Milky Way, which is one of $10^{11}$ galaxies, each containing about $10^{11}$ stars. It is interesting to hear Stuart Ross Taylor comment:

> This placing of the Earth and the Solar System, itself possibly unique, in a rather distant corner of the Universe, has implications for the position of *Homo sapiens* in the Universe which have not yet been accommodated in most philosophical, mythological or religious systems.[23]

The evolution of this complex solar system is not easy to explain. There are many chance factors, which include the initial size of the nebula, its detailed evolution, the early formation of Jupiter (a crucial part of the scenario), and the many random collisions, one of which tipped Uranus on its side, another of which stripped off a major part of the silicate mantle of Mercury, while a third formed our unique satellite, the Moon.[24]

## The birth of the universe

It was Georges-Henri Lemaître who, as early as 1927, took the implications of Slipher and Hubble's work and suggested a single primordial atom that began dividing to form the universe – beginning in an explosion. It should be noted at this point that it is space that is expanding, not the universe expanding into space. Lemaître's hypothesis not only began to explain the origin of the universe, but also the origin of the elements that made up the universe: known to be approximately 75 per cent hydrogen, 25 per cent helium and 1 per cent all other elements.

Evidence from many disciplines has come together this century: Becquerel (radioactivity), J. J. Thomson (discovery of the electron), Rutherford (structure of the atom), William Draper Harkins (the relative abundance of elements with odd and even numbers), Cecilia Payne-Gaposchkin (discovery that the Sun is almost entirely hydrogen, and that heat comes not from atomic fission but from nuclear fusion – the coming together of two hydrogen nuclei into a helium nucleus). Such nuclear fusion might explain the origin of elements. After concluding that the interior of the Sun and other stars were not hot enough to fuse light elements into an abundance of heavier elements, Carl Friedrich von Weizsacker, in 1938, suggested that this may have been achieved in a superhot primordial 'fireball'.[25]

In 1965, Roger Penrose showed that singularities are not mathematical concepts but actually exist in the real universe. He suggested the presence of 'black holes', which are the location of collapsed stars (destroyed in the explosive violence of a supernova), which leave a density so great that light cannot escape its gravitational pull. The matter of the star is compressed into a region of zero volume, so that the density of matter and the curvature of space–time become infinite. This is the nature of a singularity.[26]

Stephen Hawking realized that the reverse would also hold true and in 1970 Penrose and Hawking together postulated a physical singularity as the beginning of the universe. Penrose and Hawking suggested that the universe originated as a singularity – a boundary point at the beginning of space–time, when the whole universe was concentrated at one point. Here, the density of the universe would be infinitely large, its size infinitely small, and its energy infinitely high. This singularity is the point from which the universe has expanded following a Big Bang explosion.

In 1950, Martin Ryle had discovered radio emissions from nearby galaxies. When the distribution of radio sources in space were plotted they were not uniform, the more distant they were the more numerous they were. Thus the density of radio galaxies was greater in the past. In 1977 the differential microwave radiometer aboard a U-2 spy plane revealed that our galaxy is moving at 600 km/sec under the gravitational attraction of some distant, massive concentration of galaxies. Smoot concludes that the universe turned out to be 'much more structured than anyone had guessed, with galaxies existing as components of large conglomerations rather than being distributed uniformly through space'.[27] Yet the cosmic background radiation was seen to be smooth.

After a detective-novel-type investigation in 1992 wrinkles/fluctuations in the background radiation were identified and confirmed at the edge of the universe. When these wrinkles were mapped out Smoot was able to say:

> The big bang was correct; inflation theory (rapid expansion in early stage of universe) worked; the pattern of the wrinkles was about right for structure formation by cold dark matter; and the size distribution would yield the major structures of today's universe, under gravitational collapse through 15 billion years.[28]

The result indicated that gravity could have shaped today's universe from the tiny quantum fluctuations that occurred in the first fraction of a second after creation. The discovery of the wrinkles revealed that matter was not uniformly distributed, that it was already structured, thus forming the seeds out of which today's galaxies have developed. Smoot believes that as we converge on the moment of creation the constituents and laws of the universe become ever simpler. Cosmology – through the marriage of astrophysics and particle physics – is showing us that this complexity (of the universe) flowed from a deep simplicity as matter metamorphosed through a series of phase transitions. Travel back in time through those phase transitions and we see an ever-greater simplicity and symmetry, with the fusion of the fundamental forces of nature and the transformation of particles to ever more fundamental components.[29]

From current knowledge Barbour helpfully outlines the first three minutes of the universe's existence (see Figure 2.1).

| Time | Temperature | Transition |
|------|-------------|------------|
| 1 billion yrs | | galaxies formed (heavy elements) |
| 500,000 yrs | 2000°C | atoms formed (light elements) |
| 3 minutes | $10^9$ | nuclei formed (hydrogen and helium) |
| $10^{-4}$ seconds | $10^{12}$ | quarks to protons and neutrons |
| $10^{-10}$ seconds separate | $10^{15}$ | weak and electromagnetic forces |
| $10^{-35}$ seconds | $10^{28}$ | strong nuclear force separates |
| $10^{-43}$ seconds | $10^{32}$ | gravitational force separates |
| 0 | infinite | singularity |

Figure 2.1 [30]

We get back to a situation of the infinitely small point of energy – creation from practically nothing but not from nothing. Does this mean that we can find a 'theory of everything'? The logical answer for non-religious belief in a rational cosmos is that the laws of physics are contingent on a 'theory of everything'. A genuine theory of this kind will have to explain not only why the universe came into being, but also why it is the only type of universe in which conscious life could have developed. For we are discovering that if the initial conditions had been different then there could have been a different universe, but not one in which human life would have evolved. We have already noted similar key factors coinciding in the development of the solar system (see p. 65 above).

It is these considerations that have led some modern cosmologists to speak of 'fine-tuning', and an anthropic principle. It is often suggested that there is some guiding principle or even 'design' that has allowed complex human life to arise within the universe. There are the laws of physics, the uniformity of the expansion of the universe; its size and age – in excess of 100,000 billion, billion (km) and some 15 billion years old; and biologists see the universe as biocentric – the presence of chemicals and the laws of physics making life possible. The essential element for life, carbon, is manufactured from helium in large stars and released into the universe by supernovae explosions; if this is a mere accident it is the luckiest of coincidences. In short, science is suggesting a 'finely tuned' universe, which from the first conditions is uniquely suitable for life forms like ourselves.[31]

### Quantum worlds

So far it would appear that everything within the realm of science is entirely predictable and certain, determined by well-defined laws. This situation changed at the beginning of this century with the appearance of the quantum theory, which is the fourth of our conceptual revolutions. Max Planck suggested that light, X-rays and other waves were emitted in packets called quanta or photons. In 1926 , Werner Heisenberg showed that this simple picture leads to a surprising consequence when applied to atoms and subatomic particles. The position and velocity of these particles cannot be determined at the same time. Particles did not have well-defined positions, but a quantum state, which was a combination of position and velocity. It was also discovered that electrons do not follow a definite path around the nucleus. At the quantum level, we leave the world of objects moving along the shortest trajectory to a predetermined goal. We enter instead the quantum world of probabilities instead of certainties, which has been described by Heisenberg's Uncertainty Principle. Quantum mechanics predicts a number of different possible outcomes, and tells us how likely each possibility is. In this way it appears that unpredictability and randomness are introduced into science.

More recently has come the suggestion of 'chaos' within physical systems.[32] Chaos theory looks at complex phenomena which are beyond the grasp of a simple determinism, such as the weather, air turbulence, fluid flow, the human heartbeat, and the electrical activity of the brain. But again, when we get behind the name and look at what is meant by 'chaos theory', we find systems that appear to behave in a random fashion, but that do nevertheless obey the physical laws of the universe. The reason for the apparent chaotic behaviour is that the system is very sensitive to the factors that affect its behaviour. The unpredictability lies in our lack of complete knowledge of the initial conditions, not in the way in which the system behaves in respect to the laws of physics.

Determinism and reductionism is challenged by chaos systems, which are non-linear, and in which a very small initial change can result in a very large change at a later time. This has been called 'the butterfly effect'. Barbour observes that 'deterministic laws are strictly applicable only to closed systems; they are an approximation to reality because actual systems that are extremely sensitive to initial conditions can never be totally isolated from outside influences'. He further notes:

the unpredictability of chaotic systems is not merely a reflection of temporary human ignorance. Prediction over a long time period would require more information than could be stored on all the electrons in our galaxy, and the calculations would take longer than the phenomena we were trying to predict.[33]

## Multiverse

The hypotheses of multiverse suggest that there are billions of worlds in which by chance one has the right constants for life. The main suggestions include:

- successive cycles of an oscillating universe in which the constants vary at random through quantum uncertainties
- multiple isolated domains produced by the Big Bang – domains like expanding bubbles isolated from each other
- many-worlds quantum theory – 'every time there are alternative quantum potentialities in an atom, the universe splits into several branches'
- quantum vacuum fluctuations.[34]

Multiverse is one way of avoiding the implications of 'fine-tuning', suggesting that this is the universe in which we exist. We can say that our visible universe is part of an infinite universe, and our part is where the conditions are fine-tuned.

One view is that in a quantum world the number of universes is dependent on the quantum possibilities – billions of independent universes each different from each other. But this remains a theory as none of these other possibilities is observed.[35] John Barrow in *Impossibility: The Limits of Science and the Science of Limits*, stresses the need to distinguish between two meanings of 'universe'. There is *the Universe* with a capital U – that is, everything there is – which may be finite, or it may be infinite. But in addition there is also something smaller, which we call the *visible universe*.

> This is a spherical region centred on us, from within which light has had time to reach us since the Universe began . . . The boundary of our visible universe is called our *horizon*. It defines the boundary of observable science and its size increases steadily with the passage of time, reflecting the fact that more and more light has time to reach us.[36]

According to Barrow there is now good observational evidence that supports the idea that our visible universe underwent a surge of accelerated expansion, which is referred to as 'inflation', in its very early stages.

> Observations of the small temperature variations in the microwave radiation left over from the early stages of the Universe display the same

characteristic pattern of statistical variations that are predicted to result if we live in a vastly inflated image of a tiny primordial fluctuation.[37]

He goes on to suggest that in each inflationary area further inflation of tiny parts of themselves may take place to produce 'bubbles' within 'bubbles' with different laws, but part of the same universe.

Paul Davies, in *The Goldilocks Enigma*, suggests that the inflationary scenario automatically explains the life-encouraging features of our visible universe in terms of a physical theory, so that the anthropic explanation is abandoned. 'But,' says Davies,

> the problem isn't yet completely solved, because one still needs to assume the right level of primordial density perturbations to create galaxies, perturbations that probably arose from quantum fluctuations during the inflationary phase. Why the fluctuations in our universe have the amplitude they do is unknown. The answer might turn out to be an inevitable consequence of a future theory, or it could be that the strength of the fluctuations varies from region to region, in which case there may still be a degree of anthropic selection involved.[38]

Barrow agrees and comments further that the inflationary universe theory, in all its developments, persuades us that we should expect to find the Universe complex in its spatial structure and in its temporal development, and concludes:

> We appear likely to sit in a particular expanding bubble, unable to investigate the possibility that a Universe of elaborate never-ending complexity is blossoming beyond our horizon.
>
> The origin of even our visible part of the Universe is hidden from us. We have found that the great theories of relativity and quantum mechanics combine to provide us with an account of the universe that we see, regardless of how it began. The price we have to pay for this unexpected gift is the relinquishing of information about how, or if, the Universe began and about all its properties beyond our horizon. The Universe is not only bigger than we can know, it is bigger than we can ever know.[39]

From this perspective Davies is able to suggest that the multiverse theory shows us that what we have all been calling 'the universe' is in fact nothing of the kind. Rather, it is but 'an infinitesimal fragment of a much larger and more elaborate system – an ensemble of "universes", or of distinct cosmic regions (such as "pocket universes" that feature in the eternal inflation theory)'. We can conclude that within these universes, or regions, properties which are important for life are likely to differ, and life will only arise in those universes or regions, where the conditions are favourable for life. Universes where such conditions are unfavourable for life will be unobserved.[40] He notes that 'if these ideas are right, then the multiverse is populated by countless pocket universes in which all possible low-energy worlds – all $10^{500}$ of them – are represented somewhere'.[41]

The concept of multiverse allows cosmologists to give an explanation of our fine-tuned anthropic principle universe as one of selection, without the need to invoke the divine. The explanation for what we observe in the universe depends on features of the local cosmic environment. But Davies states that many, from both a philosophical and scientific basis, believe that the multiverse solution is based on unsound reasoning. He nevertheless notes:

> A universe which cools from an ultra-hot initial state will almost inevitably form a domain structure in which different domains will have different properties, including low-energy effective laws and values for some of the constants of nature. Although the term 'multiverse' was coined relatively recently, speculations about a multiplicity of cosmic domains based on GUTs [Grand United Theories], higher-dimensional theories and other attempts at unification have been around for three decades. In the absence of a convincing unique final theory, the default assumption is that the universe we observe is merely one fragment among a haphazard patchwork of universes.[42]

## String theory

More recent research in cosmology has sought a unification of the four basic physical forces: the electromagnetic force responsible for light and the behaviour of charged particles; the weak nuclear force responsible for radioactive decay; the strong nuclear force that binds protons and neutrons into nuclei; and the gravitational force evident in long-distance attraction between masses. Barbour maintains:

> The unification of gravity with the other three forces within one *Supersymmetry Theory* has appeared more difficult because we have no successful quantum theory of gravity. But there has been real excitement concerning *Superstring Theory*, which escapes the anomalies of previous attempts. The basic constituents would be incredibly massive, tiny, one-dimensional strings that can split or loop. With differing patterns of vibration and rotation, they can represent all known particles from quarks to electrons. There is no experimental evidence for strings; the energy required for their existence would be far beyond those in the laboratory, but would have been present at the very earliest instants of the Big Bang.[43]

The basic idea is to abandon the notion of particles altogether and replace it with flexible *strings*, moving according to the rules of quantum mechanics.

In the simplest version of the new theory, the strings form closed loops, but they are so tiny that it would take a chain of 100 billion billion of them to stretch across a single atomic nucleus. So what we previously took to be a particle – for example, an electron – is actually (according to this theory) a loop of string, only we don't see it that way because the loop is so small.[44]

One analogy for string theory is to think of a guitar string that has been tuned by stretching the string under tension across the guitar. Depending on how the string is plucked and how much tension is in the string, different musical notes will be created by the string. These musical notes could be said to be excitation modes of that guitar string under tension. In a similar manner, in string theory, the elementary particles we observe in particle accelerators could be thought of as the 'musical notes' or excitation modes of elementary strings. In string theory, as in guitar playing, the string must be stretched under tension in order to become excited. However, the strings in string theory are floating in space–time, they aren't tied down to a guitar. Nonetheless, they have tension. The string tension in string theory is denoted by the quantity $1/(2 \pi a')$, where a' is pronounced 'alpha prime' and is equal to the square of the string length scale.[45]

Paul Davies suggests that we don't ask what strings themselves are made from, but simply realize that they are primitive, indecomposable entities out of which everything else is built. He says:

> in this respect, strings are very close to the spirit of the original atomic theory of matter, but they go one better. They also explain how the particles interact without introducing a separate concept; the forces come out of string theory too because there are also string motions describing the various exchange particles such as the photons and gluons.[46]

He notes:

> The attractive thing about string theory is that you need only one sort of string to make *all* the particles: fermions and bosons [particles with integer spin, 0, 1, 2, are bosons; particles with half-integer spin, 0.5, 1.5, 2.5, are called fermions], matter particles and exchange particles – the whole lot. The string can vibrate in different patterns, each pattern corresponding to a different particle: if the string wiggles this way it's an electron, that way, it's a quark, and so on.[47]

String theories are classified according to whether or not the strings are required to be closed loops, and whether or not the particle spectrum includes fermions. In order to include fermions in string theory, there must be a special kind of symmetry called supersymmetry, which means for every boson (particle that transmits a force) there is a corresponding fermion (particle that makes up matter). So supersymmetry relates the particles that transmit forces to the particles that make up matter. Supersymmetric partners to currently known particles have not been observed in particle experiments, but theorists believe this is because supersymmetric particles are too massive to be detected at current accelerators. However, it is hoped that particle accelerators could be on the verge of finding evidence for high-energy supersymmetry in the next decade. Evidence for supersymmetry at high-energy would be compelling evidence that string theory was a good mathematical model for nature at the smallest distance scales.[48]

But Paul Davies states that strings cannot be seen and there is no direct confirmation that they exist. String theory 'deals with a rarefied domain of ultra-high energies and ultra-small distances, and doesn't so far have much to say about . . . real physics'.[49]

There are five versions of string theory, which may be united in a membrane – M theory, where M stands for membrane, or mystery, or miracle. The five string theories are 'like "five" corners of M theory where calculations can be performed, but nobody has yet written down the equations that govern the full M theory, let alone solved them'.[50] Davies concludes:

> String theory, and its further development as M theory, offers the most promising hope for unifying all of fundamental physics, but the theory remains incompletely understood and is hard to test experimentally.[51]

## Teleological arguments

George Smoot quotes Princeton physicist Freeman Dyson who said, 'The more I examine the universe and the details of its architecture, the more evidence I find that the universe in some sense must have known we were coming.'[52] Smoot himself says that 'the more we learn, the more we see how it all fits together – how there is an underlying unity to the sea of matter and stars and galaxies that surround us'.[53] Of our own solar system, geoscientist Stuart Ross Taylor[54] says that it is unlikely that such a sequence of events in the path of evolution, which led to *Homo sapiens*, would be duplicated in another planetary system. 'An unpredictable and random event such as the Cretaceous-Tertiary boundary impact (of a large meteorite), was probably crucial in clearing the scene for mammalian evolution to proceed unhindered by the giant reptiles of the Mesozoic.' A large element of chance has entered the evolution of our present system and has led to the recognition of the inherent difficulties in constructing general theories for the origin of solar system.

Jaki notes that modern scientists such as Arno Penzias (who discovered the background heat radiation of the universe in 1964) and V. F. Weisskopf have pointed to the agreement between modern cosmology and the Judaeo-Christian view of creation. He supports this conclusion with a quotation from a book on relativistic cosmology:

Most astrophysicists, cosmologists and astronomers agree that the biblical account of the beginning of cosmic evolution, in stressing 'a beginning' and the initial roles of 'void', 'light' and a 'structureless' state, may be uncannily close to the verified evidence with which modern science has already supplied us.[55]

At this point we might note the danger of linking theology to science, seen in the identification by John Robinson and Paul Tillich of views about God with, the now outmoded, steady state theory of Hoyle, Gold and Bondi.[56]

But now we are faced with the question of whether there has been a single beginning to the universe, whether the universe oscillates in and out of 'imaginary time' through a series of explosions, expansion and collapses, or whether the universe has no boundary.[57] Keith Ward believes that Stephen Hawking is wrong to suggest that if one does not have a beginning to the universe then there is no need for God. Ward correctly points out that we still need to explain the existence of space and time.

The crucial question remains: does the universe as a whole exist without having any reason or explanation, or because it has to be the way it is, or because it is brought into being and held in being at every moment by a supra-cosmic creator?[58]

Within a Big Bang model of the beginning of the universe there already existed a vast source of potential energy with a complex of quantum laws describing possible interactions of elementary particles; and the universe, according to one theory, originated by the operation of fluctuations in a quantum field in accordance with those laws. We have discussed above the possibility of multiverse resulting from such a quantum beginning to the universe.

Paul Davies notes that more recent developments in cosmology present the view that what we had previously referred to as the universe was more like a 'variegated multiverse' – 'a crazy quilt of environments with different properties and different laws of physics'.[59] He describes one aim of his book *The Goldilocks Enigma* as taking a critical look at the various responses to the fine-tuning issue, also asking whether scientists really are 'on the verge of producing a theory of everything – a complete and self-contained explanation for the entire physical universe – or whether there will always remain a mystery at the heart of existence'.[60]

Some cosmologists, irrespective of belief, continue to see humanity as an integral part of the universe – the anthropic principle. Modern cosmology, in its investigations of the universe and in the questions that those studies are raising, gives new scope to the old religious arguments about design. The discoveries of modern cosmology are not inconsistent with the conclusion that a universe whose initial conditions were finely tuned has been designed to produce human life in some part of the universe, which is conscious, aware and able to contemplate the universe. The alternative to God-given purpose is not 'brute chance' but the 'brute fact' of design itself. Yet, we note that others, like Richard Dawkins, would state that evolution mimics design.

Faced by the ultimate question of the beginning of the universe, Smoot says that science is left contemplating the question: why these conditions and not others? Or perhaps left to see the truth and treasure of the universe only in its own existence.[61] As we noted in the Introduction, for the Christian thinker more help will be found through belief in a personal God than in a theory as the final explanation. It is through the believer's encounter with God that ultimate reality is understood. However, human knowledge of God continues to be imperfect; such knowledge includes mystery. It is because God is known in this way, not because God remains unknown, that we affirm that God cannot be known fully.

## Theological implications

### Design: the anthropic principle

Barbour states that 'among the many possible universes consistent with Einstein's equations, ours is one of the few in which the arbitrary parameters are right for the existence of anything resembling organic life'.[62] Paul Davies bases his book *The Goldilocks Enigma* on the question raised by Brandon Carter in 1974: 'Suppose the laws had been a bit different from what they actually are, in this or that respect – what would the consequences be?'[63] The focus of this question was the origin of life.

> Specifically Carter's calculations suggested that if the laws had differed only slightly from what we find them to be, then life would not have been possible and the universe would have gone unobserved. In effect, said Carter, our existence hinges on a certain amount of delicate 'fine-tuning' of the laws. Like Goldilocks' porridge, the laws of physics seemed to Carter to be 'just right' for life. It looked like a fix – a big fix. Somewhat unwisely, he named this fine tuning 'the anthropic principle', giving the false impression that it concerned humankind specifically (which was never his intention).[64]

Keith Ward observes that given that 'carbon-based intelligent life exists in this universe, the fundamental physical and cosmological quantities of the universe must be compatible with this fact'.[65] He goes on to stress that a very large set of quantities need to be exactly what they are to produce intelligent life. Barrow notes that aspects of fine-tuning include:

- expansion rate – lower and the universe would collapse under gravity or higher with rapid expansion and no aggregation of material to form planets
- formation of elements – if the strong nuclear force had been weaker the universe would have been composed only of hydrogen, but if it had been stronger a helium universe would have resulted, and either way there would have been no carbon, the element necessary for living creatures
- particle/antiparticle ratio – for every 1 billion antiprotons in the early universe there were 1 billion and 1 protons – without this proportion our material universe would not exist.[66]

To these we can add what we have noted earlier in this chapter about the development of our solar system and to evolution of the mammals at the demise of the dinosaurs. Ward notes that 'what fine-tuning arguments show is that states of great value have resulted from, *and could only have resulted from*, a set of laws that are precisely adjusted in a large number of unexpected and exceedingly improbable ways'.[67] It cannot be denied that chance and necessity remain options for the atheist, but while such arguments do not provide an entirely convincing argument for design 'the fine tuning of the physical constants is just what one would expect if life and consciousness were among the goals of a rational and purposeful God'.[68]

### Chance: many-worlds theories

Some cosmologists see multiverse as an alternative hypothesis to God. There are a number of different views of multiverse:

1 quantum fluctuations
2 cycles of big bangs and big crunches
3 new baby universes born through black holes
4 inflationary hypothesis where the universe is like a bubble.

Ward says that the laws of our universe are contingent, while the laws of the multiverse are necessary. He maintains:

> For a theist, the exhaustive set of mathematical possibilities describing every possible universe and state of affairs does exist. It exists in the mind of God. The reference to God is not a superfluous addition. It has explanatory advantages. One advantage of existence in the mind of God is that the mind of God is an eternal and necessary actual being . . .
>
> A second advantage of existence in the mind of God is that God, being necessarily actual, and thus having the power of existence in the divine being, will be able to make possibilities actual.[69]

Ward believes that the hypothesis of God thus makes the multiverse hypothesis more intelligible.

> It also positively adds elements of explanation that a purely physical hypothesis does not. For the hypothesis of an ultimate creative consciousness explains the existence of finite consciousness, of creativity, and of purpose and value, in a universe that is not solely physical in nature.[70]

> The existence of a huge number of universes, all with differing fundamental forces and constants, would increase the probability that this universe would exist. That is probably the main attraction of string theory in cosmology. But something must cause the forces and constants to vary in a systematic way in order to cover the whole range of different possibilities. And something must cause the multiverse to exist, since it too seems to be ultimately contingent.[71]

In his book *Big Questions in Science and Religion*, Ward states that 'possibly the first lesson that modern science teaches is that a spiritual dimension of reality, if there is one, is likely to be unitary and intelligible'.[72] He continues:

> Science sees the universe as one interconnected set of phenomena, bound together by mathematically intelligible laws. There is a unity about it that does not suggest a plurality of spiritual powers. If there is a Spiritual Reality, it will be a mathematically inclined, unitary intelligence – we might say, metaphorically, a God of wisdom.[73]

The fact the universe originates from quantum fluctuations in a vacuum implies an origin that is both eternal and necessary. To postulate God as the ultimate reason for the existence of one or more universes becomes both rational and plausible according to Ward: 'If we turn to consider the nature of our universe in particular, the amazing fact is that this universe does possess a deep structure that seems supremely beautiful and intelligible – just what the hypothesis of God would imply.'[74]

### Chaos

Barbour notes that the holistic and anti-reductionist character of chaos theory has been described by James Gleick as follows:

> Chaos is anti-reductionist. This new science makes a strong claim about the world: namely, that when it comes to the most interesting questions, questions about order and disorder, decay and creativity, pattern formation and life itself, the whole cannot be explained in terms of the parts. There are fundamental laws about complex systems, but they are new

kinds of law. They are laws of structure and organization and scale, and they simply vanish when you focus on the individual constituents of a complex system – just as the psychology of a lynch mob vanishes when you interview individual participants.[75]

It is suggested that order emerges spontaneously in complex systems, especially on the border between order and chaos. Barbour concludes that 'too much order makes change impossible; too much chaos makes continuity impossible. Complexity at one level leads to simplicity at another level. Disorder is often the precondition for the appearance of a new form of order.'[76]

It would be a mistake to suggest that unpredictability at quantum level or in chaotic systems either rules out the existence of God or is the place where God acts in creation. From a theological perspective we can conclude that the appearance of chaos does not conflict with the belief that God can fulfil his purposes through the universe. On the one hand, if God in his omniscience knows the initial conditions of any system, he also knows what their conclusions will be. On the other hand, if God offers a real freedom to his creation, he will expose himself, and therefore make himself vulnerable, to a variety of chance variations within the universe which lead to the conclusions of a system in particular detail.[77]

### Necessity: a theory of everything

Barbour suggests that 'the values of the constants, which appear arbitrary, are in fact dictated by a more basic structure of relationships'. He says, 'perhaps there is a more fundamental theory that will show that the constants can have only the values that they have'. This is the essence of a Grand Unified Theory. But there are also the inflationary theories, which may explain why the present expansion rate is close to the critical balance, and why the microwave radiation is isotropic.[78] And Barbour concludes:

> Current theories are quite inadequate to deal with the even earlier period before $10^{-43}$ seconds when the temperature would have been so high that the fourth force, gravity, would have been united with the other three. Scientists hope to develop theories of *Supersymmetry* or *Supergravity*, which would provide a quantum theory of gravity. We saw that String Theory, in particular, may bring these diverse phenomena together. Because it would unite all the basic physical forces, it has been referred to as a Theory of Everything.[79]

In all these discussions chance and necessity are seen as alternatives to design. Barbour draws his exploration of astronomy to a conclusion with these words:

Now we know that the cosmos has included stretches of space and time that we can hardly imagine. What sort of world is it in which those strange early states of matter and energy could be the forerunners of intelligent life? Within a theistic framework it is not surprising that there is intelligent life on earth; we can see here the work of a purposeful Creator. Theistic belief makes sense of this datum and a variety of other kinds of human experience, even if it offers no conclusive proof. We still ask: Why is there anything at all? Why are things the way they are?[80]

Keith Ward writes:

> An explanation of the universe is something that makes it more probable that the universe should be as it is. Ideally, the final explanation would make the universe virtually certain. But a truly final explanation would have to explain why the explanation itself is the way it is. It would have to be self explanatory.[81]

Ward maintains that the universe needs explaining because it is contingent. If the universe had to be the way it is, necessary, then that would be the explanation, but we can think of many alternative possibilities. 'It is contingent. So if it has a final explanation, that must lie outside the universe, in some being that is necessary, to which there are no alternatives.'[82] Ward then goes on to argue that a multiverse in which all possible universes might exist can be described as both eternal and necessary, and thus any final explanation cannot have been caused. So he observes that the quantum laws and the quantum fluctuations are necessary and give the final explanation for the universe. But to believe this as a theory of everything is as much a step of faith as to posit God.

'Once you have introduced God, you have moved outside the realm of science. The mind of God may explain why this universe exists. But we have no public access to the mind of God, the hypothesis is not conclusively testable, and it gives rise to no specific predictions.'[83] He continues:

> God is not part of the scientific explanation . . . God is part of a personal explanation, which is not reducible to scientific explanation, and has a different function. Personal explanations do explain why things happen as they do – broadly, because they are intended by some consciousness to realize some purpose which that consciousness finds desirable.[84]

We are suggesting that a personal explanation includes purpose, which leads us to think of a mind behind the universe. So Ward concludes:

> the idea of God is not part of any scientific theory, and it does not block any sort of scientific search for understanding. It proposes to add a new

dimension, the personal dimension, to understanding the universe. It is therefore of great importance to take seriously, if we are not to fall into the delusion that the personal dimension simply does not exist.[85]

## Dialogue – what kind of God?

### The revival of natural theology

Modern science has revived the old design argument of natural theology, and has given it new teeth. It presents us with an understanding of the universe that includes a beginning and an end. It also demonstrates a universe that has a fine-tuning that is suggestive of purpose. From these two features is developed the anthropic principle, which proposes that the conditions for human life are written into the very fabric of the universe.

Natural theology has a long history within Christian thought, and one influential point of origin is in Greek philosophy.[86] Plato (427–347 BCE) had taught that the world that we see with our eyes and touch with our bodies was in reality only a world of shadows, which was a copy of the eternal world of Spiritual Forms to which the pure soul could attain by philosophic contemplation. Aristotle (384–322 BCE) was a member of Plato's Academy. He recognized four causes that produced all things: the full explanation of anything should say what it is made of (material cause), what it essentially is (formal cause), what brought it into being (efficient cause), and what its function or purpose is (final cause).[87] Aristotle's *Physics* sets out a good deal of theory about the workings of the universe, and includes an argument for a Prime Mover, starting from his conception of change and causation. There could be no first moment of change, he argues, as change implies existing matter. There must therefore be an Unmoved Mover. This Prime Mover, eternal, changeless and containing no element of matter or unrealized potentiality, keeps the heavenly bodies moving and maintains the eternal life of the universe.

Aristotle's concepts within the fields of science and philosophy were the basis of the thinking of many who followed, including the Christian theologians Anselm and Aquinas. In his *Monologion*, Anselm (1033–1109) begins with the experience we have of differences in degrees of value, of goodness and of being in objects around us. From this he argues for the necessary existence of an absolute standard, an absolute good, an absolute being in which the relative participates. This absolute we call God. This argument was to be more fully developed by Thomas Aquinas (1225–74), who continued the search for a rational proof for the existence of God. In line with Aristotle, he saw the world as being composed of real things which act as true causes; they are principles and goals of activity and not merely instruments or occasions for what happens. They are complete as far as they go, but must be seen in the light of the 'First Cause'. So Aquinas believed that we can arrive at the conclusion that God exists from a deeply considered acceptance of the world about us. His celebrated five ways of thinking about God's existence take up five general observations about the universe, namely its change, dependence, contingency, limited perfection and utility. He infers a changeless changer, an uncaused cause, a necessary being, a completely perfect one, and an ultimate end; all this combines to form a definition of God.

Aquinas's five ways include what later became known as the 'cosmological argument' (God as the ultimate cause of the cosmos) and the 'teleological argument' (God as the ultimate designer).[88] In all five ways he was following the principle of analogy. He argued that a dynamic world in motion must have causes; God is the single original cause. Within the world one can observe cause and effect; the sequence of cause and effect can be traced back to God as the original cause – the First Cause, Aristotle's Unmoved Mover. The existence of human beings needs the explanation of another order of Being; we are contingent (we do not necessarily need to be here) and so we must owe our existence to a necessary Being (who owes his existence to nothing outside himself). Moreover, human attributes such as truth, goodness and nobility must have their origin in a being who has these attributes perfectly. Finally, the universe shows evidence of design; there must be a designer, for how else have things come into existence at all?

While Aquinas presents his five ways as if they are proofs of the existence of God, Alister McGrath argues that they were not intended to prove the existence of God from rational argument, but were designed to provide a rational defence of an already existing faith in God.[89]

### Natural theology in dialogue with science

Alongside the great scientific discoveries of the seventeenth and eighteenth centuries there was the flourishing of rational philosophy, which was focused on the world rather than on God. René Descartes (1596–1650) saw rational argument as the only source of truth. Seeing the mechanistic view of the universe proposed by science, he divided the universe into object and observer; matter and mind; the scientific world of the physical universe, and the philosophical world of the mind with its values, beliefs and emotions (including the soul). John Locke (1632–1704) took this a stage further, suggesting that knowledge comes through the physical senses: observation, analysis, and deduction according to reason. Revelation is demoted or discarded in favour of reason.

David Hume (1711–76) believed that truth or falsehood could only be learned from experience, and that the only field of demonstrative reasoning was mathematics. In his *Dialogues Concerning Natural Religion* he acknowledged that the argument from design was the strongest of the traditional 'proofs', but then proceeded to undermine it by some devastating arguments. First, he observed that the universe was more like a living organism than an artefact that had been made, so that order could be said to be immanent in nature itself, rather than being derived from a designer. It was as if the universe was just 'growing' by itself according to its own internal guidelines. Second, he pointed out that for any universe to exist it must be ordered, and so it will be bound to look as if it were designed. Third, we know that a watch is designed because we have other mechanisms to compare it with; but the universe is unique and incomparable. Fourth, we cannot deduce from a finite, imperfect world that there is an infinite, perfect creator; the design argument can only indicate a creator who is one degree different and more clever than we are.[90]

Hume's criticisms of natural theology were taken further by Immanuel Kant (1724–1804). Kant considered that the teleological argument, or argument from design, was acceptable, but not logically compulsive. Following Hume he pointed out that it only proves the existence of an architect of the universe whose powers may be remarkable, but not necessarily infinite.[91]

Science largely presents mechanistic and reductionist ideas of creation, which see the universe as a great machine, understood by reduction to its basic parts. The machine idea changes our relationship to the world, as we become observers, analysts, managers, seeing and operating from outside nature. So this is a dualistic model par excellence. The alternative would be an organic and holistic world-view. It is the current ecological crisis that is forcing us to rethink our views of creation and our relationship to it. This reflection can take different forms: scientific or mystical, classical or New Age, religious or postmodern. Ecology is stressing the connectedness of all things, touching on the mystery of life itself. The concepts of Gaia, Mother Earth, Mother Nature, World Soul, which disappeared with Enlightenment rationalism, have now resurfaced with ecology.

Paul Davies believes that while science usually leads in the direction of reliable knowledge, the breathtaking answers of science still leave the question 'Why?'[92] The universe may well show astonishing ingenuity in its construction, and human beings certainly appear to be part of the scheme of things, but we are left with the question of whether the chain of explanation ends with God or some superlaw.

Paul Davies has suggested that such an understanding of the universe, uncovered by physicists, provides us with a surer path to God than religion.[93] Albert Einstein earlier expressed the view that the very fact that the universe was comprehensible is a miracle,[94] and such is the apparent order of the universe that Sir James Jeans described God as a mathematician.[95] Though without making an appeal to religious belief, Fred Hoyle urged that 'when by patient enquiry we learn the answer to any problem, we always find, both as a whole and in detail, that the answer thus revealed is finer in concept and design than anything we could ever have arrived at by a random guess'.[96]

## A revived argument from design

The main features of the modern design argument are:

- An ordered universe.
- The nature of the universe as an interrelated organism. From a scientific perspective we see that under the diversity and complexity of the universe there is an underlying unity, an interconnectedness in its fundamental forces and principles. This would suggest one unifying source of creativity or origin.
- The anthropic principle – our universe has to take account of our presence.
- The amazingly tiny changes in many of the fundamental constants of nature in the initial state of the universe, noted earlier, that would have prevented the existence of atom-based life of any sort.
- The mystery of personality; even for some biologists the appearance of *Homo sapiens* is a surprise. There is a distinctiveness in personhood.

In the conclusion of *The Goldilocks Enigma*[97] Paul Davies summarizes the various positions that scientists take with regard to the universe:

1 *The absurd universe* – the majority position among scientists – the universe is as it is, mysteriously, and it just happens to permit life. No God, no designer , no teleological principle, no destiny. 'The fact that life exists, seemingly against vast odds, is attributed to an extraordinary accident', as is the evolution of a mind able to understand the universe.[98]

2 *The unique universe* – belief in a deep underlying unity to be revealed sometime by physics: maybe string/M theory, a theory of everything. This position holds the dream of having a complete understanding of our physical existence. 'Because the theory fixes everything, it is unexpected good fortune that this fix turns out to be consistent with life and mind (not to mention understanding).'[99]

3 *The multiverse* – supported by a growing number of scientists – a multiplicity of cosmic domains, such as bubble universes, pocket universes, variegated cosmic regions, all resulting from the big bang. The view that every possible universe is therefore possible leads to attacks from all sides: the religious see it as a desperate attempt to avoid a god, and the string/M theory purists who see it as abdication in the face of mathematical difficulties.[100]

4 *Intelligent design* – the design of God, the natural explanation for those who believe in God. But this has the drawback of providing no explanation of how or why God did it. The other clear disadvantage that Davies spots is one well known to theology – such a designer need not be the personal relationship-building God of the Bible, but merely a superpower or supercomputer.

5 *The life principle* – the universe emerges from an overarching principle that constrains towards life and mind. This builds purpose into the workings of the universe. The problem is how such a principle came to be built into the physical laws that explain how everything comes about. It also fails to explain why life and mind are singled out as the goal of cosmic evolution. Where does the life principle come from?[101]

6 *The self-explaining universe* – a closed explanatory causal loop, where the universe explains/creates itself. But we are still left to ask 'Why?'

> Perhaps existence isn't something that gets bestowed from outside, by having 'fire breathed' into a potentiality by some unexplained fire-breathing agency (i.e. a transcendent existence generator), but is also something self-activating. I have suggested that only self-consistent loops capable of understanding themselves can create themselves, so that only universes with (at least the potential for) life and mind really exist.[102]

7 *The fake universe* – a simulation, a sham.
8 *None of the above.*

Davies concludes that he favours 5 or 6 – 'I do take life, mind and purpose seriously, and I concede that the universe at least *appears* to be designed with a high level of ingenuity' – although he refuses to settle for a 'god' or for a 'mystery'.[103] While Davies denies being 'crypto-religious', he does believe that

> life and mind are etched deeply into the fabric of the cosmos, perhaps through a shadowy, half-glimpsed life principle, and if I am honest I have to concede that this starting point is something I feel more in my heart than in my head. So maybe that is a religious conviction of sorts.[104]

He concludes that most scientists stick with 1 and leave the rest to philosophers and theologians.

### Some provisional conclusions

John Barrow, in his *New Theories of Everything*, concludes that mathematics cannot be an explanation of everything – there are those phenomena that are 'illusive' and intrinsically 'non-mathematical':

> Not every feature of the world is either listable or computable. For example, the property of being a true statement in a particular mathematical system is neither listable nor computable. One can approximate the truth to greater and greater accuracy by introducing more and more rules of reasoning and adding further axiomatic assumptions, but it can never

be captured by any finite set of rules. These attributes that have neither the property of listability nor that of computability – the 'prospective' features of the world – are those which we cannot recognize or generate by a series of sequence of logical steps.[105]

He suggests that beauty, simplicity and truth are prospective features (pointing beyond themselves, looking to the future): 'there is no magic formula that can be called upon to generate all the possible varieties of these attributes'.

The restrictions of mathematics and logic prevent these prospective properties falling victim to mere technique even though we can habitually entertain notions of beauty or ugliness. The prospective properties of things cannot be trammeled up within any Theory of Everything. No non-poetic account of reality can be complete.[106]

The scope of Theories of Everything is infinite but bounded; they are necessary parts of a full understanding of things but they are far from sufficient to reveal everything about a Universe like ours . . . There is no formula that can deliver all truth, all harmony, all simplicity. No Theory of Everything can ever provide total insight. For, to see through everything, would leave us seeing nothing at all.[107]

Ward does not believe that science has rendered religion obsolete. He rightly concludes:

The religious believer can say that we know consciousness exists and that agents know, envisage, choose, enjoy, and have ideals, values, and purposes. Any adequate account of reality must include those as primary and irreducible facts. So, Ultimate Reality cannot be simply unconscious and indifferent. Somehow the factors of consciousness and value must be included in any account of Ultimate Reality. And this coheres well with the most basic religious belief that consciousness and value are at the heart of reality.[108]

So we have to ask: what kind of universe can be the context for the evolution of beings such as us? Yet these scientific arguments have the same fundamental problems as the philosophical arguments of Anselm and Aquinas. They can be pointers to, but not proofs of, the existence of God.

There are scientific arguments that oppose the conclusions of fine-tuning. Richard Dawkins would take a quite different view from John Barrow, drawing attention to the nature of chance and uncertainty in the universe in general, and in the evolution of life in particular. However, rather than denying chance, we might then try to incorporate it into the design. Polkinghorne attempts to do this, arguing that chance and necessity give a world with ragged edges, where order and disorder interlace with each other; chance then leads both to systems of increasing complexity and new possibilities, and also to imperfectly formed, malfunctioning systems.[109] 'Natural evil' (which we will discuss in Chapter 7) is thus seen as a kind of untidiness and disorder.

A further problem with the design argument appears to be the opposite to the challenge of chance. There is a difficulty of keeping freedom really in view the more that design is stressed; consequently there is a problem with the kind of God that scientific arguments seem to lead to. Cosmologists can look for one superlaw, a theory of everything, without reference to God, because all their talk about design is merely an expression of how they observe the universe. Most scientists are certainly not looking to prove or to disprove the existence of God, but simply to understand the universe scientifically. So religious believers (including some scientists) can build a picture of 'God' on scientific models and present God as a divine 'mathematician' or an infinite 'computer programmer'; the resulting defect, from a truly theological point of view, is that a logically consistent universe which is the creation of a supreme mathematician or programmer seems to leave no room for freedom. No freedom means no relationship, and therefore no personal involvement of a personal God.

We have to ask what sort of God is being implied by our scientific discoveries. Although the modern arguments for design are far stronger than those of Anselm and Aquinas, they still have the same inherent problems. John Hick is right to draw a number of conclusions.[110]

- The argument from design does not establish divine existence, but poses the question to which one answer can be God.
- One cannot suggest that the existence of an eternal creative Mind is self-explanatory, while a universe that exhibits the fundamental laws it does exhibit, is not.
- While we all perceive the physical world around us, our beliefs about that world will depend on the information and experience available to us. For a Christian, belief in a purposeful creator is seen to be completely reasonable in the light of scientific research, but for a non-Christian there may be other explanations for the nature of the universe.

The conclusions of scientists like Paul Davies, who take no account of revelation or religious experience, will take us no further than some power or force, a kind of demiurge, behind the universe. Scientists are likely to avoid the theological implications of their conclusions, and so will not recognize the ways in which human sinfulness will prejudice their views. Basing a religious belief mainly on science can therefore lead to an anthropocentric view of God who, having been discovered as the author of life, is reduced to a being or mind just like us.

## Key texts

John Barrow, 2008, *New Theories of Everything: The Quest for Ultimate Explanation*, Oxford: Oxford University Press.

Paul Davies, 2007, *The Goldilocks Enigma: Why is the Universe Just Right for Life?* London: Penguin Books.

Malcolm Jeeves and R. J. Berry, 1998, *Science, Life and Christian Belief*, Leicester: Apollos/InterVarsity Press.

George Smoot and Keay Davidson, 1993, *Wrinkles in Time: The Imprint of Creation*, London: Abacus.

David Wilkinson, 2001, *God, Time & Stephen Hawking: An Exploration into Origins*, London: Monarch.

## Further reading

Michael Arthern, 2004, *Mountains on the Moon: A Stroll through History, with a Fresh Look at Scientists and Faith*, Birmingham: Crossbridge Books.

Ian G. Barbour, 2005, *Religion and Science: Historical and Contemporary Issues* (a revised and expanded edn of *Religion in an Age of Science,* 1998), London: SCM Press.

John Hedley Brooke, 1991, *Science and Religion: Some Historical Perspectives*, Cambridge: Cambridge University Press.

Gwen Griffith-Dickson, 2005, *SCM Core Text: Philosophy of Religion*, London: SCM Press.

Stephen Hawking, 1988, *A Brief History of Time*, London and New York: Bantam Press.

John Polkinghorne, 1998, *Science and Theology: An Introduction*, London: SPCK.

——1994, *Science and Christian Belief*, London: SPCK.

——2001, *The Work of Love:Creation as Kenosis*, London: SPCK.

Keith Ward, 1996, *God, Chance & Necessity*, Oxford: One World.

——2008, *Big Questions in Science and Religion*, Pennsylvania: Templeton Foundation Press.

——2008, *Why There Almost Certainly Is a God: Doubting Dawkins*, Oxford: Lion.

## Notes

1 T. S. Eliot, 1961, *Selected Poems*, London: Faber & Faber, pp. 97–8.

2 Stephen W. Hawking, 1988, *A Brief History of Time*, London and New York: Bantam Press, p. 175.

3 Paul Davies, 1992, *The Mind of God*, New York and London: Simon & Schuster, p. 232.

4 Quoted by Peter W. Francis, 'Exploration of the Solar System', in G. C. Brown, C. J. Hawkesworth and R. C. L. Wilson (eds), 1992, *Understanding the Earth: A New Synthesis*, Cambridge: Cambridge University Press, p. 3.

5 George Smoot and Keay Davidson, 1993, *Wrinkles in Time: The Imprint of Creation*, London: Abacus, p. 2.

6 Smoot and Davidson, *Wrinkles*, p. 9.

7 Stanley L. Jaki, 1992, *Genesis 1 through the Ages*, London: Thomas More Press, p. 182.

8 Paul Thagard, 1992, *Conceptual Revolutions*, Princeton NJ: Princeton University Press, p. 3.

9 For use of the term 'paradigm shift', see T. S. Kuhn, 1962, *The Structure of Scientific Revolutions*, Chicago and London: Phoenix Books.

10 Thagard, *Conceptual Revolutions*, p. 6.

11 John Hedley Brooke, 1991, *Science and Religion: Some Historical Perspectives*, Cambridge: Cambridge University Press, p. 18.

12 Brooke, *Science and Religion*, p. 28.

13 Smoot and Davidson, *Wrinkles*, p. 24.

14 David Wilkinson, 1993, *God, the Big Bang and Stephen Hawking*, Monarch: Tunbridge Wells, p. 43.

15 Angela Tilby, 1992, *Science and the Soul*, London: SPCK, p. 70.

16 Einstein, quoted in Tilby, *Science and the Soul*, p. 72, and Davies, *The Mind of God*, p. 148.

17 Thagard, *Conceptual Revolutions*, pp. 223–4.

18 Smoot and Davidson, *Wrinkles*, p. 36.

19 Smoot and Davidson, *Wrinkles*, p. 51.

20 For a full discussion, see Roger Penrose, 1989, *The Emperor's New Mind*, Oxford: Oxford University Press, pp. 302–47.

21 Stuart Ross Taylor, 'The Origin of the Earth', in Brown, Hawkesworth and Wilson, *Understanding*, p. 26.

22 See John Polkinghorne, 1986, *One World: The Interaction of Science and Theology*, London: SPCK, p. 56.

23 Taylor, 'The Origin of the Earth', p. 27.

24 Taylor, 'The Origin of the Earth', p. 43.

25 For further discussion on these discoveries, see Smoot and Davidson, *Wrinkles*, pp. 58–60.

26 Hawking, *Brief History*, pp. 49–50.

27 Smoot and Davidson, *Wrinkles*, pp. 272–3.

28 Smoot and Davidson, *Wrinkles*, p. 278.

29 Smoot and Davidson, *Wrinkles*, p. 291.

30 Ian G. Barbour, 1998, *Religion and Science: Historical and Contemporary Issues*, London: SCM Press, p. 197.

31 For a fuller discussion of these points see: Davies, *The Mind of God*; and 2007, *The Goldilocks Enigma: Why is the Universe Just Right for Life?* London: Penguin Books; Penrose, *The Emperor's New Mind*; John Barrow, 1990, *Theories of Everything*, Oxford: Oxford University Press; and 1999, *Impossibility: The Limits of Science and the Science of Limits*, London: Vintage; and my own works, 1994, *In the Beginning God: Modern Science and the Christian Doctrine of Creation*, Oxford: Regent's Park College and Macon: Smyth & Helwys; and 1999, *Earthshaping: Earthkeeping. A Doctrine of Creation*, London: Lynx/SPCK.

32 For chaos theory, see J. Gleick, 1988, *Chaos: Making a New Science*, New York: Viking. Also see I. Stewart, 1989, *Does God Play Dice?* Oxford: Blackwell;

and J. T. Houghton, 1990, 'New Ideas of Chaos in Physics', *Science and Christian Belief*, vol. 1, pp. 41–51.

33 Barbour, *Religion and Science*, p. 183.

34 Barbour, *Religion and Science*, p. 206.

35 David Wilkinson, 2001, *God, Time & Stephen Hawking: An Exploration into Origins*, London: Monarch, p. 93.

36 Barrow, *Impossibility*, pp. 159–60.

37 John Barrow, 2008, *New Theories of Everything: The Quest for Ultimate Explanation*, Oxford: Oxford University Press, p. 40.

38 Davies, *The Goldilocks Enigma*, p. 173.

39 Barrow, *Impossibility*, p. 189.

40 Davies, *The Goldilocks Enigma*, p. 172.

41 Davies, *The Goldilocks Enigma*, p. 194.

42 Davies, *The Goldilocks Enigma*, p. 196.

43 Barbour, *Religion and Science*, p. 196.

44 Davies, *The Goldilocks Enigma*, pp. 126–7.

45 http://superstringtheory.com

46 Davies, *The Goldilocks Enigma*, p. 127.

47 Davies, *The Goldilocks Enigma*, pp. 126–7.

48 http://superstringtheory.com

49 Davies, *The Goldilocks Enigma*, pp. 127–8.

50 Davies, *The Goldilocks Enigma*, p. 129.

51 Davies, *The Goldilocks Enigma*, p. 131.

52 Smoot and Davidson, *Wrinkles*, p. 293.

53 Smoot and Davidson, *Wrinkles*, p. 296.

54 Taylor, 'The Origin of the Earth', pp. 25–43.

55 Benjamin Gal-Or, 1981, *Cosmology, Physics and Philosophy*, New York: Springer Verlag, p. 5.

56 The steady state theory gave an eternal ground to the existence of the universe and it has been suggested that it was one of the background cultural influences that led theologians like John Robinson to regard God less as personal than as 'the ultimate reality', and Tillich to suggest that God was not exterior to the universe but 'the ground of our being'. There is a warning here for all theologians, that they should take care in aligning theology with scientific theories, which are constantly being revised as new facts come to light.

57 For Hawking (*A Brief History of Time*), to be left with merely a 'singularity' as the solution to the beginning of the universe would be a frustration, as a singularity is the ultimate unknowable. The real philosophical problem with the Big Bang is that it is a one-off happening, an anomaly. It is impossible to get behind it or before it. Scientists have tried to cope with this dilemma by suggesting cycles of bangs and crunches, or parallel universes. There is a widespread desire to get away from an idea of uniqueness. This desire is the motivation behind the search for a unifying of the four forces that govern the universe: gravity, electromagnetism and the weak and strong nuclear forces. Such a grand unifying theory is believed by some to be the ultimate answer.

58 Keith Ward, 1996, *God, Chance & Necessity*, Oxford: One World, pp. 16–17.

59 Davies, *The Goldilocks Enigma*, p. xi.

60 Davies, *The Goldilocks Enigma*, p. xii.

61 Smoot and Davidson, *Wrinkles*, p. 295.

62 Barbour, *Religion and Science*, p. 204.

63 Brandon Carter, 'Large number coincidences and the anthropic principle in cosmology', in M. S. Longair, 1974, *Confrontation of Cosmological Theories with Observation*, Dordrecht, Holland: Reidel, p. 291.

64 Davies, *The Goldilocks Enigma*, pp. ix–x.

65 Keith Ward, 2008, *Big Questions in Science and Religion*, Pennsylvania: Templeton Foundation Press, p. 236.

66 Barbour, *Religion and Science*, pp. 204–5.

67 Ward, *Big Questions*, p. 238.

68 Barbour, *Religion and Science*, pp. 205–6.

69 Keith Ward, 2008, *Why There Almost Certainly Is a God: Doubting Dawkins*, Oxford: Lion, p. 70.

70 Ward, *Why There Almost Certainly Is a God*, p. 70.

71 Ward, *Why There Almost Certainly Is a God*, p. 72.

72 Ward, *Big Questions*, p. 231.

73 Ward, *Big Questions*, p. 231.

74 Ward, *Big Questions*, p. 236.

75 James Gleick in closing address, 1990 Nobel Conference at Gustavus Adolphus College, quoted by Steven Weinberg, 1992, *Dreams of a Final Theory*, New York: Random House, p. 60.

76 Barbour, *Religion and Science*, p. 184.

77 See Paul S. Fiddes, 1992, *The Creative Suffering of God*, Oxford: Oxford University Press, pp. 61, 63ff.

78 Barbour, *Religion and Science*, p. 207.

79 Barbour, *Religion and Science*, p. 208.

80 Barbour, *Religion and Science*, p. 220.

81 Ward, *Why There Almost Certainly Is a God*, pp. 53–4.

82 Ward, *Why There Almost Certainly Is a God*, p. 54.

83 Ward, *Why There Almost Certainly Is a God*, p. 61.

84 Ward, *Why There Almost Certainly Is a God*, p. 62.

85 Ward, *Why There Almost Certainly Is a God*, p. 62.

86 It is held by many that this is the only point of origin, but I will argue through the course of this book that natural theology also has its origins in the Jewish and Christian Scriptures.

87 J. O. Urmson, 1960, *The Concise Encyclopaedia of Western Philosophy and Philosophers*, London: Hutchinson, pp. 28–51.

88 C. Brown, 1969, *Philosophy and the Christian Faith*, Leicester: Tyndale, p. 26.

89 A. E. McGrath, 1992, *Bridge-building: Effective Christian Apologetics*, Leicester: InterVarsity Press, p. 60.

90 David Hume, *Dialogues Concerning Natural Religion (1779)*, Part VII, ed. N. K. Smith, 1947, *Hume's Dialogues Concerning Natural Religion*, London: Nelson.

91 See Immanuel Kant, *Critique of Pure Reason*, trans. and ed. N. K. Smith, 1933, London: Macmillan, Second Division, Book II, chapter III, sections 4–6, (pp. 500–25); and John Hick, 1971, *Arguments for the Existence of God*, London: Macmillan, pp. 82–3.

92 Davies, *The Mind of God*.

93 Paul Davies, 1983, *God and the New Physics*, London: Dent, p. xi.

94 Quoted in Davies, *The Mind of God*, p. 148, and Tilby, *Science and the Soul*, p. 72.

95 Quoted in Davies, *The Mind of God*, p. 140.

96 Fred Hoyle, 1960, *The Nature of the Universe*, New York: HarperCollins, p. 103.

97 Davies, *The Goldilocks Enigma*, pp. 295–303.

98 Davies, *The Goldilocks Enigma*, p. 296.

99 Davies, *The Goldilocks Enigma*, p. 297.

100 Davies, *The Goldilocks Enigma*, p. 299.

101 Davies, *The Goldilocks Enigma*, pp. 300–1.

102 Davies, *The Goldilocks Enigma*, p. 301.

103 Davies, *The Goldilocks Enigma*, p. 302.

104 Davies, *The Goldilocks Enigma*, pp. 302–3.

105 Barrow, *New Theories of Everything*, p. 245.

106 Barrow, *New Theories of Everything*, p. 245.

107 Barrow, *New Theories of Everything*, pp. 245–6.

108 Ward, *Big Questions*, p. 242.

109 John Polkinghorne, 1988, *Science and Creation*, London: SPCK, pp. 47–8.

110 Hick, *Arguments*, pp. 33–6, 46, 108–16.

# 3

# Evolution and the Origin of Life

## Overview

### Before Darwin

In the world today there are more than 350,000 species of plants, of which approximately 250,000 are flowering plants, 10,000 are ferns and trees, and 60,000 are algae and fungi. There are 1,200,000 species of animals of which about 900,000 are arthropods (mostly beetles and insects), 120,000 are molluscs (snails, winkles, oysters and other shells), and 45,000 are chordates, which include us. Fossil evidence of life is distributed over more than 120 kilometres of sedimentary rocks, which have accumulated in many ocean basins through geological time. It appears then that this fossil record should give vital clues to understanding the rich variety of species that we see around us today, but the history of palaeontology is marked by constant conflict with scientific and ideological dogmas and authorities, including those of the Christian Church.

At first fossils seemed to verify the deluge of the Noah Flood described in Genesis 7, for the finding of sea animals in the rocks underlying present-day land confirmed that this land was once covered by the sea. In 1484 Leonardo da Vinci was put in charge of a project to build canals in northern Italy, around Milan. He unearthed mussels, snails, oysters, scallops, shattered crabs, petrified fish and countless other species. But there was no sea in the vicinity of Milan, and he wondered how these remains of marine life had found their way into the soil of Lombardy and how they had become petrified.

Greek scientists and philosophers had made the same discoveries in the sixth century BCE, and Herodotus saw only one explanation, namely that the region in question must have at one time been covered by the sea, with these fossils once living there. Leonardo was a brilliant scientist, far ahead of his time, not only in making basic designs for aeroplanes and submarines, but also in geology. He denied the possibility that fossils could have had their origin in a flood like the biblical deluge, as rivers would have carried the dead to the sea, rather than sucking up the dead from the sea to the mountains. For Leonardo, as for the ancient Greeks, fossils were seen to be the remains of once living creatures.

However, during the period of the Middle Ages and the Renaissance, others considered that fossils were the creation of mysterious forces emanating from the stars, and there are many occult stories that relate to fossil finds in England. There were some who would later suggest, in trying to answer the evolution debate, that fossils were placed in the rocks by the devil to confuse human beings. This is only one step removed from an even more dreadful suggestion also made, that God placed fossils in the rocks to test the belief of human beings concerning creation. It seems bizarre that people who wished to hold to the literal truth of Scripture should suggest such devious activity on the part of the God revealed in those Scriptures.

In 1750 Georges Louis Leclerc, Comte de Buffon (1707–88), worked out that if the Earth had cooled from a molten ball it would have taken at least 75,000 years. In 1787 he suggested that within its cooling history there had been many periods with many different floras and faunas, and that there had been many deluges and catastrophes. Twenty years later, Buffon's disciple, Jean-Baptiste de Monet, Chevalier de Lamark (1744–1829), spoke bravely of 'boundless ages, thousands, indeed millions of centuries'.[1] Lamark became Professor of Zoology at the Musee Nationale d'Histoire Naturelle in 1794, and in 1801, like Buffon before him, sought to trace all forms of animal life to a common origin. He anticipated Darwin in conceiving of the idea of organic evolution, suggesting that living organisms were always trying to improve themselves. Having suggested that present-day forms had developed out of forms now preserved as fossils, Lamark then looked for a possible mechanism. He suggested that new environmental conditions compelled animals to adjust, and that during this process new organs developed and ones that were not used disappeared. Like Darwin, he wrongly believed that characteristics acquired in an individual's lifetime were passed on to its offspring.

In the early nineteenth century Georges Dagobert, Baron Cuvier (1769–1832), the French naturalist, founded the science of palaeontology. He related the various forms of parts of animals to their particular function; for example, when he found fossil feathers he stated that this indicated that the animal involved could fly. He pioneered comparative anatomy and zoological classification. While he recognized both evolution and extinction within fossil groups, he maintained that the biblical flood was the last great catastrophe or geological revolution to affect our planet.

The theory of evolution continued to be regarded as a crank notion among most scientists, who held to the notion that the fauna and flora of the Earth had changed radically between 25 and 30 times in the course of its geological history. God, or an unknown natural force, it was argued, had periodically committed mass slaughter of all organisms and then, after total catastrophic destruction, recreated a new set of animals and plants.[2]

Charles Lyell (1797–1875), a Scottish geologist, who laid the foundations of all modern geology, completed the first edition of his three-volume

*Principles of Geology* in 1830–33, and subsequently revised this work 12 times up to his death in 1875. Lyell demolished the catastrophe theory of Cuvier and cited numerous examples of his own view of a step-by-step transformation of landforms in the geological past. He recognized slow cumulative changes in the surface of the Earth over a long period of time. He demonstrated the operation of agents such as rivers, volcanoes, earthquakes and the sea in past geological periods, and developed the concept of uniformitarianism, whereby the processes acting in the present were the key to understanding the way in which those same types of process operated in the past.

The first edition of his work was read by Darwin as he set out on the *Beagle* expedition, and it had a profound effect on his thinking. However, up to the ninth edition of his work, Lyell clung on to Cuvier's theory that plant and animal species were immutable. His only concession to Lamark was to grant that minor adjustments of species to their environment might take place. But nevertheless his recognition of slow cumulative changes in aspects of the crust's development was to have an impact on Darwin's thinking.

### Darwin and his successors

Charles Darwin (1809–82) was born in Shrewsbury. He attended Edinburgh University in 1825 to study medicine but, not wanting to follow in his father's footsteps as a doctor, went to Cambridge in 1827 to study classics, with a view to becoming a clergyman. Throughout this time at university Darwin maintained an interest in geology and botany, being influenced by Adam Sedgwick, Professor of Geology, and the Revd John Stephen Henslow, Professor of Botany. Henslow recognized that Darwin's calling was not to the priesthood and persuaded him to accompany Capt. Robert Fitzroy, as a naturalist on the *Beagle*. So at the age of 22 Darwin set sail on a 5-year voyage of exploration and discovery, which took in the east coast of South America, Terra del Fuego, the Falkland Islands, the west coast of South America, the Galapagos Islands, Tahiti, New Zealand, Australia, the Cape of Good Hope, Bahia, and home. Darwin's first publications were the results of his geological studies: *The Structure and Destruction of Coral Reefs* (1842), *Geological Observations of Volcanic Islands* (1844), and *Geological Observations on South America* (1846).

Darwin took Charles Lyell's uniformitarianism as the basis of his explanation of biological phenomena, but radically changed it to include the principle of natural selection, which explained progressive change and indeed made it inevitable. By the end of the *Beagle*'s voyage, Darwin had become convinced that species were not immutable and that they could be transformed into new species. This was his conclusion from observing finches on the Galapagos Islands (volcanic islands 1000 kilometres west of Ecuador, in the Pacific) and the armadillo-like creatures of South America. On the voyage Darwin had noted the mutation of species in changed environments, and also their changing development through the physical isolation of species, which he observed on either side of the Andes and on the islands of the Galapagos archipelago.

Darwin's theory of evolution by natural selection (*On the Origin of Species by Means of Natural Selection, or the Preservation of Favoured Races in the Struggle for Life*, published in 1859) was a direct challenge to the dominant scientific theory of the early nineteenth century. Most scientists of Darwin's day held that species were individual creations of God, even though geologists were beginning to suggest a very old Earth.

The book's first edition was sold out on the day of publication. It was reviewed for *The Times* newspaper by a marine biologist and vertebrate palaeontologist, Thomas Henry Huxley (1825–95), who when he had read Darwin's theory, exclaimed, 'How extremely stupid not to have thought of that!' The *Origin* had a notable list of supporters. It included Huxley, the major zoologist of his time, Hooker, the finest botanist, and Lyell, the greatest geologist. Also in support were Herbert Spencer, Sir John Lubbock (later Lord Avebury), Canon Tristram, who had studied the animals recorded in the Bible, Alfred Newton, the ornithologist, and Charles Kingsley, clergyman and novelist.

Darwin was opposed by the naturalist Philip Gosse, who was a member of the Plymouth Brethren, by the geologist Adam Sedgwick, and by the comparative anatomist and palaeontologist Richard Owen. There was a growing opposition from the side of the Church, which had recognized that Darwin's conclusions were incompatible with a doctrine of creation deduced from a literal understanding of Genesis. Owen was the scientific mind behind the religious opposition to Darwin at the Oxford Meeting of the British Association in 1860. But while Bishop Wilberforce's largely scientific arguments were attacked by Huxley, it was the Bishop who won the support of the audience.

In 1809 Jean Lamark had suggested the transmutation of species, based on a model of increasing complexity and a capacity to inherit acquired characteristics that were useful to the particular environment. Although Darwin did not reject such inheritance, he considered that evolution was change that resulted from random variation and natural selection. Darwin rejected Lamark's ideas because they did not explain, for example, why tree frogs should climb trees. Reading Malthus's essay on population growth (1838) led Darwin to recognize that 'only organisms well adapted to their environments and to reproduction would survive the struggle for existence'.[3]

The conceptual revolution comes through the view that there is a commonality of descent through evolution rather than a hierarchy of taxa (plant and animal groups). One dominant view at the time was represented by William Paley[4] who maintained that the complexities of fossil and living species were explained as individual works of the divine creator. Darwin's main hypotheses, that organic beings undergo natural selection and that species of organic beings have evolved, enabled him to explain a host of facts, from geographical distribution of similar species to the existence of vestigial organs. Thagard is right to point out that

> Darwin's theory does not strictly contradict the existence of God, since one can always maintain that it was God who created the universe with laws that eventually resulted in natural selection and biological evolution ... however, Darwin's theory decisively undermined a powerful argument for God's existence based on the adaption of organisms.[5]

In 1863 Huxley published *Evidences of Man's Place in Nature*, and in 1871 Darwin published *The Descent of Man*. These two works laid the basis for the belief that human beings lie at the end of an evolutionary tree that stretches back into the depths of geological history. Darwin deduced that human beings had probably originated in Africa, a conclusion that found support in the twentieth century through the work of the Australian anatomist Raymond Dart, who found a human-like skeleton at Taung in southern Africa in 1924, and called it *Australopithecus*. Further confirmation has come from the British archaeologist and anthropologist Louis Seymour Bazett Leakey (1903–72), who found fossil hominids in the region of Olduvai Gorge, Tanzania. This work has been followed up, through the 1970s and 1980s, by Richard Leakey's discoveries in Kenya.

The conceptual revolution marked through the work of Darwin is of commonality of descent through evolution rather than the kind-hierarchy of taxonomy, whereby human beings are one kind in a list of animals. Paley's view was that a divine creator explained the complexities of the world, including all the individual species of animals and plants. Darwin's main hypotheses, that organic beings undergo natural selection and that species of organic beings have evolved, enabled him to explain a host of facts, from geographical distribution of similar species to the existence of vestigial organs.

| Paley's model | Darwin's model | |
|---|---|---|
| Watchmaker | Malthus's theory | ↓ |
| ↓ | struggle for existence | ↓ |
| ↓ | natural selection | ↓ |
| ↓ | evolution | ↓ |
| watch | variety of species | |

Figure 3.1

The concept of evolution began with Lamark, but Darwin provided the theory of a natural mechanism by it which it might be actualized. Yet neither Lamark nor Darwin was able to show how characteristics of the favoured species were passed on from one generation to another. The answer was found in the mid-nineteenth century by the Abbot of Brunn, Gregor Johann Mendel (1822–84), in Moravia, through the breeding of garden peas in a monastery garden, but did not become known until the end of the century. By crossing pea plants he arrived at the concept of dominant and recessive genes, and formulated the laws of heredity. His results lay unnoticed until 16 years after his death. Mendelian genetics combined with Darwinian natural selection provided the means by which evolution might be understood to progress.

The last 50 years have seen dramatic progress in molecular biology, which is that part of biology that applies the methods of physics and chemistry to living things. Important for our discussion of evolution is the research into macromolecules: the proteins, nucleic acids and the polysaccharides. These are long chain polymers composed of linear strings of smaller molecules, and among them it is the nucleic acids which make up the genes. Their principal function is to store and transmit information. There are two kinds of nucleic acid: deoxyribonucleic acid, known by the shorthand DNA, and ribonucleic acid, RNA. In 1953 Francis Crick (1916–2004) and James Watson (b. 1928) discovered the double helix structure of DNA. For this work they shared with M. H. F. Wilkins the Nobel Prize for Physiology or Medicine in 1962. Watson wrote up his personal account of the research in 1968 in a book entitled *The Double Helix*.

### The process of evolution

The Modern Synthesis has brought together population genetics and evolutionary theory. Evolution takes place slowly due to the accumulation of small changes, many of which are brought about by environmental change. In this case mutations that are suitable to the environment give an advantage in reproduction. It has also been recognized that both competition and co-operation may be seen, for example, in the symbiotic relationship of species.

In the 1930s Goldschmidt and others challenged the assumption that evolution develops through accumulated small changes. More recently Stephen Jay Gould and Niles Eldredge expressed the view that there are long periods of stasis with little change interspersed with rapid speciation during short periods. They noted that 'speciation could occur rapidly if a small population was geographically isolated'.[6] There are also nonadaptive changes that do not necessarily give advantage – sometimes the by-product of other genetic changes. Barbour cites as an example the development of large antlers in the Irish elk, which are unwieldy, but are a by-product of a stronger skeleton.

Barbour draws attention to the active role of genes. He observes:

In neo-Darwinism, random mutations and the recombination of genes provide the raw material of change, but the directionality of evolution is entirely the result of natural selection . . . But some biologists suggest that genes play a more active role in their own evolution. For one thing, the mutational repertory of a gene is a function of its structure, which limits the operation of change. Some changes are the result of the transposition of genes, and transposability is a function of gene structure. Some enzymes also promote mutation. The ability to evolve faster depends on internal as well as external factors. A species can in effect learn to evolve, using strategies successful in the past.[7]

## Scientific aspects

### The structure and age of the earth

Most of the largest planetesimals (planetary fragments) within our solar system coalesced about 4500 million years BP (before present), with most of the 100 km-sized and smaller objects being accreted in the next 500 million years, and completed by about 3800 million years BP. This is known from the dating of the last great collisions on the Moon, dated from samples collected by the Apollo mission. The oldest rocks on Earth are dated at 3960 million years BP. The noble gases (helium, neon, argon, krypton and xenon) and hydrogen are strongly depleted in the earth relative to their solar abundances. It appears that by the time Earth, Venus, Mars and Mercury accreted, the gaseous components of the solar nebula were gone.

There is no evidence for a primitive atmosphere of Earth composed of gases from the solar nebula.[8] Most of the primitive volatiles originated from degassing of the molten mantle in the first 500 million years. The presence of water is a problem, as little appears to have been available in the zone of the nebula where the Earth formed. Temperatures would not have been low enough for water-ice to exist closer than the present asteroid belt, which exists between the orbits of Mars and Jupiter. It is known that the carbonaceous chondrites (a type of meteorite) contain 20 per cent by weight water, and it seems likely that most terrestrial water was derived from late accretion of such planetesimals between 4400 and 3800 million years BP. However, this raises a further problem, the disruptive effect of such impacts would remove earlier atmospheres and hydrospheres. During the early stages of accretion the Earth heated up and became molten through a number of factors, including the decay of short-lived radioactive isotopes, and the continuing impacts of accreting planetesimals. These impacts explain the lack of rocks older than 3960 million years on Earth, after which the crustal plates began to form.[9]

The major geological revolution of the twentieth century was the developing theory of plate tectonics. At the beginning of the century, Alfred Wegener (1880–1931), a German geologist and meteorologist, suggested that the continents had once been together and had drifted apart through time. Wegener suggested that 200 million years ago the continents of Africa, South America, Australia and India were united with Eurasia and North America to form a single super continent that he called 'Pangea'. He made his suggestion based on a study of the rocks, the fossils, the indications of past climatic conditions preserved in the rocks (palaeoclimatology), and the major fault and mountain structures he observed at the edges of these continents. Although he was ridiculed in his lifetime, he has been completely vindicated by the research into plate tectonics in the last 50 years. Wegener put forward his ideas for drifting continents in a lecture in 1912 and a book first published in 1915, which was translated into English in 1924, entitled *The Origin of Continents and Oceans*.

He suggested that the continents were collected together at the North Pole and that their movement away from the pole was the result of gravity. Wegener's mechanism of tidal forces and *Polflucht* (meaning flight from the pole), gravitational slip from the pole, was seen as inadequate. Wegener's opponents saw contraction of the crust, producing lateral forces, as the explanation for major geotectonic features. The distribution of fossil fauna was explained by land bridges; continental and oceanic crusts were considered to be of the same composition; and vertical movements took place through isostacy.

Wegener's theory of drifting continents remained on the fringe until the 1960s. The production of sea-floor maps during the 1950s by the US Navy led to the recognition of the mid-ocean ridges and subsequently the hypothesis of sea-floor spreading, the widening of the ocean basins caused by the up-flow of mantle material to form new oceanic crust. This was a very different explanation to that of Wegener. In 1965, the recognition of symmetrical stripes of reversed and normal magnetism in the sea-floor supported the sea-floor spreading hypothesis.

The paradigm or supermodel of plate tectonics was independently conceived by Dan McKenzie and Jason Morgan in 1967. 'It grew out of the application to a spherical earth of sea-floor spreading with its two corollaries – the mid-oceanic ridges with their symmetrically magnetized strips of ocean floor (the Vine-Matthews-Morley hypothesis) and transform faults (Tuzo Wilson, 1965).'[10] The mid-oceanic ridges are recognized as the surface expression of mantle convection.

When all of the information from the sea floors, together with the stratigraphic, palaeontological and palaeoclimatic data that had supported continental drift, was put together, tectonic plates were recognized, bounded by oceanic ridges (where new crust was being formed), ocean trenches (where one plate descended beneath another and was absorbed into the Mantle) and transform faults (where the plates slipped side by side). Finally the geo-physical evidence of rigid crustal plates, a plastic layer below the crust, and the subduction of the crust below ocean trenches, confirmed plate tectonics as a credible hypothesis.

The plate tectonics model proposes that the entire surface of the Earth comprised a series of rigid, but relatively thin plates, 100–150 kilometres thick, see Figure 5 in the Introduction. The size of these plates is variable. Six major plates cover most of the Earth's surface: Eurasian, African, Indian, Pacific, Antarctic and American plates. These plates are seen to be in contin-uous motion, moving apart, or towards, or alongside each other at rates of between 1 and 3 cm per annum. This movement is taking place in the more 'plastic' layers below the brittle upper layers of the crust. When the brittle upper crust moves it fractures and an earthquake occurs. If we consider, as an example, that the Pacific plate has been moving north-westwards relative to the American plate at some 3 cm per annum for more than a century, along the line of the San Andreas Fault, and that that movement has yet to be seen on the surface of the crust, we recognize that a major earthquake is going to occur.[11]

Three types of plate margin have been recognized: a constructive margin, such as the mid-Atlantic ridge, where the plates are moving apart and new material is added to the crust in the form of volcanic rock; a destructive plate margin, such as the oceanic trench of the Aleutian arc (between Alaska and the former USSR), where one plate is sliding under another; and a con-servative plate margin, such as the San Andreas Fault line, where two plates are sliding past each other, with no material added or lost. These plate mar-gins are the site of almost all the earthquake and volcanic activity seen in the world today.

On a global scale the whole crust of the Earth has changed and developed through geological time. On a smaller scale, the rocks along the coastline of Great Britain or in the mountains, river valleys, quarries and mines, present a similar picture of change and development through time. These rocks show the development of different environments and climates, from arctic to equatorial; periods that were quiet, when sediment was slowly laid down in calm seas; and times of large-scale disruption, when the sea floor was thrown up and folded to form mountains, accompanied by earthquakes and violent volcanic activity. There has been a complex development of the rocks that make up the Earth's crust.

The evidence from the study of the Earth's crust demonstrates, as clearly as is possible, that our planet has had a long history. It was realized by Rutherford and Holmes in England and Boltwood in America, early in the twentieth century, that the decay of unstable isotopes to produce stable (radiogenic) isotopes could be used to date rocks and minerals. These unsta-ble radioactive isotopes, over time, decay (change by loss of protons and/or neutrons) to stable isotopes of another element. The development of better mass-spectrometers in the 1950s allowed the measurement of the quantities of such isotopes, and this has led to methods of the measurement of geological time known as radiometric dating. Relatively (relative to the time-scale involved) precise and accurate methods of dating are based on the radioactive decay rates of isotopes. Figure 3.2 shows examples of half-lives (time taken for half of the unstable isotopes to decay).

| parent | daughter | half life |
|--------|----------|-----------|
| $^{14}C$ | $^{14}N$ | 5730 years |
| $^{87}Rb$ | $^{87}Sr$ | 4.88 billion years |
| $^{40}K$ | $^{40}Ca$ | 1.40 billion years |
| $^{40}K$ | $^{40}Ar$ | 110 million years |
| $^{147}Sm$ | $^{143}Nd$ | 108 billion years |
| $^{234}U$ | $^{230}Th$ | 248,000 years |
| $^{235}U$ | $^{207}Pb$ | 704 million years |
| $^{238}U$ | $^{206}Pb$ | 4.468 billion years |

Figure 3.2[12]

Radiometric dating has established the age of the Earth (c. 4550 million years BP), and of the major changes in its history, and in so doing it has revolutionized our understanding. Through such dating we find that microbial colonies have left fossil records (stromatolites) of life since 3500 million years BP, the first vertebrates appeared about 530 million years BP, the first land fossils occur at the end of the Silurian (c. 395 million years BP), and hominoid species first appeared a mere 4 million years BP.

There are, however, limitations for our study of the Earth's crust, which have implications for the conclusions we might draw. We cannot directly observe past events in the geological history of the Earth, stretching back some 4550 million years, nor can we directly observe the deeper reaches of the crust and the Earth's interior, thousands of kilometres below our feet. We also recognize that, through geological time, periods of crustal movement, marine erosion, metamorphism, and igneous intrusion and extrusion have destroyed large parts of the record in the rocks. This means that some geological theories and hypotheses, including that of evolution, are described as models that best fit the facts as we know them.

## The fossil record

The development of life on planet Earth has been influenced by the development of the atmosphere, and in particular the oxygen content of that atmosphere. It is widely held that most of the gases of the present atmosphere were derived from gases given off during volcanic eruptions, early in the Earth's history. If they were similar to those of modern volcanoes, water vapour and carbon dioxide ($CO_2$) would have made up the bulk of the volatiles, followed by hydrogen sulphide, carbon monoxide, hydrogen, nitrogen, methane, ammonia, hydrogen fluoride, hydrogen chloride, and argon. The lack of molecular oxygen in modern volcanic exhalations has led to the conclusion that the atmosphere in the Archaean (4500–2500 million years BP) was anoxygenic, the free oxygen that we see today having evolved subsequently. The oxygen must have been derived from dissociation of oxides such as $CO_2$ or $H_2O$; solar radiation providing the energy source for two possible photochemical reactions, inorganic (photodissociation) and organic (photosynthesis).[13]

Ultra violet radiation breaks down water vapour to $H_2$ and $O_2$. It is assumed that some of this free oxygen helped to form the ozone layer of the primitive atmosphere, which acted as a barrier to further ultraviolet radiation and enabled early life forms to evolve enzymes to deal with toxic oxygen. Larger amounts of oxygen are produced through photosynthesis: low energy light provided the energy for primitive organisms to produce carbohydrates by photosynthesis from water and $CO_2$, releasing oxygen as a by product. This reaction occurred in green plants and cyanobacteria (formerly termed blue-green algae).

Although from 4000 to 2000 million years BP most of the oxygen produced was used in oxidation or became fixed in carbonate deposits, such as stromatolites, it is generally accepted that free oxygen became abundant in the atmosphere between 2500 and 2000 million years BP. Large quantities of organic carbon were buried in oxidized form as limestones in the period 900–600 million years BP, which indicates that oxygen probably increased substantially during this period. Fossil charcoal from the Devonian suggests a level of 13 per cent for atmospheric oxygen. It is calculated that oxygen levels rose significantly during the Permo-Carboniferous (350–250 million years BP), because of the rise of vascular land plants and the widespread burial of organic matter in vast coal swamps. Oxygen abundance increased to near present-day levels during the Cretaceous and early Tertiary periods (135–25 million years BP).[14]

There is a close relationship between oxygen levels and the development of life forms. The progressive increase in the molecular oxygen content of the atmosphere triggered off major biological innovations that enabled life to advance and diversify. By about 2000 million years ago oxygen reached 10 per cent of present atmospheric level; by 1500 million years BP it had increased to such an extent that the first oxygen-employing eukaryotes (organisms whose cells contain a nucleus within which lie the chromosomes) appeared in oxygenated waters. By 700–600 million years BP the first Metazoa appeared (*Ediacara* – jellyfish, worms and sponges), complex multicellular organisms that require oxygen for their growth. During the Cambrian period (570–510 million years BP) skeletal eukaryotes usurped the function of prokaryotes (single-celled organism with no distinct nucleus, such as bacteria and blue-green algae) in removing the $CO_2$ greenhouse gas through the precipitation of calcium carbonate.[15]

It appears then that the fossil record should give vital clues to understanding the rich variety of species that we see around us today. But what is the origin of this diverse life that is found in the rocks and in the world today? How did it begin? Why did it develop in the sea first and then on the land and in the air? The origin of carbon-based life has been a puzzle that has intrigued biologists and palaeontologists.

Life as we observe it today is the end product of cosmic and terrestrial evolution over the last 15,000 million years. Cesare Emiliani maintains that 'far from being a miracle, life is a *necessary* and *inevitable* consequence of the way the world originated and evolved'.[16] He suggests that life may have begun a number of times during the early turbulent period 4500 to 3800 million years ago, each new start wiped out by the latest asteroidal impact. Life took hold when these impacts ceased, about 3800 million years BP. He believes that life originated when methane was the dominant gas in the atmosphere, as demonstrated by the Urey-Miller experiment, which produced amino acids.[17] However, while amino acids are important building blocks, in order to have the simplest forms of life many other organic compounds must be present, and conditions favourable for their interaction must exist. This leads Morris to comment that 'there is an immense gulf between this soup of relatively simple molecules and a cell capable of division and replication'.[18] Interest more recently has focused on clay minerals as possible templates for coding of information; and the possible role of hydrothermal systems connected with oceanic spreading plate margins, in the origin of life on earth.

What happened in the first 800 million years of Earth history is shrouded in uncertainty. Nitrogen, water vapour and $CO_2$ were the major components of the early atmosphere, the $CO_2$ preventing the new Earth from freezing, for without its 'greenhouse effect' the less luminous Sun of 4000 million years BP would have been unable to warm the planet sufficiently (more fine-tuning). The earliest known fossil life that has been found is bacterial and algal material, together with the presence of amino acids, in rocks as old as 3200 million years BP. However, the bulk of present-day mammals have developed in the last 20 million years.

From that starting point in the primordial ocean we now need to consider how and why life developed as it did. By 600 million years BP the ozone level would have been sufficient to cut out the DNA-inactivating ultraviolet radiation. This would have opened up the oceans to the development and growth of photosynthesizing phytoplankton, which would in turn lead to a large increase in the amount of oxygen in the atmosphere. Plant life on dry land only existed from about 420 million years BP. It was only at this stage that the lethal ultraviolet levels were cut out by the atmosphere, so allowing plant life to develop. Berkner and Marshall[19] suggest that the evolution of life on Earth is related to critical levels of oxygen in the evolving atmosphere. The growth of land plants leads to further, more rapid, increase in oxygen levels. It has been suggested that at this time the oxygen level had reached more than 10 per cent of its present-day level.[20] This gave rise to an immediate evolutionary response with many groups of land plant and animal species developing from their marine counterparts.

Lovelock says, 'The climate and chemical properties of the earth now and throughout its history seem always to have been optimal for life. For this to have happened by chance is as unlikely as to survive unscathed a drive blindfold through rush-hour traffic.'[21] His concept of Gaia draws on the same supporting fine-tuning as we discussed in consideration of the anthropic principle in Chapter 2.

We need to remember at this stage in our discussion the limits of our knowledge of the fossil record, and therefore of the information in support of the theory of evolution. The earliest life forms were mostly microbial. One problem in interpretation is that 'organisms with radically different biochemistries, tolerance of oxygen, ability to utilize substrates and so forth are often morphologically indistinguishable'.[22] Thus radical evolution may not be observable (the 'Volkswagen Syndrome', where the outer shell remains unchanged but under the bonnet there are significant changes). Long-term evolution cannot be investigated experimentally, but hypotheses can be tested against the fossil evidence.

One important new proposition is that of punctuated evolution,[23] whereby most morphological evolution was limited to small, geographically isolated populations, undergoing rapid divergence from their parent populations, while large well-established species populations remained morphologically static. It is also clear that much morphological evolution is too rapid to be faithfully registered in the fossil record: the latter yields only the vague outlines of highly dynamic patterns. The conclusions of palaeontologists are therefore restricted by the morphology and limited preservation of fossils. While the fossil record is often incomplete and complete evolutionary lineages cannot be shown, there is sufficient evidence of changes from one species to another in successive rock layers to demonstrate that mutation in response to environmental change does take place. Such mutation would form the basis of natural selection.

Jerry Coyne[24] outlines the limitations of the fossil record, estimating that of the 17 million to 4 billion species that ever lived we have discovered 250,000 different fossil species, that is, about 0.1–1 per cent of all species. Nevertheless, Coyne maintains that 'we can now show continuous changes within lineages of animals; we have lots of evidence for common ancestors and transitional forms . . . and we have dug deep enough to see the very beginnings of complex life'.[25] Such transitional forms, absent from Darwin's view, have now been found spanning the gap between different kinds of living organisms. One of the most recent discoveries, made in 2004, was *Tiktaalik roseae*, a transition from fish to amphibian, dating from about 375 million years BP.[26]

Coyne explains that the same is true for birds and for whales. He states:

> While we may speculate about the details, the existence of transitional fossils – and the evolution of birds from reptiles – is fact. Fossils like *Archaeopteryx* and its later relatives show a mixture of bird-like and early reptilian traits, and they occur at the right time in the fossil record. Scientists predicted that birds evolved from theropod dinosaurs, and sure enough, we find theropod dinosaurs with feathers.[27]

Coyne concludes that the fossil record confirms the predictions of evolutionary theory, demonstrates that transitional forms appear where they should, and evolutionary change is remodelling the old into the new with no need of special creation.

## DNA and the human genome

The fundamental mechanism for evolution has been explored and demonstrated through the study of DNA. It was in 1944 that microbiological experiments by Avery, MacLeod and McCarty demonstrated that DNA rather than protein was capable of transferring inherited characteristics.

In 1953 Crick and Watson recognized the double strand of DNA, and realized that in the way that the nucleotides[28] in the two strands touched each other there was the possibility of a copying mechanism for the genetic material. In the 1960s it was recognized that double helical DNA unwinds and is copied into complementary strands of RNA. The sequence of nucleotides in the RNA determines the sequence of amino acids in the protein chains. Barbour notes:

> At regular intervals along each strand is a projecting nucleotide base (one of four bases, abbreviated A, C, G, and T), which is linked to a base in the opposite strand. The base pairs form cross links like the rungs of a ladder. An A base will link only with a T base, and C only with G. Here was a mechanism for one of the crucial properties of genes: *replication*. If the two strands separate, every base in each strand will attract a new partner base (from the surrounding fluid) and build up a new partner-strand identical to the old one, with A, C, G, and T units in exactly the same order. Mutations are apparently caused by damage to a portion of the DNA molecule or by defective replication.[29]

The other important property of genes is the control of developmental processes. All living organisms are composed of *protein chains* built out of simpler building blocks, the 20 amino acids. The DNA remains in the cell nucleus, but its distinctive sequences are copied on single strands of messenger RNA and carried to other parts of the cell, where amino acids are assembled into protein chains. It was found that there is a *genetic code* in which a distinctive group of three bases corresponds to each of the 20 amino acids. The order of the triplets in the DNA determines the order in which the amino acids are assembled into protein chains.

Barbour observes:

> In the DNA, then, an 'alphabet' of just four 'letters' (A, C, G, and T bases), grouped in three-letter 'words' (each specifying one of the amino acids), is arranged in 'sentences' (specifying particular proteins). Thousands of sentences of varying length and word order can be made from the twenty basic words, so there are thousands of possible proteins. Long paired strands, made of exactly the same four bases in various sequences, constitute the genes of all organisms, from microbes to human beings. In all known organisms, the same code is used to translate from DNA to protein, which seems to indicate a common origin for all living things.[30]

James Watson, who oversaw the first two years of the Human Genome Project, summarizes the magnitude of the discoveries:

> The genome is the entire set of genetic instructions in the nucleus of every cell. (In fact each cell contains *two* genomes, one derived from each parent: the two copies of each chromosome we inherit furnish us with two copies of each gene, and therefore two copies of the genome.) Genome sizes vary from species to species. From measurements of the amount of DNA in a single cell, we have been able to estimate that the human genome – half the DNA contents of a single nucleus – contains some 3.1 billion base pairs: 3,100,000,000 As, Ts, Gs, and Cs.[31]

Francis Collins comments:

> Investigations of many organisms, from bacteria to humans, revealed that this 'genetic code', by which information in DNA and RNA is translated into protein, is universal in all organisms . . . GAG means glutamic acid in the language of soil bacteria, the mustard weed, the alligator, and your aunt Gertrude.[32]

Commenting on this process, Andrew Miller, Professor of Biochemistry at Edinburgh, writes: 'The DNA double helix suggests the mechanism whereby genes are passed on through generations. In order to work adequately the copying mechanism must be of high fidelity.'[33] However, errors do creep in, altering the amino acid sequence in the proteins. These produce mutations, some of which may bring about a situation whereby the organism cannot survive; others may be neutral; and some give a reproductive advantage. This throws a lot of light on what may be going on in evolution.

To these observations Collins adds his view that the components of living things turn out to be marvellous, intricate and aesthetically pleasing,

> from the ribosome that translates RNA into protein, to the metamorphosis of the caterpillar into the butterfly . . . Evolution, as a mechanism, can be and must be true. But that says nothing about the nature of its author. For those who believe in God, there are reasons now to be more in awe, not less.[34]

To summarize: the primary gene products are the direct consequence of a rather simple chemical process that has been worked out in the revolution of molecular biology begun in 1953 with the elucidation of the structure of DNA by James Watson and Francis Crick. At this level, inherited characters can be said to be determined by the genes carried by an individual. Once we leave the primary gene product level, however, the occurrence, speed and direction of chemical processes in the body are affected to varying extents by environmental influences.[35]

Starting with the recognition of the defective genes that led to the common genetic illness of cystic fibrosis, Collins recounts the work of the human genome project, including the competition that came from Celera, a private research operation which threatened to make the map of the human genome only available by payment. The first announcement of the success of the project was made on 26 June 2000 and, as Collins is pleased to record,

> In April 2003, in the month that marked the fiftieth anniversary of Watson and Crick's publication on the double helix, we announced the completion of all the goals of the Human Genome Project. As the project manager of the enterprise, I was intensely proud of the more than two thousand scientists who had accomplished this remarkable feat, one that I believe will be seen a thousand years from now as one of the major achievements of humankind.[36]

### The origin of life

Francis Collins notes that all evidence currently available suggests that the Earth was not conducive to life for its first 500 million years. The planet was under constant bombardment from giant asteroids and meteorites, one of which actually tore the Moon loose from Earth. It is therefore not surprising that rocks dating back 4 billion years or more show absolutely no evidence of any life forms. 'Just 150 million years later, however, multiple different types of microbial life are found. Presumably, these single-celled organisms were capable of information storage, probably using DNA, and were self-replicating and capable of evolving into multiple different types.'[37]

But how did self-replication organisms arise in the first place? Collins maintains that no current hypothesis explains how 'in the space of a mere 150 million years, the prebiotic environment that existed on planet Earth gave rise to life'.[38] Stanley Miller and Harold Urey's experiments in the 1950s suggested that it might be possible for complex organic molecules to arise from natural processes in the universe (see note 17). Collins notes that neither DNA nor RNA can be produced through such experiments and that the conclusion of Francis Crick that life forms arrived on earth from outer space 'simply forces that astounding event to another time and place even further back'.[39] Others have observed that self-replicating clay particles may have reduced the gap between non-living and living forms, but we are still a long way from the origin of DNA.

Given the lack of a solution to the origin of life some theists have suggested that God initiated the appearance of DNA and RNA. But this is another case of the 'God of the gaps' argument, which may be doomed to failure as science advances. Collins is right to observe that 'There are good reasons to believe in God, including the existence of mathematical principles and order in creation. They are positive reasons, based on knowledge, rather than default assumptions based on (temporary) lack of knowledge.'[40]

## Evolution

Barbour quotes Jeffrey Wicken: 'Nature produces itself hierarchically – one level establishing the ground of its own stability by utilizing mechanisms made available by lower levels, and finding functional contexts at higher levels.' [41] Barbour goes on to note:

> here is a clue as to how evolution can exhibit both *chance* and *directionality*. Chance is present at many levels: mutations, genetic recombination, genetic drift, climatic variations, and so forth. Evolution is an unrepeatable series of events that no one could have predicted; it can only be described historically. Yet history has seen an ascent to higher levels of organization, a trend toward greater complexity and sentience. The dice are thrown, but the dice are loaded; there are built-in constraints. In particular, modular structures are *relatively stable*, and so the advances are conserved.[42]

But it is precisely at this point that a number of questions arise. Miller raises some of them, and he himself finds these questions to be at least suggestive of the grounds for Christian belief. Why do organisms metabolize, reproduce and evolve? Can life be explained fully in terms of physics and chemistry?

Can the apparent self-determination and goal-orientation of organisms be accounted for fully by physics and chemistry? He concludes by stating that 'Molecular biology will always be more than just physics and chemistry . . . there will be essential boundary conditions. Contingency will be evident.'[43]

Although Richard Dawkins[44] begins with an entirely reductionist view, which sees life merely in terms of its chemical and physical components, he concludes that there must be some guiding mechanism in the otherwise chance development of complex life forms. When faced with the question of how something so complex as the human eye could evolve, his answer is that it has done so by one small step at a time through the immensity of geo-logical epochs. Dawkins concludes that the essence of life is statistical improbability on a colossal scale. Thus, whatever the explanation for life might be, 'it cannot be chance', by which he means 'pure naked chance'. Cumulative selection, he maintains, is a different form of chance, 'chance at every step'; it is what he calls 'tamed chance'. To 'tame' chance means to break down the very improbable into less improbable small components arranged in series. However, he also states that there must be a 'mechanism' for guiding each step in the same particular direction; otherwise 'the sequence of steps will career off in an endless random walk'. This guiding mechanism for Dawkins is the urge for survival, and so a 'non-random' aiming at a target of survival at every step.[45]

We have every right, however, to question the explanatory power of this theory. Is such small-scale non-random survival really sufficient to explain the convergence of evolutionary patterns on the separated continents of Eurasia-Africa, North-South America, and Australia, whereby similar species have developed in isolation from each other over the last 200 million years? It is significant that Dawkins is looking for an immanent principle by which evolution takes place. He finds it in gradual natural selection alone, but for a Christian believer the guiding mechanism will be expressed as the involvement of the immanent God with creation. The heart of this issue is not whether natural selection through non-random survival takes place, but whether it is a *sufficient* mechanism to lead to the development of conscious self-aware human beings. We might then suggest that the immanent purpose of the Creator, working *through* natural selection and non-random survival, appears to be more reasonable than chance, even if it is a 'tamed' kind of chance.

## Dialogue

### Evolution and creation

Julian Huxley, grandson of Thomas Henry Huxley, comments that Dar-win's voyage on the *Beagle* was to change not only his attitude to life, his beliefs and basic concepts, but it was to provide food for thought for millions of people, it was to produce schisms in the church and a century of argument among scientists. It was also to lay the most important foundation-stone for a fuller understanding of living things and the world we live in.[46]

In discussion of the foundation laid by Darwin's theory we can explore the findings of a variety of biologists both those with a Christian belief and those with none.

There is little doubt in the scientific community that the neo-Darwinian synthesis of natural selection and genetic inheritance is the explanation for the development and distribution of all animal and plant life on the planet. Geneticist Jerry Coyne (not a Christian), notes that evolution is 'a mechanism of staggering simplicity and beauty' and if there was ever a question over the theory it was in the nineteenth century, when the evidence for a mechanism of evolution was unclear.[47] Christians working in various fields of biology are agreed in their view that evolution is true, inasmuch as it is the best explanation of the facts that we find in palaeontology, anthropology and genetics. Coyne asks why it is that people today still doubt this theory, and comments, 'We don't doubt in the existence of electrons or black holes, despite the fact that these phenomena are much farther removed from everyday experience than is evolution . . . What's *not* a problem is the lack of evidence.'[48]

Denis Alexander, who is the Director of the Faraday Institute for Science and Religion, Cambridge, states that

the purpose of Darwinian theory is to explain the biological diversity that we see all around us on our planet . . . we're looking at a world of immense diversity in which we are accustomed to encountering hundreds of different biological species in the normal course of everyday life.[49]

Evolutionary theory seeks to explain where the 10–20 million living species have come from. Biological evolution is a slow process taking place over billions of years since early after the formation of the Earth some 4566 million years ago.

Evolution is based on two principal ideas: diversity in the genome, for example mutation resulting in differences of ability to survive and reproduce; and natural selection, that is, genomes generating organisms with slightly better or slightly poorer survival. Differences in genomes are accumulated through mutation, sexual reproduction and gene flow. Alexander comments that natural selection takes place through successful reproduction which ensures that the individual's genes are passed on to the next generation, and that 'natural selection therefore acts as a rigorous filter to reduce the amount of genetic variation in the population'.[50]

Evolution is not a smooth curve from the very simple to the very complex. As we noted earlier, Stephen Jay Gould and Niles Eldredge observed long periods of stasis with little change interspersed with rapid speciation during short periods, where Barbour notes, 'speciation could occur rapidly if a small population was geographically isolated'.[51] Evolution has also been affected by changes in the earth's environment. For example, by the changing composition of the atmosphere, especially with the increasing oxygen content.

Alexander comments that biological diversity is late in the Earth's history, as before the Cambrian (c. 600 million years ago) most living creatures were rarely more than a millimetre across.[52] During the succeeding eras mass extinctions have played an important part in triggering new waves of species diversification. More than 99 per cent of all species that have ever lived on this planet are now extinct. About 65 million years ago, at the Cretaceous/Tertiary boundary, about 60–75 per cent of all species (including the dinosaurs) became extinct, probably as a result of an asteroid collision.[53]

As a geneticist Alexander goes on to make an important point:

> unlike the fossil record, there are no gaps in the genetic record. By that I do not mean that we have a complete record of all the genome sequences of every species that ever lived – of course we do not and never will have because 99% of them are no longer around to get DNA samples. Nevertheless, in the 1% that remains we have a DNA record, including disused genetic fossils that take us back to the dawn of life.[54]

By genetic fossils Alexander means that 'all genomes of organisms that have evolved recently are littered with ancient genes, still in use, that we can identify as going deep back into evolutionary time. But in addition they are replete with relics of genes no longer in use', which are signatures of evolutionary histories.[55]

Alexander expresses his view of evolution that 'virtually no biologist in the research community actually doubts [whether evolution happened], but about mechanisms, interpretations, classification disputes there are debates. Evolution is no "holy cow" – it is every biologist's dream to make discoveries that would upset some cherished theory' – your career would be made.[56] In answer to those anti-evolutionists he challenges them to understand that 'really serious objections to evolution, if there are any, have to be presented the tough but proper way, by publication of solid results in respectable scientific journals'.[57] Once we see evolution as God's chosen way, it ceases to be a 'bogey man'.[58]

Both Alexander and Sam Berry,[59] former Professor of Genetics, University College London, note the significant genetic relationship between human beings and our closest animal relative, the chimpanzees. Berry notes that the DNA difference between the two species of chimpanzee – *Pan troglodytes* and *Pan paniscus* – is 0.7 per cent, and between chimpanzees and human beings 1.6 per cent. He then draws attention to the fact that the difference between the two extant species of gibbon is 2.2 per cent, which is greater than the difference between human beings and chimpanzees.[60] Alexander draws the inescapable conclusion that human beings are directly related to the rest of animal life, unless God has planted misleading evidence, or set out to deceive us.[61] His preferred model to understand human beings as God's creation is *Homo divinus*. He sees Genesis as proto-history, in which God reveals himself to a couple of Neolithic farmers in the Near East, as a result of which they become spiritually alive.[62]

### Can we find a consensus in the views about evolution?

Alister McGrath quotes the late Stephen Jay Gould, an atheist, who stated that 'either half my colleagues are enormously stupid, or else the science of Darwinism is fully compatible with conventional religious beliefs – and equally compatible with atheism'.[63] Richard Dawkins on the other hand would not disagree with the biological evidence discussed above, but would be diametrically opposed to the conclusions drawn:

> I am continually astonished by those theists who . . . seem to rejoice in natural selection as 'God's way of achieving his creation'. They note that evolution by natural selection would be a very easy and neat way to achieve a world full of life. God wouldn't need to do anything at all![64]

Dawkins is astounded that any scientist might invoke the divine in discussion of evolution, and has even less time for the biblical literalist.

My own view is that evolution is a process within the universe's history. This history is not a chance process but is constrained by the physical (God-given) parameters of the universe's beginnings and by its (God-given) laws. I believe that we should recognize that this is the way in which God has brought the universe and life of planet Earth into being, and through this recognition praise God for his faithfulness, his creativity, and every aspect of his grace that we find for our lives in this world.

### Finding a satisfactory conclusion

Alister McGrath, in his Christian critique of Richard Dawkins' position, notes that 'Dawkins holds that the explanatory force of Darwinism on the one hand, and the aesthetic, moral, and intellectual failings of religion on the other, lead the honest person directly and inexorably to atheism.'[65]

He summarizes Dawkins' hostility towards Christianity as:

1 the Darwinian world-view makes God unnecessary
2 religion is based on faith with no rigorous evidence to support it

3 religion offers an impoverished view of the world
4 religion leads to evil.

But we will want to observe that Dawkins does not engage with alternative views. There are important questions to ask about what sort of God Dawkins finds to be redundant or discredited. For example, in *River out of Eden*, he says that 'the universe we observe had precisely the properties we should expect if there is, at bottom, no design, no purpose, no evil, and no good, nothing but blind pitiless indifference'.[66]

The problem with this argument is that Dawkins, like many creationists and those who subscribe to intelligent design, places Darwinism and God in opposition. Science is not the field of intellectual discourse in which God can be proved or disproved. The view that since Paley's watchmaker God has been disposed of by Darwin's thesis, God does not exist, is almost laughable. The concept of God the watchmaker has long been rejected by theology. The critique of the teleological argument presented by David Hume still holds true.[67]

McGrath takes Dawkins to task over his view that faith is blind trust in the absence of evidence.[68] He notes that Dawkins moves from 'not proven' to 'therefore equals false', which is in itself a bad argument. Dawkins' use of 'improbable' to describe God has no rational support and is, in McGrath's words, 'a populist swashbuckling rhetorical exaggeration'.[69] John Lennox supports this view when he observes that when Dawkins suggests that evolution and God are mutually exclusive alternatives, he implies that God and evolution belong to the same category of explanation.[70]

McGrath maintains with historians, such as John Brooke, the view that conflict between science and Christianity is a piece of Victorian propaganda and relates to a time at the end of the nineteenth century when 'professional scientists wished to distance themselves from their amateur colleagues', mostly clergymen, and so become independent of the Church.[71]

Far from a case of small-mindedness, McGrath confirms that the Christian approach recognizes an immediate sense of wonder at the beauty of nature; a derived sense of wonder from the mathematical representation of reality; and a derived sense of wonder at what the natural world points to. We can agree with his opinion that 'if anything, a Christian engagement with the natural world adds a richness which I find absent from Dawkins' account of things, offering a new motivation [for us all] for the study of nature'.[72]

Spencer and Alexander suggest that the attacks on faith by Darwinian fundamentalists do not help people to understand and accept evolution, and in fact drive them into the hands of the creation science movement.[73] However, the arguments presented by those who ascribe to creationism and its newer version, intelligent design, are likewise unhelpful. They treat evolution as an anti-religious philosophy rather than science. Their views move away from the immanence of God, leave us perilously close to a 'God of the gaps' argument, and in an attempt to protect Scripture's final authority devalue scientific investigation, while also denying the significance and authority of God's revelation in the created world.[74] This is far removed from early scientists like John Ray who spoke of holding the book of God's word in one hand and the book of God's works in the other.

## Intelligent design

This is a form of episodic creationism. Some of its supporters hold to an old Earth, but many of their arguments are similar to those held by creationists, for example in their denial of macroevolution. A key exponent of this position, William Dembski,[75] is concerned that modern theology, mistakenly, has a theodicy and theology of nature that rules out intervention. Intelligent design is defined as design that is due to an actual intelligence. In further defining intelligent design, as opposed to the design argument, the author suggests that we need to distinguish between design that may be the result of natural causes and that which exhibits features characteristic of intelligence. This raises the same concern that we have noted elsewhere of separating God from nature, as if God were not the author of natural processes.

Dembski consistently places intelligent design in opposition to Darwinism, suiting his theological thesis, which seeks to exclude evolution as a principle in theological debate. He states that if it is not excluded we find that the unchanging God of traditional theology gives way to the evolving God of process theologies. Thus traditional theism, with its strong transcendence, is ousted by panentheism, with its modified transcendence wherein God is inseparable from and dependent on the world. Dembski's position here runs the danger of being contrary to Scripture, where God is clearly seen to be active within creation.

Alexander notes that Michael Behe,[76] another advocate of intelligent design, proposes that some entities are so complex that they could not have appeared by chance. One such entity that Behe identifies is the bacterial flagellum. It is an example of an irreducible complex system. But Alexander observes that 'most of the components of the flagellum have roles and functions that are widely known and are widely spread through living organisms', and the evolution of the flagellum has now been demonstrated.[77] Alexander recognizes that intelligent design is proposing an 'ill-defined designer in the gap of our present ignorance',[78] which is a version of the 'God of the gaps' argument.

In discussing naturalism Dembski concludes that the naturalist is likely to posit Nature (writ large) or the Universe (also writ large) or mass-energy or superstrings or some such entity as the final resting place for explanation, and that Darwinism conduces towards naturalism whereas intelligent design, at least in contemporary Western culture, conduces towards theism.

Alexander addresses one of the fundamental theological flaws in the intelligent design position, when he poses the question, where does DNA come from? He believes that it really doesn't matter as this is God's work in creation. He points out that the intelligent design and creationist literature speaks of

> the impossibility that life could emerge out of chemicals by sinister sounding 'blind materialistic, naturalistic forces.' But wait a minute these are God's chemicals, God's materials, that are being talked about here. A mystery bigger than the origin of life is why Christians should ascribe pagan-sounding characteristics to God's world.[79]

Coyne rightly recognizes that the heart of the problem is the fact that evolution raises profound questions of purpose and morality, and the emotional consequences of facing this fact. Yet he does not believe that evolution leaves us in such a barren naturalistic and materialistic world. He observes: 'Yes, certain parts of our behaviour may be genetically encoded, instilled by natural selection in our savanna-dwelling ancestors. But genes aren't destiny.' He states that 'there is no reason . . . to see ourselves as marionettes dancing on the strings of evolution. One lesson that all geneticists know, but which doesn't seem to have permeated the consciousness of the public, is that "genetic" does not mean "unchangeable".'[80] He recognizes that while the world is full of selfishness, immorality and injustice, we also find kindness and altruism.

### Entering into dialogue

Nancy Murphy develops a model for thinking about the relation of theology, ethics, the natural sciences and the human sciences, which understands them as hierarchically ordered and intrinsically interconnected. It is the level of explanation that is important. Her central thesis is that biological evolution requires the higher level of explanation which only theology can give. Humankind, created in God's image, is created to participate in God's creativity, in its splendour and its suffering.

When she considers God's action in the natural world, Murphy considers the modern views under three headings: deism – activity restricted to initial creation; interventionism, where God's continuing action is one of intervention through specific events; and immanentism, where it is seen that if God works in the universe then every event in some sense is an act of God – so God acts through nature and history. The discoveries of science – Newton's laws of motion, evolution, the fine-tuning of an expanding universe, and the anthropic principle – push us in the direction of immanentism.

In a later work[81] she rightly points out that the conflict between science and biblical faith is an argument about the ways in which God acts. She then states that, for example, in opposing creationism our arguments should not centre on proving evolutionary theory (which only some are equipped to do) but rather on the creationist's view of divine action.

We can propose a move away from the interventionist model of God's action found in the creationist and intelligent design arguments and explore an understanding of God's immanent action within creation, which is more securely biblical. Here we find the God who accompanied the people of Israel as pillar of cloud and pillar of fire, who directed them through his servants the prophets, who was incarnate in Christ, and who is ever present as Holy Spirit.

Murphy examines attacks on evolution that emphasize waste and suffering, and affirms that evolution requires death. For example, we needed to be meat-eaters to develop the metabolism to support large brains. She also asks why we should be concerned that species die out. Do we want the dinosaurs around now? She also notes that pain is necessary if there are to be animals that exhibit complex behaviour, and that we need pain in order to protect ourselves from self-destruction. She concludes:

> If God is to create life, and this means real life, life that actually lives in its environment in an ecosystem and not just toy creatures that have to be kept alive by constant divine action, then the biological world has to be very much the way it is. Most of the suffering in nature (that is not caused by us) is *natural*; it simply needs to be present in order for there to be life at all, especially for there to be life like ourselves.[82]

Coyne concludes:

> We are the one creature to whom natural selection has bequeathed a brain complex enough to comprehend the laws that govern the universe. And we should be proud that we are the only species that has figured out how we came to be.[83]

This can be a true conclusion for both the scientist and for the Christian seeking to understand God's world.

### Somewhere to stand

It is a problem when words are hijacked – I am a 'creationist' inasmuch as I believe that God is the creator of all that exists or has been or will be in this universe. The sadness of the modern Creation Science Movement is that they cut themselves off from the revelation of God in scientific research, and they fail to find the depth of God's revelation in Scripture by treating Genesis 1 as if it were a divinely dictated text. As John Polkinghorne observed: 'Mistaking poetry for prose can lead to false conclusions. When

Robert Burns tells us his love "is like a red, red rose", we know that we are not meant to think that his girlfriend has green leaves and prickles.'[84]

Richard Dawkins exploited the more extreme views surrounding evolution in his 2008 television series, which explored the life and work of his hero Charles Darwin.[85] The media find the conflict model an easy one to present, whereas the dialogue between Christianity and science, explored by many writers,[86] is far more complex and time-demanding.

For many theistic evolutionists today, Polkinghorne's summation of Charles Kingsley's reaction to the *Origin of Species* is a helpful position to hold:

> Kingsley said that no doubt God could have created a ready-made world, but it had turned out the Creator had done something cleverer and more valuable than that, in creating a world so endowed with potentiality that creatures 'could make themselves' through the shuffling explorations of natural selection. The God who is the Creator of nature can as properly be seen to be at work through natural processes as in any other way.[87]

## Theological implications

### Biblical considerations

In the biblical accounts of creation we understand that we are linked to natural creation: created on the same day (Gen. 1), and of the same substance (Gen. 2). But we are also distinct: *imago Dei* (Gen. 1), and with God's spirit/breath (Gen. 2).[88] Berry has sought to consider whether or not a special creation of human beings 'in the image of God' is possible. He considers the later stages in the development of hominids. *Homo erectus* was widely distributed in the Upper Pleistocene, about 1 million years BP; an upright walker, meat-eater, tool-maker, belonging to the 'great hand axe' culture. They did not differ greatly from *Homo sapiens* and seem to have overlapped with them. There are a number of well-documented intermediary forms, from 300 to 150,000 years BP, including *Swanscombe* (lower Thames valley), *Vertessozollos* (Hungary), *Steinheim* (Germany), and *Montmaurin* and *Fontechevade* (France).

Berry states that the gene pool of any species is the result of the interactions of the past individuals of that species with all their previous environments. If human beings were instantaneously created, it follows that all their behaviour, reactions and relations would be the consequence of God's intention, Adam's sin, and the short time since the Garden of Eden. Although possible, Berry maintains that this is almost certainly untrue and also that it raises theological difficulties: first, God does not use the whole of his creation for his purpose; and, second, it requires our relationship with God to be controlled genetically, as genes must be created to enable response to God. Berry concludes:

There are three possible views about human origins: as 'nothing but' a highly evolved ape; as 'nothing but' a special creation of God made complete in every respect; or as an ape inbreathed by God's Spirit, with an evolutionary history but with a unique relationship with the Creator. Only the last can incorporate both a sensible understanding of Scripture and the findings of science . . . [and do] justice to the God of the Bible, who is both creator and sustainer.[89]

There comes a stage in the development of hominids when they are conscious of, and able to relate to, the creator. The biblical account would suggest that this is an act of God's self-revelation, when human beings have developed to a point when such a revelation might be received.

## Options for belief

Humankind, created in God's image, is created to participate in God's creativity, in its splendour and its suffering. God's action in the natural world is seen to be one of being immanent. Murphy is anxious that we do not fall into the trap of simply suggesting that God puts a 'rubber stamp' on all the natural happenings of the universe or the trap of thinking that God approves of everything that happens. She therefore suggests three essential features of divine action in the human realm:

- God creates individuals with his or her own integrity, power, capacities, who participate in creation
- God respects human freedom
- God accepts the cost of respecting the individuality and freedom of human creatures.[90]

Barbour stresses that there is a pervasive role of chance in evolution – mutation, environmental changes. He states that 'Evolutionary history is irreversible and unrepeatable. Potentialities that were present at one point were permanently excluded by particular lines of development. Most mutations are harmful to the organism, or even lethal.'[91] Monod believes that such blind chance makes design a non-starter.

There are a number of theological responses to chance noted by Barbour:

- God controls events that appear to be random, although this does not explain blind alleys
- God designed a system of law and chance, which is an expression of God's overall design of the universe
- God influences events without controlling them, which is the view taken by process theology.[92]

Murphy progresses her argument to include every action of God at every level of existence in the universe. She believes that the indeterminacy at sub-atomic particle level, while not being the same as free will, does nevertheless provide a valuable analogue for free will in an account of divine action. Here is the answer to evil, suffering and natural disasters. God co-operates with, rather than overpowers, such indeterminacy or free will.

Exploring ethics, Murphy asks where we should look for moral guidance in such a universe? She suggests that we look not at the *products* of divine creative action, but rather to the *moral character* of that action. The moral character of God's action includes constant *involvement* – not a distant deistic indifference. So, God respects the integrity of creation and accepts the cost of withholding power – the inefficiency, waste and even suffering that may result.[93]

She concludes that the ethic of creation is an ethic of non-violence – persuasive but not coercive. As in Christ, it is suffering through to something higher. She maintains that 'God counts it worth the cost of sin to have creatures who respond freely to divine love'; and, 'If the death of Jesus is the ultimate act of God's withholding of power, then Jesus' resurrection is the promise and foretaste of final victory.'[94]

Francis Collins provides an admirable summary of the options that are open to us at this point. He considers that agnosticism is a 'cop out'; it simply has not bothered to survey all the evidence for the great faith traditions of the world. In criticism of creationism he points to the fallacy of literal translation of poetic and metaphorical texts, while at the same time observing that if God created a universe to appear to be old then such a God would be a deceiver. In demolishing intelligent design he notes that it does not hold up scientifically, 'providing neither an opportunity for experimental validation nor a robust foundation for its primary claim of irreducible complexity'. But it also fails theologically, giving a 'God of the gaps' answer to the aspects science currently cannot explain.[95]

His own position is to maintain that we need a harmony between science and faith. He testifies to his own position:

The need to find my own harmony of the worldviews ultimately came as the study of genomes – our own and that of many other organisms on the planet – began to take off, providing an incredibly rich and detached view of how descent by modification from a common ancestor has occurred. Rather than finding this unsettling, I found this elegant evidence of relatedness of all living things an occasion of awe, and came to see this as the master plan of the same Almighty who caused the universe to come into being and set its physical parameters just precisely right to allow the creation of stars, planets, heavy elements, and life itself.[96]

For Collins, the God of the Bible is the God of the genome.

**Key texts**

Denis Alexander, 2008, *Creation or Evolution: Do we have to choose?* Oxford: Monarch.

Francis Collins, 2007, *The Language of God: A Scientist Presents Evidence for Belief*, London: Simon & Schuster/Pocket Books.

Alister McGrath, 2007, *Dawkins' God: Genes, Memes, and the Meaning of Life*, Oxford: Blackwell.

James Watson, 2004, *DNA: The Secret of Life*, London: Arrow Books.

**Further reading**

Ian G. Barbour, 1998, *Religion and Science: Historical and Contemporary Issues*, London: SCM Press.

R. J. Berry, 1996, *God and the Biologist: Faith at the Frontiers of Science*, Leicester: InterVarsity Press/Apollos.

G. C. Brown, C. J. Hawkesworth and R. C. L. Wilson (eds), 1992, *Understanding the Earth: A New Synthesis*, Cambridge: Cambridge University Press.

Jerry A. Coyne, 2009, *Why Evolution is True*, Oxford: Oxford University Press.

Richard Dawkins, 1986, *The Blind Watchmaker*, London: Longmans.

——1989, *The Selfish Gene*, Oxford: Oxford University Press.

——1996, *River out of Eden: A Darwinian View of Life*, New York: Basic Books.

Steve Jones, 2000, *The Language of the Genes: Biology, History and the Evolutionary Future*, rev. edn, London: Flamingo/HarperCollins.

Nancey Murphy, 2002, *Religion and Science: God, Evolution, and the Soul*, Proceedings of the 2001 Goshen Conference on Religion and Science, ed. Carl S. Helrich, Kitchener, Ontario: Pandora Press.

Paul Thaggard, 1992, *Conceptual Revolutions*, Princeton NJ: Princeton University Press.

**Notes**

1 Quoted in H. Wendt, 1970, *Before the Deluge*, London: Palidin, p. 81.

2 Wendt, *Before the Deluge*, p. 130.

3 Paul Thaggard, 1992, *Conceptual Revolutions*, Princeton NJ: Princeton University Press, p. 133.

4 For Paley's understanding of individual divine design of animals and plants, the finding of a watch while walking on the heath indicating a watchmaker, see William Paley, *Natural Theology* (1802), repr. in R. Lyman (ed.), 1925, *The Works of William Paley*, London.

5 Thaggard, *Conceptual Revolutions*, p. 136.

6 Ian G. Barbour, 1998, *Religion and Science. Historical and Contemporary Issues*, London: SCM Press, p. 224.

7 Barbour, *Religion and Science*, p. 225.

8 Stuart Ross Taylor, 'The Origin of the Earth', in G. C. Brown, C. J. Hawkes-

worth and R. C. L. Wilson (eds), 1992, *Understanding the Earth: A New Synthesis*, Cambridge: Cambridge University Press, pp. 36–7.

9 Brian F. Windley, 1995, *The Evolving Continents*, Chichester: John Wiley, p. 1.

10 Windley, *The Evolving Continents*, p. 6.

11 A minor movement (a couple of millilitres or less) along a fracture in the Earth's crust will produce a major earthquake. The last major movement along the San Andreas Fault was the great San Francisco earthquake of 1906. From 1906 to 2010 is 104 years, which at 3 cm/year is over 3 metres. There is a major earthquake waiting to occur!

12 Chris J. Hawkesworth and Peter van Calsteren, 'Geological Time', in Brown, Hawkesworth and Wilson, *Understanding the Earth*, p. 135.

13 Windley, *The Evolving Continents*, p. 418.

14 Windley, *The Evolving Continents*, p. 422.

15 See Windley, *The Evolving Continents*, pp. 426–7, and Simon Conway Morris, 'The Early Evolution of Life', in Brown, Hawkesworth and Wilson, *Understanding the Earth*, pp. 437–9 for a fuller discussion of these points.

16 Cesare Emiliani, 1992, *Planet Earth: Cosmology, Geology, and the Evolution of Life and Environment*, Cambridge: Cambridge University Press, p. 371.

17 In the 1930s, J. B. S. Haldane suggested that organic compounds formed in the early atmosphere of the Earth and eventually found their way into the oceans, which formed a hot 'soup' where these compounds could grow. This would form a non-oxidizing or reducing environment. The great leap forward in the study of the origin of life came with the work of S. L. Miller in 1953, who demonstrated in an experiment that the amino acids, purines and pyramidines could be produced naturally in such a reducing environment. Miller applied electrical discharges to a mixed 'atmosphere' including methane, ammonia and water vapour, and produced a number of organic compounds. It was considered that as a result there would be a build-up of organic compounds in the oceans, which would provide a 'nutrient broth' in which the first living organisms developed. This led scientists to believe that the Earth's primitive atmosphere was a reducing one, with carbon present in the form of methane. However, though today no one doubts the validity of Miller's experiments there is now considerable doubt over the composition of the atmosphere that was assumed.

18 Morris, 'The Early Evolution of Life', p. 438.

19 L. V. Berkner and L. C. Marshall, 'Oxygen and Evolution', in I. G. Gass, P. J. Smith and R. C. L. Wilson (eds), 1971, *Understanding the Earth*, Sussex, Open University: Artemis Press, pp. 143–9.

20 Berkner and Marshall, 'Oxygen and Evolution', pp. 143–9.

21 J. E. Lovelock, 1987, *Gaia: A New Look at Life on Earth*, Oxford: Oxford University Press, p. 10.

22 Morris, 'The Early Evolution of Life', p. 439.

23 Stephen Jay Gould, 1990, *Wonderful Life: The Burgess Shale and the Nature of History*, London: Hutchinson Radius, through his work on the Cambrian (530 million years BP) Burgess Shale of British Columbia, draws attention to the wide variety of classes and phyla that are present in the Burgess Shale, leading him to suggest that 'the maximum range of anatomical possibilities arises with the first rush of diversification . . . Later history is a tale of restriction, as most of these early experi-

ments succumb and life settles down to generating endless variants upon a few surviving models' (p. 47). Gould says that Darwin saw competition under natural selection, with the better-adapted species winning, and so for Darwin contingency is the primary support to evolution (p. 300). Yet Gould maintains that nature was not as smoothly ordered as Darwin suggested, that large-scale catastrophic changes in environment have left their mark. He concludes that the Burgess Shale suggests a pattern of maximum diversity at the bottom, with contingency leading to proliferation along certain lines only – a 'Christmas tree, bottom heavy, evolutionary tree'.

24 Jerry A. Coyne, 2009, *Why Evolution is True*, Oxford: Oxford University Press, pp. 23–4.

25 Coyne, *Why Evolution*, p. 28.

26 Coyne, *Why Evolution*, pp. 38–9.

27 Coyne, *Why Evolution*, p. 50.

28 A nucleotide is a chemical compound that consists of three portions: a heterocyclic base, a sugar, and one or more phosphate groups. In the most common nucleotides the base is a derivative of purine or pyrimidine, and the sugar is the pentose (five-carbon sugar) deoxyribose or ribose. Nucleotides are the monomers of nucleic acids, with three or more bonding together in order to form a nucleic acid. Nucleotides are the structural units of RNA, DNA and several cofactors – CoA, flavin adenine dinucleotide, flavin mononucleotide, adenosine triphosphate and nicotinamide adenine dinucleotide phosphate. In the cell they have important roles in metabolism, and signalling. http://en.wikipedia.org/wiki/Nucleotide

29 Barbour, *Religion and Science*, p. 226.

30 Barbour, *Religion and Science*, p. 226.

31 James Watson, 2004, *DNA: The Secret of Life*, London: Arrow Books, p. 165.

32 Francis Collins, 2007, *The Language of God: A Scientist Presents Evidence for Belief*, London: Simon & Schuster/Pocket Books, p. 104.

33 A. Miller, 'Biology and Belief', in R. J. Berry (ed.), 1991, *Real Science, Real Faith*, Eastbourne: Monarch, p. 82.

34 Collins, *The Language of God*, p. 107.

35 R. J. Berry, 1996, *God and the Biologist*, Leicester: InterVarsity Press, p. 60.

36 Collins, *The Language of God*, p. 122.

37 Collins, *The Language of God*, p. 89.

38 Collins, *The Language of God*, p. 90.

39 Collins, *The Language of God*, p. 91.

40 Collins, *The Language of God*, p. 93.

41 Jeffrey Wicken, 1987, *Evolution, Thermodynamics and Information*, New York and Oxford: Oxford University Press, p. 177.

42 Barbour, *Religion and Science*, p. 230.

43 Miller, 'Biology and Belief', pp. 85–6.

44 Richard Dawkins, 1986, *The Blind Watchmaker*, London: Longmans.

45 Dawkins, *The Blind Watchmaker*, pp. 317–18.

46 Julian Huxley and H. B. D. Kettlewell [1965], 1975, *Charles Darwin and his World*, London: Book Club Associates/Thames & Hudson Ltd, pp. 5–6.

47 Coyne, *Why Evolution is True*, p. xv.

48 Coyne, *Why Evolution is True*, p. 242.

49 Denis Alexander, 2008, *Creation or Evolution: Do We Have to Choose?* Oxford: Monarch, p. 48.

50 Alexander, *Creation or Evolution*, p. 82.

51 Barbour, *Religion and Science*, p. 224.

52 Alexander, *Creation or Evolution*, p. 88.

53 Alexander, *Creation or Evolution*, p. 104.

54 Alexander, *Creation or Evolution*, p. 119.

55 Alexander, *Creation or Evolution*, p. 108.

56 Alexander, *Creation or Evolution*, p. 130.

57 Alexander, *Creation or Evolution*, p. 131.

58 Alexander, *Creation or Evolution*, p. 182.

59 R. J. Berry, 1996, *God and the Biologist. Faith at the Frontiers of Science*, Leicester: InterVarsity Press/Apollos.

60 Berry, *God and the Biologist*, p. 30.

61 Alexander, *Creation or Evolution*, p. 213.

62 Alexander, *Creation or Evolution*, pp. 236–43.

63 Stephen Jay Gould, 'Impacting a Self-Appointed Judge', *Scientific American* 267, no. 1, 1992, pp. 118–21, quoted in Alister McGrath, 2007, *Dawkins' God: Genes, Memes, and the Meaning of Life*, Oxford: Blackwell, p. 80.

64 Richard Dawkins, 2007, *The God Delusion*, London: Transworld/Black Swan, p. 143–4.

65 McGrath, *Dawkins' God*, p. 11.

66 Richard Dawkins, 1996, *River out of Eden: A Darwinian View of Life*, New York: Basic Books, p. 133.

67 See David Hume, *Dialogues Concerning Natural Religion (1779)*, Part VII, ed. N. K. Smith, 1947, *Hume's Dialogues Concerning Natural Religion*, London: Nelson; and my summary argument in John Weaver, 1994, *In the Beginning God: Modern Science and the Christian Doctrine of Creation*, Macon: Smyth & Helwys, Oxford: Regent's Park College, pp. 131–2.

68 Richard Dawkins, 1989, *The Selfish Gene*, Oxford: Oxford University Press, p. 198.

69 McGrath, *Dawkins' God*, p. 91.

70 John Lennox, 2007, *God's Undertaker: Has Science Buried God?* Oxford: Lion, p. 87.

71 McGrath, *Dawkins' God*, p. 142. See also John Hedley Brooke, 1991, *Science and Religion: Some Historical Perspectives*, Cambridge: Cambridge University Press.

72 McGrath, *Dawkins' God*, p. 149.

73 Nick Spencer and Denis Alexander, 2009, *Rescuing Darwin: God and Evolution in Britain Today*, London: Theos, p. 37, also available as pdf from www.theosthinktank.co.uk

74 Vincent E. Bacote and Stephen R. Spencer, 'What are the Theological Implications for Natural Science?' in Dorothy F. Chappell and E. David Cook, 2005, *Not Just Science*, Grand Rapids MI: Zondervan, p. 73.

75 William A. Dembski, 2004, *The Design Revolution: Answering the Toughest Questions about Intelligent Design*, Downers Grove IL: InterVarsity Press.

76 Michael J. Behe, 1996, *Darwin's Black Box: The Biochemical Challenge to Evolution*, New York: Free Press.

77 Alexander, *Creation or Evolution*, p. 299.

78 Alexander, *Creation or Evolution*, p. 305.

79  Alexander, *Creation or Evolution*, pp. 332–3.

80  Coyne, *Why Evolution is True*, pp. 250–1.

81  Nancey Murphy, 2002, *Religion and Science: God, Evolution, and the Soul*, Proceedings of the 2001 Goshen Conference on Religion and Science, ed. Carl S. Helrich, Kitchener, Ontario: Pandora Press.

82  Murphy, *Religion and Science*, p. 54.

83  Coyne, *Why Evolution is True*, p. 254.

84  John Polkinghorne, 'Shining a light where science and theology meet', http://www.timesonline.co.uk/tol/comment/faith/article4790446.ece?print=yes&randnum

85  *The Genius of Charles Darwin*: Richard Dawkins examines the legacy of Charles Darwin. Three-part series broadcast on Channel Four at 8 p.m. on Mondays 4, 11 and 18 August 2008. Produced by the same team that created *Root of All Evil?* and *The Enemies of Reason*.

86  See for example: Barbour, *Religion and Science*; Berry, *God and the Biologist*; Celia Deane-Drummond, 2001, *Biology and Theology Today*, London: SCM Press; Malcolm Jeeves, 1997, *Human Nature at the Millennium*, Leicester: InterVarsity Press/Apollos; Malcolm Jeeves and R. J. Berry, 1998, *Life and Christian Belief*, Leicester: InterVarsity Press/Apollos; Alister E. McGrath, 1999, *Science and Religion: An Introduction*, Oxford: Blackwell, and 1998, *The Foundations of Science and Religion*, Oxford: Blackwell; Nancey Murphy, 1997, *Reconciling Theology and Science*, Kitchener, Ontario: Pandora Press; Ted Peters and Gaymon Bennett, 2002, *Bridging Science and Religion*, London: SCM Press; John Polkinghorne, 1998, *Science and Theology: An Introduction*, London: SPCK, and 2001, *The Work of Love: Creation as Kenosis*, London: SPCK; Christopher Southgate, 1999, *God, Humanity and the Cosmos: A Textbook in Science and Religion*, London: T&T Clark; Keith Ward, 1996, *God, Chance and Necessity*, Oxford: One World, and 1998, *God, Faith and the New Millennium*, Oxford: One World, 1998; Fraser Watts (ed.), 1998, *Science Meets Faith*, London: SPCK, and 2002, *Theology and Psychology*, Farnham: Ashgate.

87  John Polkinghorne, 'Shining a light where science and theology meet'.

88  Berry, *God and the Biologist*, p. 31.

89  Berry, *God and the Biologist*, p. 54.

90  Murphy, *Religion and Science*, pp. 35–6.

91  Barbour, *Religion and Science*, p. 237.

92  Barbour, *Religion and Science*, pp. 239–40.

93  Murphy, *Religion and Science*, pp. 39–40.

94  Murphy, *Religion and Science*, pp. 42–3.

95  Collins, *The Language of God*, p. 193.

96  Collins, *The Language of God*, pp. 198–9.

# 4

## The Human Brain and the Development of the Mind

### Overview of the field of study

#### Growing understanding of the nature of the brain

The human brain is not like the heart or liver, fixed and predictable in its function within the body, but rather it is in constant dialogue with the outside world, influenced and constantly being updated through the experiences of the senses.

The Greek philosophers considered that the soft substance of the brain was the perfect location for the soul, while thinking and feeling were associated with the heart and lungs.[1] This view changed with the discovery of the connection of the eye to the brain by Alcmaeon of Croton (c. 550–450 BCE), and was confirmed by the observations of the Egyptian anatomists Herophilus (c. 335–280 BCE) and Erasistratus (c. 304–250 BCE) who traced what we now know to be nerves connecting the whole body to the brain.

The brain can be held in one cupped hand and has the consistency of raw egg. It is divided into two hemispheres that sit around a 'stalk', the brain stem, which tapers down into the spinal cord. At the back is a 'cauliflower-shaped' extension, the cerebellum, which protrudes from the main brain, the cerebrum. The brain sits in a fluid, the cerebrospinal fluid, which is constantly renewed and contains salts, sugars and proteins.

The physical structure of the brain shows that it is composed of $10^{12}$ neurons; the female brain weighs 1.25 kg and the male 1.45 kg. Each neuron is about 40,000ths of a millimetre in diameter. They each have two kinds of branches extending from them: the tree-like dendrites, which collect electrical impulses, and the longer single strand axon, which conveys the signal away from the cell. Specific chemicals play a significant part in neuronal communication. Communication between neurons takes place at the 'gap' or synapse between axons and dendrites. Here the electrical charge is converted into a chemical transmitter. There are some 100 billion neurons in our brains, each with thousands of connections. The brain is fundamentally a chemical system – even the electricity it produces comes from chemicals.

When we consider the chemical structure of the brain we discover that there are 54 different chemical substances, the transmitters, which allow nerve cells to 'talk' to each other. One individual nerve cell may receive chemical information from 1000 nerve cells in its vicinity, which defines its activity. It is this that leads to mood, drive, motivation, pleasure, pain, impulsiveness.

Susan Greenfield uses analogies of relationships, networking and conversations for neurons (brain cells), which she states have their own internal life support systems, so that they can adapt to change, and are in close association with others most of the time. She notes:

> neurons don't really make contact with each other but are separated by a gap called the synapse, and the electrical blip just cannot breach across this tiny void. An intermediary is necessary to cross between one neuron and another, so a chemical messenger or transmitter is released from one cell and activates the next . . . The ultimate building-block of brain operations, and therefore the basis of our uniqueness, is this chain of electrical-chemical-electrical events.[2]

In the analogy that Greenfield is using, the synapse can be seen as the relationship and the transmitter as the language.

The outer layer of the brain is called the cortex. Greenfield observes:

> An important clue to brain function is that in more sophisticated animals the cortex is folded – convoluted – so that its surface area has been able to increase while respecting the confines of a relatively small skull. Flattened out, the rat cortex would be the size of a postage stamp, that of a chimp would be the size of standard typing paper, while the human brain would be four times greater still! . . . The more extensive the cortex, the more an animal will be able to think for itself.[3]

The cortex is about two millimetres thick and has areas that have specific functions: the motor cortex, which controls the muscles; and the visual cortex and auditory cortex, which process signals from the eyes and ears. However, states Greenfield, other regions of the cortex cannot be so clearly classified:

> For example, a region toward the back of the head at the top (posterior parietal cortex) receives input from the visual, auditory, and somatosensory systems. Thus, the function of such a region is less obvious. Patients with damage to the parietal cortex display a wide range of impairments, according to the exact area and extent of the lesion.[4]

Symptoms including sight, touch, apraxia (being clumsy), or the confusion of left and right (spatial skills) result from problems in the co-ordination of the senses. There can also be problems of disassociation – 'that's not my arm'.

This suggests that the parietal cortex, like other 'association' areas of cortex, must be responsible for the most sophisticated and elusive functions of all: thinking, or, as neuroscientists prefer, *cognitive processes*.[5]

Of all regions of the brain the prefrontal cortex has shown the most significant change between species in mammalian evolution: 3 per cent greater in cats, 17 per cent in chimpanzees, and 29 per cent in human beings. The observation of patients who have suffered brain injury has demonstrated that this part of the cortex controls the more sophisticated parts of our minds – not motor skills, senses or basic survival, but personality. This leads Greenfield to observe that 'our characters, which we think of as fairly fixed and inviolate aspects of ourselves, are really at the mercy of our physical brain: they *are* our brain'.[6]

Modern brain-scanning techniques – PET (positron emission tomography), MRI (magnetic resonance imaging) and MEG (magnetoencephalography) – are able to identify when particular areas of the brain are active, by identifying the additional oxygen, proteins or electrical activity. In this way it is possible to identify areas associated with hearing words, seeing words, speaking words and generating verbs. This leads Greenfield to conclude that 'the brain is made up of anatomically distinct regions, but these regions are not autonomous minibrains; rather, they constitute a cohesive integrated system organized for the most part in a mysterious way'.[7]

The brain operates throughout our lives, 24 hours a day, 7 days a week, monitoring, among other things, the dips and surges of glucose in our blood, the distension of our stomachs, the pressure in our bowels, and the beat of our hearts. Every single moment it's co-ordinating the interplay of our vital organs, interfacing with our immune and hormonal systems, and orchestrating the tens of thousands of chemical reactions and interactions that enable us not just to stay alive but to run for a bus, dream, remember, reason, plot, grieve, fantasize and love. Above all, it is our brain that gives us that unique consciousness that no one else is party to, and on top of that a self-consciousness, which is a continuing experience of our own special identity.[8]

Greenfield explains that just as we are constantly evolving as people, changing as a result of the subtle, all-important interplay between our genetic predisposition and the diverse events in our environment, so too do the individual neurons in our brain respond and change, according to the type, strength and frequency of inputs. We are at

> our most impressionable when young, and have the most changeable shifts in quantity and quality of relationships in early childhood. As with people, so it is with neurons. In the young brain, the branches (dendrites) are themselves growing and thus will be most malleable according to whatever inputs are most hard-working and in whatever brain areas . . .

The dynamics of environment and neuronal malleability give rise to an ever-evolving identity, one that is unique and individual, yet an individuality that is constantly transforming.[9]

## The mind and the field of psychology

Malcolm Jeeves[10] notes that linking the mind and brain raises questions about the 'soul', and evidence from behaviour genetics raises questions about human nature and animal nature. He discusses the warfare model in psychology, where Freud 'explained away' religious beliefs; and B. F. Skinner, following on from Freud, took a 'nothing buttery' approach, nothing but our neurons, to behaviour and religious beliefs. As in the physical and biological sciences, according to some interpretations, the Christian faith is in conflict with psychological discoveries. Jeeves suggests that integration between psychology and Christian belief is difficult because much of modern psychology deals in mathematical equations. However, he believes that dialogue is possible through research into the mind–brain unity, which underlines the unity of the human person.

Jeeves with Berry bemoans the fact that

almost all scientific psychologists are methodological determinists. If they did not aim to identify regularities in human behaviour that would enable them to explain and hence predict it, there would be little point in their whole enterprise . . . If the tentative application of a methodological determinism turns out to be reasonably successful, then the next step is to assume that we can predict particular behaviours.[11]

They believe that problems arise when we move from this to a metaphysical determinism which assumes that this is totally the result of chemical processes in a tightly linked mind–brain. This then raises the theological question of freedom of choice.

Jeeves and Berry follow the view of Donald MacKay in considering the dual aspect of mind–brain as *comprehensive realism*, where mental activity and correlated brain activity are seen as:

inner and outer aspects of the same complex set of events which together constitute conscious human agency . . . The irreducible duality of human nature is, on this view, seen as duality of aspects rather than duality of substance.

They continue by noting that 'the mind determines brain activity and behaviour. But in a complementary fashion mental activity and behaviour depend upon the physically determinate operations of the brain, which is a physico-chemical system.[12] They regard mental activity as being embedded in brain activity, as demonstrated when the system goes wrong. They believe that it would be wrong to consider the mind–brain as a monist identity, as, quoting Roger Sperry, the laws of biophysics and biochemistry are not adequate to account for the cognitive sequencing of a train of thought. Similarly they quote J. Z. Young: 'the brain contains programmes, which operate as a *person* makes selection among the repertoire of possible thoughts and actions'. It is the person and not the brain that makes this selection.[13] All our knowledge and understanding of mind and brain comes through our experience as conscious agents, and thus we can say that the conscious agent has ontological priority.

## The spiritual dimension

In discussing the search for the God gene, Robert Winston believes that the greatest legacy of human evolution is our relatively huge brain. *Australopithecus afarensis* had a cranial capacity of 450 millilitres, *Homo erectus*, 1 million or so years later, 900 millilitres, but *Homo sapiens* 1450 millilitres, 'and with this increase came an unsurpassed cerebral cortex – the seat of the imaginative and thinking powers'.[14] He maintains that while the evolutionary causes of this larger brain are uncertain, group interaction, toolmaking, walking upright, patterns of hunting and changes in diet may all have played their parts.

Human beings were especially vulnerable as babies, but also as adults to climate and to predators. Therefore ingenuity and ability to master their environment was key in survival. But these characteristics 'would also have helped them to live a rich imaginative life, to consider the mysteries of their existence and develop a set of answers that we call religion'.[15] As a Christian I would want to add the contribution to our understanding that comes from the biblical witness to God's revelation of the nature of the universe, life and the place of human beings within it.

From an evolutionary perspective the communal nature of religion would have given hunter-gatherers a stronger sense of togetherness, but, asks Winston, is there a 'Divine Idea' that is carried into our genes? He notes:

> While nobody has identified any gene for religion, there are certainly some candidate genes that may influence human personality and confer a tendency to religious feelings. Some of the genes likely to be involved are those which control different levels of different chemicals called neurotransmitters in the brain. Dopamine is one neurotransmitter which we know plays a powerful role in our feelings of well-being; it may also be involved in the sense of peace that humans feel during some spiritual experiences.[16]

Certainly he recognizes that shared religious belief and a sense of moral code would lead to a growing together and caring for one another. Maybe a 'morality module' is activated in the brain at an early age. Winston has noted that certain brain areas become activated when we engage in co-operation with others, and that these areas are associated with feelings of pleasure and reward. It also seems that certain areas of the brain are brought into action in situations where we feel empathy and forgiveness.[17]

Considering personality and spirituality, Jeeves and Berry draw attention to a number of significant issues. They suggest that if we accept that on balance the evidence for a genetic influence on personality traits such as extroversion and neuroticism is broadly correct, there will be implications for Christian behaviour. For example, those who prefer more boisterous expressions of their faith in congregational worship may be manifesting an outworking of their biologically inherited extraversion, while those who prefer quieter, more private and reflective worship may be manifesting their biological tendency to neuroticism. Those sharing the same creedal beliefs may at the same time, for genetic reasons among others, express them differently.[18]

With regard to senile dementia they assert that the disorganization of psychological processes evident in dementia cannot truly affect a person's objective relationship with God, though it may well affect their subjective experience of that relationship. Some people suggest that this relationship is maintained through ways and channels that transcend the experience of the body, but Jeeves and Berry observe that the experiences of Christian believers in the terminal stages of some forms of dementia refute this.[19] There is a need to recognize the harrowing spiritual journeys of many of these patients and to affirm from a biblical perspective that while the patient has no relationship with God, God continues to hold such a person in a loving relationship.

They conclude:

There are changes in our brains which occur through no choices of our own; Alzheimer's disease is a classic case. On the other hand, what we do to ourselves may affect the workings of the neural substrate of our minds. Increasing self-knowledge has the potential to make us more responsible for our own actions and more attentive to those who, through no fault of their own, suffer diseases of the mind . . . We ought to regard *ourselves* as agents responsible for our actions, albeit ready to entertain the possibility that *others* have been abnormally subject to their biology and/or outside influences.[20]

These will include the social, environmental and cultural contexts in which we live.

## Scientific aspects

### *The evolving brain*

Reflecting on our human origins we know from molecular biology and from fossil discoveries that human beings and modern African apes are probably descended from common ancestors. African chimpanzees and gorillas share 99 per cent of their DNA with human beings, which is comparable with the genetic kinship of foxes and dogs or of zebras and horses, as we noted in Chapter 3. We can trace hominids from 4 million years BP, with *Homo habilis* 2 million years BP making primitive stone tools, and *Homo erectus* 1.6 million years BP who probably used fire. *Homo sapiens* dates from about 500,000 years BP. We may suggest that evolution resulted in the development of brains capable of asking the right questions.

In the 1960s Francis Crick moved into neurobiology to examine the ways in which DNA affected the brain. James Watson points out that while we have fewer genes than a mustard plant, 25,000 against 27,000, intelligence is based on genetic switches. Our brains give us sensory and neuromotor capabilities beyond other forms of life. He suggests:

> Vertebrate complexity may also be enhanced by sophisticated genetic switches that are typically located near genes . . . It is here that regulation occurs, with regulatory proteins binding to the DNA to turn adjacent genes on or off. Vertebrate genes seem to be governed by a much more elaborate set of switching mechanisms than those of simpler organisms.[21]

Watson downplays the role of nurture in development of the mind, when he states:

> A fertilized egg containing a chimp genome still inevitably produces a chimp, while a fertilized egg containing a human genome produces a human. No amount of exposure to classical music or violence on TV could make it otherwise . . . the greatest part of what each individual organism will be is programmed ineluctably into its every cell, in the genome.[22]

In considering gene expression Watson notes that while on the basis of their close relationship humans and chimpanzees are close to each other for both blood cells and liver, the gene expression in the brain tells a totally different story. The human brain is very different from that of the chimpanzee, with an inventory of the genes whose expression differs. He thinks that the critical differences (about 1 per cent of DNA) will lie not in the genes themselves but in their regulation. 'Humans, I suspect, are simply great apes with a few unique – and special – genetic switches.'[23]

As we noted in Chapter 3, Francis Collins would see this somewhat differently, as he states that our similarities with other species is elegant evidence of the relatedness of all living things, and is an occasion of awe – part of the master plan of the same God who brought the universe into being and set its physical parameters just precisely right to allow the creation of stars, planets, heavy elements and life itself.[24]

Through the evolutionary story we recognize the development of the brain. There is the base of our brain which controls respiration, cardiovascular system and instinct, which we share with reptiles and birds. The midbrain or limbic system controls hormones and emotions, and this we share with other animals. Finally there is the neocortex (outer layer), which controls perceptual, cognitive and communicative processes, which we share with higher mammals.[25] While chimpanzees are able to communicate with symbols and have some self-awareness, human beings have a greater self-consciousness, including memory, anticipation, meaning, imagination and symbolic worlds, and creativity, rational reflection and responsibility for moral choices.

Biological evolution considers genetic survival and tends to be reductionist in its assumptions. Altruism is explained away as a response towards survival of the genes. Cultural evolution is more significant according to Barbour, where variability is the result of deliberate and directional innovations. 'New ideas, institutions, and forms of behavior are often creative and imaginative responses to social problems and crises.' The transmission of information takes place through 'memory, language, tradition, education, and social institutions rather than through genes'. Such changes are deliberate and more rapid.[26]

### Brain structure

The brain is vital in processing and co-ordinating the information that floods in through our senses, with the outputs of the brain often expressed through movements. Brains are only required by life forms that move, as Greenfield observes:

> The whole point is that for an animal moving around, there is an interaction with an environment that is incessantly changing. You need a device to tell you very quickly what is happening and, most importantly, to enable you to respond to what is happening, to get out of the way of predators or to chase after prey.[27]

Signals are sent to muscles along the spinal cord, but sometimes the spinal cord can function more or less autonomously, without control from the brain. These movements are reflexes, which are defined as a fixed response to a particular trigger. Greenfield notes that there are four 'brain motorways' in the spinal cord from the brain stem which have differing roles. One such pathway is for semi-reflex rhythmic movements like swimming; one co-ordinates movement with visual and sensory information; one is for balance; and the forth mediates the moving of individual limbs.[28]

There is a fifth form of movement, distinctive to human beings, which is for the fine movement of the fingers, human dexterity. The messages for this do not come from the brain stem but from the top of the brain, from the motor cortex. Greenfield observes that the more precise the movement, the greater the part of the brain that is used, and adds:

> The motor cortex is pivotal to the generation of movement: not only does it have direct control of some of the muscles controlling the hands, and hence of precision movements, but it also exerts a hierarchical influence over the other four movement motorways.[29]

Yet these are not the only parts of the brain that are involved. For example, the cerebellum is important for movements where there is a continuous feedback from our senses, which in turn trigger or influence the next type of movement, as for example in tracing or playing a musical instrument. There are also the 'ballistic' movements associated with the basal ganglia. We see that there is no single part of the brain that controls movement. 'The generation of movement is the net result of many brain regions acting together as individual instruments do in a symphony. The type of movement being made, and whether it requires conscious control, determines exactly which brain region is involved.'[30]

The somatosensory system carries signals along the spinal cord related to pain and touch to the somatosensory cortex, which is located behind the motor cortex. Different neurons in this cortex correspond to touch in different parts of the body. Large portions of the cortex are involved in the movements of the hands and the mouth, which are important for basic human activities of feeling and eating, and which dominate in young babies.

Visual information is collected on the retina and sent via the optic nerve to the visual cortex, the outer layer at the back of the head.

> [The] private inner world of one's own consciousness is influenced by sensory input pouring in and reflected in an outward movement. By being able to receive detailed and incessant information about our environment, and responding quickly and appropriately to each individual situation, we are in constant dialogue with the outside world.[31]

Recognizing the complexity of the brain, Greenfield maintains that

> it is hard to match up familiar events in the outside world exclusively with actual events in a single brain region. Different parts of the cortex, such as the motor cortex and the somatosensory cortex, clearly have different functions, and association areas such as the prefrontal cortex and

parts of the parietal cortex must each have their own type of specialized roles. But contrary to the phrenologists' vision, these roles do not correspond on a one-to-one basis with the obvious aspects of our character and specific activities in the real world. It is one of the biggest challenges in neuroscience today to understand the relationship between what is actually going on within certain brain regions and how such internalized physiological events are reflected in outward behaviour.[32]

A clear example is seen in the case of Parkinson's disease, which is caused by the failure of cells in the *substantia nigra* of the middle part of the brain to produce the chemical dopamine. Dopamine is delivered to another part of the brain, the striatum. But then, we ask, what is the function of dopamine in the striatum? This leads Greenfield to observe:

> The anatomy of the brain does not directly match up with the chemistry of the brain: there is no one chemical exclusive to any one brain region. Rather the same chemical is distributed over many different brain regions while each brain region makes and uses many different brain chemicals. It is therefore very hard to say what is most important when considering brain damage – the brain region concerned or the change in the chemical balance in the brain.[33]

An examination of the effects and recovery from strokes indicates another aspect – neuronal plasticity. A stroke occurs when the blood supply is cut off to part of the brain. Recovery from strokes and some brain damage demonstrates that brain functions do not belong exclusively to one area or particular population of neurons. It appears that other brain cells gradually learn to take over the role of the damaged cells.

### Use and misuse of drugs

Gradually, in each young human, the brain becomes personalized by unique experiences to become a unique entity. It is this personalization of the brain that is the 'mind'. But taking drugs can affect our minds through affecting brain function. Drugs have one essential feature in common: 'all drugs that affect brain function do so by interfering with the finely tuned operations of a chemical messenger, a transmitter, at the synapse'. The result is that the 'normal, carefully tuned sequence of events which enables a transmitter to be released from one neuron and activate another – is thrown into disarray'.[34]

- Nicotine mimics the transmitter acetylcholine, resulting in raised heart rate and blood pressure.
- Amphetamine prolongs the action of dopamine and noradrenaline, which as they are active in the synapse far longer than they should be, increase

arousal levels, heart rate and blood pressure and lead to the dangers of stroke.
- Cocaine, on the other hand, slows down their removal.
- Ecstasy (3,4-methylenedioxymethamphetamine, MDMA) triggers the explosive release and subsequent depletion of serotonin. It is a hallucinogen because it gives a feeling of disembodiment, euphoria and causes hyperactivity. 'The flooding of the brain with serotonin results in dramatic effects on metabolism, on how temperature is regulated.' The release of serotonin may also cause the death of some neurons, for example those which regulate basic functions such as sleep.[35]
- Cannabis, which, unlike alcohol, is only slowly removed from the body, impairs driving ability, as well as perceptual motor skills, for up to five days after taking the drug. Cannabis works on specific target proteins (receptors) in the brain and can therefore modify synapses, and hence neuronal plasticity and hence the mind. Its use can demotivate us, disrupt the memory and shorten attention span. 'A user may not realize their natural intellectual potential and may arguably be a different person compared to the one they would have been if they had never [smoked].'[36] It may also trigger a predisposition to schizophrenia or depression.
- Heavy-duty tranquillizers block the connection between a transmitter and its usual target protein, a receptor.

Drugs work as caricatures of natural transmitters. A further example considered by Greenfield is morphine (heroin). She notes:

The side effects of heroin include constriction of the pupils, constipation, and suppression of the coughing reflex. In fact, because of these last two actions it used to be sold as an effective ingredient in anti-cough and anti-diarrhoea medications.
    A pernicious action of morphine and heroin is to slow down the respiration rate by a direct inhibitory action within the basic part of the brain, the respiratory centre in the brain stem, just above the spinal cord, which controls breathing. Sometimes this action can be so severe that breathing stops and the person dies. In fact, inhibition of breathing is the most common acute cause of death in heroin abuse.[37]

At the level of the synapse, the way morphine works is to mimic natural transmitters. The drug can fool the target neuron that is being activated by its natural chemical messenger. The danger is that a drug such as morphine or heroin can act on all possible brain areas at the same time, at each and every respective synapse: it will swamp the normal receptor sites. The receptor site becomes accustomed to higher amounts of the chemical, with the result that more and more of the drug is required to gain the desired effect, and this leads to addiction. Greenfield comments that in a fast-developing technological world making people confused and inadequate, 'how welcome the hazier world of a drug-induced wellbeing, which in turn reduces the cognitive competence and curiosity required in order to adapt to modern life'.[38]

## Mental illness and mental health problems

The mind operates through neuronal connections. A human baby has a brain the same size as a chimpanzee, but in the first two years of life the development of the synapses is astounding. The rapid growth in neuronal connections matches the growth in the development of physical functions – related to the cortex. The second phase of brain development lasts until adolescence and is characterized by the development of a great number of 'easily forming' connections; some early connections remain and some are lost. In later adolescence further pruning of the connections takes place, up to 50 per cent. In children, for example, there is a mixing of sight and sound so that they may 'see' a sound and 'hear' a colour, something lost in adults, where there is a focusing of the mind. Also there is a locating of activity: we know language and grammar with the left hemisphere of our brain, whereas we sense the meaning of sentences with the right hemisphere.

We have little memory of childhood events; it is a time when we face a deluge of disconnected events, whereas in adult life our memories and current experiences develop into a narrative of our personal conceptual framework. When the reverse takes place – losing touch with particular things, places, people, faces – when everything becomes a blur of generic faces and abstract sensations, we become as confused, disorientated and frightened as a toddler: this is dementia.[39] The dendrites die back and brain development is reversed, leading to the experience of a series of disconnected events.

Jeeves and Berry are certain that the link between mind and brain is seen clearly in sufferers of Alzheimer's dementia, which is caused by damage to brain cells.

> Neurofibrillary tangles develop in the brain; granulovascular deterioration becomes evident in the brain cells. In addition, there are neurochemical changes, most often a deficiency of the neurotransmitter acetylcholine. One result is that previously patterned circuits of nerve signals become scrambled and the brain can no longer sustain its normal psychological functions.[40]

Turning to mental illness Greenfield observes that 'although the neurotic who suffers from agoraphobia or claustrophobia or obsessive-compulsive behaviour is leading a severely compromised life, their perception of the world is normally similar to that of almost everyone else'. On the other hand, 'the schizophrenic is not a divided person, but a person divided from reality'.[41]

Mental illness is a disorder of brain chemistry. Mood and impulsiveness are controlled by cirotonine; drive and motivation by noradrenaline; pleasure by dopamine. Many of the best characterized genetic disorders affect mental performance. They have also attracted the interest of gene mappers, particularly bipolar disease (BPD) and schizophrenia. A genetic link has been demonstrated in these two illnesses: 80 per cent of bipolar identical twins and 50 per cent of schizophrenic identical twins in research studies had the disease. However, it should be noted that diagnosis is based on symptoms that may have a number of genetic causes. 'Thus the genes underlying schizophrenia may differ from one case to the next,' and the genetic culprits of mental illness have 'so far proved particularly elusive'.[42]

Watson notes that 'a recent study reveals that as many as twelve chromosomes – half the total – have been shown through mapping analysis to contain genes contributing to schizophrenia'. Perhaps there are some genes responsible for the overall organization and structure of our brains. 'Malfunctions in these genes may be the cause of delusional or hallucinatory episodes common to both BPD and schizophrenia.'[43]

Greenfield draws attention to the parallels between the thinking of young children and people with schizophrenia and concludes:

> The crucial point, then, is that the schizophrenic, like the child, is living in the present, responding to the inputs of the moment rather than fitting them into the internalized conceptual framework that enables us to make sense of the world, along with all the benefits and losses which that facility brings. In one scenario it is a case of being 'out' of one's mind; in the other the mind has yet to develop fully.[44]

Schizophrenia cannot be explained in terms of one cause such as a faulty gene or at the level of brain organization on a macro level or at synaptic level. 'Whatever the initial trigger, one of the widely acknowledged features of the schizophrenic brain is that somehow an excess of the transmitter dopamine plays an important and immediate role in the psychotic experience, in the loss of mind.'[45]

Dopamine emanating from the brain stem plays an important role in the prefrontal cortex, which is involved in the more sophisticated higher cognitive processes. Recorded examples of damage to the prefrontal cortex have shown personality change, recklessness and living for the moment, amnesia and a dream-like loss of touch with time and reality. The excess of dopamine in the prefrontal cortex might render the region inactive, as if damaged. Greenfield believes that 'the incoming dopamine would inhibit the cells in the prefrontal cortex and thus impair their normal networking with local amino acids'.[46]

But Greenfield observes that we can go beyond drugs and psychoses to everyday life and find instances when we let ourselves go through other excesses. These have the common features of an 'absence of self-consciousness, extreme emphasis on the sense *per se*, high emotion and loss of the "reason"', a loss of the checks and balances that characterize the mature human mind. 'The respite from having a mind, an identity, seems – except for the extreme example of psychosis – desirable as an intermittent state.' She continues with the further observation:

> It is an interesting paradox of human beings that many of us are hugely attracted to hedonistic experiences that allow us to leave our minds behind in the here-and-now of drugs and sex and rock and roll, yet at the same time most of us would shun and disparage engaging in such (literally) 'sensational' activities all the time, in favour of retaining our self-conscious identities.[47]

Ever since human beings evolved, every individual brain has been unique, with our own narrative, experience and evaluation. People might lose their minds through drugs, drink, ecstasy or mental illness, but what is actually missing? It will not be the loss of consciousness, for we are still in touch with our first-hand subjective experiences. We can see that the mind is bound up with the physical brain, yet is distinct from it.[48] Greenfield states:

> holistic brain function does not have a simple one-to-one correspondence with any one synapse or class of transmitters . . . One way of looking at the brain simultaneously from the top-down and bottom-up perspectives is to consider the action of drugs. We can see how drugs influence behaviour while they also change chemical communication at the single synapse. After all, a seemingly individual and unchanging mind is completely at the mercy of our physical brain, our neurons.[49]

### Artificial intelligence

Artificial intelligence (AI) raises issues about the nature of the human person that are closely intertwined with those raised by neuroscience. Both are the source of a 'nothing but' reductionism about the human person, which sits uneasily with Christian views. However, whereas neuroscience is physicalist, AI is more dualist in assuming that intelligence can be replicated independently of the human body. There are three strands to AI:

- a practical strand, which is the development of computers to think for us
- a theoretical strand, which is essentially the interpretation of the way in which cognitive processes work, which in turn liberates psychology from

behaviourism through considering the language of the computer program instead
- an ideological strand, represented by the popularist views of the brain as merely a computer, and what computers will be able to do in the future.

A consideration of AI assists Christian thinking about mind–brain and consciousness/personhood, because it helps us to identify the algorithmic and non-algorithmic aspects of mind–brain function.

Significant progress has been made in computer development: for example, there are computers that can successfully play chess, but they play it in a different way. Computers are programmed to look for predictability, whereas chess masters look at patterns of play in an intuitive way. However, we need to be careful in setting boundaries that computers will never cross, for example suggesting that computers will never be able to learn or create as these boundaries have already been crossed in some respects.

We might look at *intentionality*, and recognize that computers do not know the meaning of the symbols they operate with. We might also consider *inner experience*, such as human emotions. Some emotions can be predicted and programmed, but the computer, for example, has no experience of anger. There are *connectionist* computers that allow a number of programmes to run at the same time, and we have seen the development of computers with bodies, which offers the recognition that human intelligence is 'embodied intelligence'.

Computers can be claimed to have 'intelligence', but this is a concept that has been redefined by scientists. It is always an analogy; the actual similarities between the human mind and computers are limited. Some suggest that you might programme the personality of someone into a computer, thereby preserving their soul! Computer scientists might find this exciting because they have power and control, but would such a computer have freedom? If they don't, they are not human. If the computers did have freedom then the computer scientists would have no control, and would in effect be acting as God (this would be an act of self-emptying – *kenosis* – similar to God's self emptying of sovereign control in the creation of human beings with free will, and in becoming a human being in the incarnation), giving control and freedom to their creation.

Penrose does not believe that true intelligence could actually be present unless accompanied by consciousness. He maintains:

when I assert my own belief that true intelligence requires consciousness, I am implicitly suggesting (since I do not believe the strong AI contention that the mere *enaction* of an algorithm would evoke consciousness) that intelligence cannot be properly simulated by algorithmic means, that is by a computer, in the sense that we use that term today.[50]

He believes that there is a non-algorithmic aspect to consciousness. He draws this conclusion from the human characteristics of aesthetic appreciation, wonder, together with many distinctly human emotions.

## Theological implications

### Who are we from the perspective of neuroscience?

Greenfield presents the idea that inside our heads there is endless upheaval: circuits of neurons ceaselessly shifting their allegiances and their balance of power with their neuronal neighbours, both nearby and more distantly throughout our nervous systems. Since drugs and disease, and now the newer technologies, all intervene at the level of this neuronal networking, it is hardly surprising that the resultant 'mind' is so vulnerable. Greenfield maintains:

> Throughout each normal day the world, and living in it, is leaving its mark on the effectiveness of your synapses, the levels of neurotransmitters, the activated and silenced genes, new neurons and newly dead ones. Yet despite the endless and spectacular dynamism of your brain – one that we have just seen may be increasingly and dramatically manipulated and accelerated in the future – there is none the less usually a reassuringly consistent theme that is *you*: your identity.[51]

We see this through the perspective of mind (how we see ourselves) or personality (how others see us). Our personalities may differ in different contexts and with the different people with whom we meet – friends, family, a night out, a business meeting. Moment to moment events change our brain and our mind within it. 'So we cannot think of an individual as an isolated entity, but rather as a provisional product of what has happened in that person's brain to date, combined with what is happening to change that brain right now.'[52]

Identity lasts a lifetime, and will encompass all those transformations to our neuronal landscape as our minds broaden and narrow as the result of living in the world. Nevertheless, there is an irrefutable sense that we are a unique and continuous first-person consciousness. Emphasizing self-consciousness and self-realization Greenfield maintains that the Industrial Revolution brought upward social mobility dependent on personal ambition and initiative. People were not defined by their place or function in society. This was reflected in the appearance of the novel as a literary genre. She notes that 'the essential feature common to both the novel and consciousness is one of a private state – an inner world, therefore, that differs from that of all other individuals'.[53]

Greenfield identifies the inner subjective state and the objective narration of events, where subjectivity may even eclipse reality. For her, the life narrative is a clue for insights into a first-person perspective – daily life experience leaving its mark on the brain as the physical connections between neurons become personalized and reflect experience. She thus draws a distinction between consciousness and self-consciousness. She believes that consciousness is variable and depends on what is happening in the brain at any moment – it is the result of internal chemical factors combined with external features of the outside world. 'The more extensive the neuronal assembly, the more tens of millions of neurons are involved, the greater the possibility for self-consciousness.'[54]

Reflecting on modern information technology, ID cards and security cameras, Greenfield regrets that our mental inner sanctum, so vital to our sense of identity, is under threat. She notes that statistics reveal that 8- to 18-year-olds are spending upwards of 8.5 hours per day using electronic media, yet often with little understanding of its reliability as a source of information. She notes the increasing popularity of social networking sites such as MySpace and Facebook and asks: 'What might this increasingly dominant screen socializing mean for the way future generations interact in relationships?' She notes that research suggests that there is a consequent risk to family life, the risk of a marked decline in verbal communication skills, and the danger for impressionable young minds of exposure to sexual and violent images. She also notes the influence in becoming consumers leading to 'fashion and early sexualization for girls, "domination" and "mastery" for boys', which are the themes of many products.[55]

Being familiar with the malleability of the human brain, Greenfield predicts that spending so much time in cyberspace will inevitably lead to minds very different from any others in human history, and that we cannot assume that our brains are inviolate. We may end up in a world in which our key values are lost for ever.[56] Thinking is a key value. Unthinking can be seen when emotions of rage and lust or drugs focus on the immediate feeling. Thinking may be expressed as a journey, a narrative, a sequencing of propositions – the placing of people, objects, facts, words into a serial sequence, a temporal narrative of some sort. Beyond just thinking in time sequences, she adds thinking 'metaphorically'. Cave art, language itself and the use of tools are examples of thinking 'metaphorically' as they involve the use of symbols. Greenfield notes the importance of reading, of the symbols of words, of entering worlds of imagination and reflection, and wonders whether a screen-orientated generation will be missing out.

She maintains that exposure to fast-paced images of screen before the age of four diminishes a child's attention span in later life. This leads to the need for more stimulation within shorter periods of time, and puts reading books in jeopardy. It is suggested that a child growing up needs a three-way conversation between him- or herself, the parent and the real world. Screen 'does little for the inner imagination, nor is it an outer real life'. On screen you watch an ever-changing visual image – such images are arresting, fast paced, and invite you to interact. The problem begins when the screen image has no pre-existing conceptual framework in which to understand metaphor – it is merely the here and now.[57]

Greenfield continues her warning as she observes that in traditional childhood games imagination played an important role – be it football, cowboys and Indians or boxes that were cars or castles. 'But with the advent of toys that are computer games, or that link TV shows to console games, the emphasis has shifted towards taking the world at face value with little need to question or understand it, let alone create it for yourself.'[58] There are associated problems of all stimulation being visible, and also the failure to understand risk – if all activity is seen in a virtual world. From a Christian perspective this leaves us with a false perception of a fulfilled and fulfilling life and a created world that have their origin in God. Our lives and this world begin to lose meaning and may fail to make sense to us. Through an emphasis on the immediacy of the present, we may lose the value of history and past experience, and fail to be open to the future and to hope.

### Who are we psychologically and biblically?

A person is a human being in relationship with other human beings. The personal is that which distinguishes the human from the non-human, that is, from animals and machines that may perform some of the same features as human beings. For example, we might consider the exploration of the ability to love and be loved, seen as an essential human characteristic in the film *Artificial Intelligence AI*.[59] The tag line of the film is 'David is 11 years old. He weighs 60 pounds. He is 4 feet, 6 inches tall. He has brown hair. His love is real. But he is not.' He is not human.

> In the plot it is a time when natural resources are limited and technology is advancing at an astronomical pace. Where you live is monitored; what you eat is engineered; and the person serving you is not a person at all. It's artificial. Gardening, housekeeping, companionship – there is a robot for every need, except love. Emotion is the last, controversial frontier in robot evolution. Robots are seen as sophisticated appliances; they are not supposed to have feelings. But with so many parents not yet approved to have children, the possibilities abound.
>
> Cybertronics Manufacturing has created the solution – his name is David (Haley Joel Osment); a robotic boy, he is the first programmed to love. David is adopted as a test case by a Cybertronics employee (Sam Robards) and his wife (Frances O'Connor), whose own terminally ill child has been cryogenically frozen until a cure can be found. Though he gradually becomes their child, with all the love and stewardship that

entails, a series of unexpected circumstances make this life impossible for David.

Without final acceptance by humans or machines, and armed only with Teddy, his supertoy teddybear and protector, David embarks on a journey to discover where he truly belongs, uncovering a world in which the line between robot and human being is both terrifyingly vast and profoundly thin.[60]

So how do we define being human? Human behaviour can be analysed in terms of our social roles. However, there is a danger in thinking that this is all a person is. We can choose between roles and decide how to act when roles conflict, for example the roles of loving care, provision and discipline in a parent when a child acts in a dangerous or selfish way.

From Descartes onwards it has been acceptable to define a person by their rational thought. But if we do this we separate thinking from emotion and from the source of action. For example, I understand 'fear' and 'in pain' as states of mind that reflect my personal experience, but I am only able to discern a similar state of mind in others by their behaviour. Our concept of a person is thus a social concept.

Some behaviours and actions can be explained causally, for example the speedy withdrawal of a hand from a hot surface. But some are the result of a decision to follow a particular course of action. Thus we recognize that human beings have intentions and purposes, make choices and solve problems. They perceive and act in the world in a way that is interpreted by the concepts and beliefs they hold.

From a psychological standpoint, Sigmund Freud believed that people were driven by three basic biological instincts: survival – the need to breathe, eat, drink; sex – the need for heterosexual genital intercourse; and death. According to Freud, these instincts (the id) are universal and ultimately motivate everything we do. But we can satisfy them only in a social context, which sets limits on our freedom to satisfy them. We cannot eat whatever we want whenever we wish, nor can we have intercourse whenever and with whomever our instinct bids us. The result would be chaos and our instincts would be less well satisfied than they are.

In the interests of maximizing instinctual satisfaction the individual becomes a calculator (the ego), forming rules regarding what behaviour does or does not succeed. But case-by-case calculation to maximize satisfaction is inefficient. It is better to 'internalize' in our emotions (the super-ego) in the face of society's approval and disapproval. Thus we become unconsciously afraid of our instincts, and defend ourselves against them by intellectualizing them, denying them, or projecting them. These defences form our traits of personality.

Carl Jung perceived a synthesis of two dimensions: the conscious or finite ego, and unconscious or infinite self. In most people the conscious and the unconscious are isolated from one another. The goal of life is for these to become integrated – the conscious ego to be aware of what is in the unconscious and the unconscious to become the possession of the particular ego. Where this integration has not taken place a person may be restless, dependent on others and subjected to their emotions, whereas integrated people are serene, self-possessed and objective about their emotions.

Christianity takes the biblical material as an account of fundamental human nature from which a list of ideal personality traits, the Christian virtues, can be derived. Human beings are created in the image of God, for joyful obedience and dependence on God, and for loving fellowship with their fellow human beings. This presupposes a fundamental human desire for God. The word 'person' does not figure in biblical anthropology, but the Hebrew holistic view is fundamental to biblical thinking. The Hellenistic view was to divide the rational (spiritual) from the physical, and this dualistic view coloured much of Western thought. The perspective of personhood that we have been exploring in this chapter tends to reflect a biblical holistic view.

The biblical story is throughout about the relationship of God to a community, to a family, tribe or nation, but certain individual persons have a special place in it. The story is about such matters as God's choice of them, God's covenantal relationship with them, their response in action, and how God respects their personhood by holding them responsible for the choices and decisions they make, corporately and individually. God is seen as a living God, who is in the business of forming and deepening community and enabling persons to grow through the encounter with God in their history and experience. Personal life of individuals or communities is constituted in the biblical perspective by the address of the divine Word; the Word is finally and fully revealed as a person, Jesus Christ. It means that God is so personal that we see what God is only in a personal life. God can become a human being because a human being is a person and because God is personal.

Nancey Murphy deals with the doctrine of the human soul in the light of research in neuroscience, the understanding of God's involvement in a universe that contains violence and suffering, and in the face of division and disbelief in Christian understanding of evolution. Murphy considers that one key question concerns whether we see human beings in a dualist, holistic or physicalist way. She rightly observes that evolution and dualism do not sit happily together, and in exploring the more recent work of neuroscience she states that 'all the human capacities once attributed to the immaterial mind or soul are now yielding to the insights of neurobiology'.[61] She argues that when humans are seen as part and parcel of nature, then, and only then, can communion with God be seen as the *telos* (completion) of the whole evolutionary (and cosmic) process. In emphasizing the holistic nature of persons, Murphy encourages her own students to consider the extent to which their own experience of God is actually made up of bodily experiences: joy, tears and the urge to worship. We move away from the false division between saving souls and caring for people's bodily needs.

## Human dignity – imago Dei

Greenfield, after her assessment of early twenty-first-century Western culture, asks if there is an alternative to the 'Somebody' of unfettered consumerism and the 'Nobody' of depersonalized screen hedonism. She observes that we can define ourselves by various groups of which we are a part – age, nationality, ethnicity, sex, marital status, social status – but we can also perceive of ourselves as individuals. Greenfield states that 'in order for a collective identity to take a real hold something more is needed: a shared belief system'.[62] This is her 'Anyone' scenario, where we are not swept up in the crowd, but are shaped by the values and outlook of our belief system.

Theology and philosophy can provide a conceptual framework; anthropology identifies general patterns of belief, its acquisition and maintenance; psychology allows us to quantify the dimensions of our beliefs in terms of personality; and these combined prepare the ground for neuroscience to identify the physico-chemical mechanisms that subserve systems in the brain.

Greenfield looks at strong collective fundamentalist ideologies (which she states are not the same as religious faith) that control every aspect of life from eating, dress, thoughts and views, such as the Nazis, some modern-day cults, al-Qaeda or the Taleban. The non-believer is an enemy who might invade our brain, infiltrate the mind and influence what we believe, and in doing so jeopardize our very identity.

> Interestingly enough, this is precisely the vocabulary that is also employed by the renowned atheist Richard Dawkins, who has developed non-belief into a belief system all of its own and who persistently refers to religion as a 'virus': 'Like computer viruses, successful mind viruses will tend to be hard for their victims to detect. If you are the victim of one, the chances are that you won't know it, and may even vigorously deny it . . .'[63]

Intolerance and a closed mind are characteristics of such a position.

Central in our concern with the human mind will be how we perceive truth, the various models we use to describe our understanding of the world, and, for Christians, a personal relationship with God and the place of the human soul. After disposing of both the dualist view of two distinct substances – body/soul, and the reductionist, nothing buttery – only atoms and molecules – Jeeves and Berry explore the Hebrew/Christian pictures of human nature.[64] They examine the biblical use of *nepes* (Hebrew) and *psyche* (Greek) for 'soul', concluding that these words normally refer to the whole person, and most frequently carry the meaning 'life'. A similar examination of *ruah* (Hebrew) and *pneuma* (Greek) for 'spirit' shows this to be a life principle, that which makes us alive and conscious. They affirm that we are biological machines, but that we are also in the image of God. They assert that we are not controlled by our genes; virtually all human behaviour (and associated characters like intelligence) can be unintentionally or consciously influenced by the environment.

As there is now a greater emphasis on the unity of the human person, mind–brain, or behaviour–brain, theologians must be careful of not falling into the same mistake over the 'soul' with neuroscientists as they did with Galileo and concern over a heliocentric rather than geocentric universe. Jeeves urges care not to read theological language as biological language, for example 'flesh' in Romans 7.14ff. He believes that the New Testament provides support for the view of the person as a psychophysical or somato-psychic unity in the present earthly life, and for looking forward to a new form in life beyond death.

Jeeves concludes that spirituality is 'a relationship of our embodied selves to God that has the natural and irrepressible effect of making us alive to the Kingdom of God here and now in the material world'.[65] The crucial clues for the Christian seeking the distinctiveness of humankind are to be found in the biblical witness to our capacity for a personal relationship with the Creator. The Hebrew/Christian doctrine of creation is not anthropocentric with human beings as the cream of creation, but is theocentric, which sees creation as the expression of God's greatness and majesty in the cosmos (see Psalms 8 and 104). The special status of human beings is not to be found in differences of brain structure or of psychology, but in the incarnation, where humanity becomes the mode of existence of God (John 1.1–18; Phil. 2.6–11; Heb. 4.14–16).

While behaviour is dependent on genetic endowment, early upbringing, social, cultural and physical environment, we are still free to make choices and to respond as one person to another. We are also free to respond to God. Christians are encouraged to develop attitudes and behaviour based on their experience as well as on revelation and doctrine, with these experiences being illuminated by a redeemed perception of the world; always remembering Nancey Murphy's contention that there are boundary questions which science is unable to answer, but to which theology may provide some positive insights.

### Mental capacity and spirituality

The human brain is the most complex system in the natural world: 100 billion neurons connected with thousands of others through synaptic junctions numbering 100 trillion or so. Electrical signals transmitted through these lead to sensory and motor activity. But we know little of how this works. We understand the difference between the right (intuitive, imaginative, holistic thought) and left (analytical, systematic and abstract thought) sides of our brains. We know that physical or chemical intervention affects both consciousness and behaviour, such as drugs that influence mood and behaviour – mental life is strongly dependent on physical events in the brain.

This once again forces us to consider the materialistic and dualistic views about the mind–brain. B. F. Skinner, as we noted earlier, states that science should concentrate on objective events such as the correlation of a stimulus and a behavioural response. Dualism on the other hand does not allow for anything intermediate between matter and mind, so everything except mind is assumed to be totally devoid of sentience, subjectivity or interiority.[66]

Human beings take about 16 years to mature into an adult, and so it may be helpful to look at the development of the brain in this process. By the end of the first month of gestation a primitive brain has been formed in the embryo. By the fifth week in the womb it is possible to identify two bulges at the front that are the foundation of our hugely developed cerebral hemispheres, as well as certain regions below the cortex, such as the basal ganglia, which are important for movement. Amazing growth takes place, with 250,000 new neurons produced per minute through cell division.[67]

By nine months' gestation, we have most of the neurons in our brains that we are ever likely to have, and once born the brain continues to grow as the head expands. At six months the head will be half its adult size and by two years three-quarters its adult size. Even within the first month a baby already has some reflexes, for example a primitive grasping reflex, and picking up objects develops by the end of the first year, with independent movement of individual digits a little later.

Consciousness develops after birth in response to the environment. While the brain of the chimpanzee does the majority of its growing in the womb, the greater part of the human brain's development takes place after birth. Although most of the neurons are in place at birth, the development of synaptic communications develops after birth. All the time in the new brain, the axons are now growing out from the neurons to connect them to other neurons. Much of the spectacular increase in brain size after birth is attributable to the development of these processes acting as lines of communication between neurons, rather than simply the addition of more neurons.[68]

Greenfield is keen to point out that an enriched environment for brain development is not a matter of possessions or physical activity, but rather the key factor is the stimulation of the brain. Human stimulation is largely the result of those things that involve learning and memory: 'Human stimulation can be achieved informally outside the schoolroom by lively conversations, meaningful relationships, crossword puzzles, and incessant reading, irrespective of whether such events occur in an inner city or on a beach in the Caribbean.'[69] We are fashioning neural connections to give an individual brain.

By middle age we are fairly fixed in personality, and our brain processes are slowing down, although still evolving and reacting to the environment, sometimes learning new skills such as driving or using a computer. Better nutrition, fitness and health care keeps us alive to greater and greater age, although by 75 years there is a 5 per cent loss, and by 90 years a 20 per cent loss, in brain weight.

Alongside the neurological understanding of what is happening in our brains we can add the observations of behavioural scientists such as James Fowler, who considers the development of faith in human beings. For Fowler, faith involves both rationality and passionality. Fowler speaks of the 'logic of connection' and the 'reasoning in faith'. He then stresses the importance of imagination in knowing, and the power of symbols. He also associates moral reasoning with faith in his recognition of seven stages of faith.[70] These stages are pertinent not only to the development of faith but to adult development in general, so it is worth looking at some of them in a little detail.

At his stage 3, *Conforming Faith* (12–19 years), Fowler suggests that adolescents need 'mirrors' – to reflect their changes in appearance and new looks. So the views of others become important for the image of self. They worry about being accepted socially and sexually. For these people God is seen as having inexhaustible depths and is capable of knowing the mysterious depths of self and others. Faith is synthesized rather than analysed. Faith concepts are grasped but the person will go along with the faith crowd. Transition to the next stage comes through noticing contradictions in the lives of valued leaders, or through a break, such as leaving home. But Fowler recognizes that some adults never in fact pass beyond this stage at all.

Stage 4, *Choosing Faith* (18–40 years), includes taking seriously the burden of responsibility for commitments, lifestyle, beliefs and attitudes. At this stage tensions develop between self-fulfilment and self-actualization as a primary concern on the one hand, and service to other people and being for them on the other hand. Many adults do not reach this stage and for others it does not arrive until their 40s. Beliefs are analysed, compared and contrasted. Reactions can be pluralistic or fundamentalist.

Stage 5, *Balanced Faith* (midlife), is a time of reworking and reclaiming the past, an opening to the voices of the 'deeper self'. There is in faith a willingness to live with paradoxes and inconsistencies. The views of other faith traditions are appreciated as enriching rather than threatening.

Finally stage 6, *Selfless Faith* (maturity), is – according to Fowler – a rare stage, which he identifies with Martin Luther King's non-violence, Ghandi's selflessness, or Mother Teresa's self-sacrifice on behalf of others. These persons embody costly openness to the power of the future; they create liberation and shock waves. We might suggest that they are Christlike and challenge us in our calling as his disciples.

The identification of such stages in the behaviour and the perceptions of how children and adults learn and grow in understanding are generalizations based on observation. They are neither laws nor even principles, but they do inform our understanding about the ways in which people think.

## Dialogue

### *Individuality and personhood*

In distinguishing a male from a female brain, the best we could achieve would be educated guess work. Recognizing kindness or a sense of humour would be impossible. Each brain has the same basic ground plan, but circuitry is influenced greatly by environment. Identical twins are clones of each other. They are two people with identical genes because the single fertilized egg split into two; but are they identical people? They will show distinct perceptions and thoughts that define unique consciousness even though they are genetically the same. It is our experiences that are a key factor in shaping the micro circuitry of the brain.

We might, for example, have the potential of being a linguist, but if we are never exposed to a variety of languages the potential will not be realized.

> Our character continues to adapt as we respond to, and recoil from, the incessant experiences thrown in our path. For experiences to have any lasting significance in this way, they need to be remembered. The essence of the individual thus lies in no small part with what he or she can remember.[71]

Greenfield recognizes that memory is clearly a product of the physical brain, but compared to more explicit sensory or motor functions, it would be readily regarded as an aspect of the mind. The stored memories, prejudices and previous experiences would serve as a counterweight to the flood of everyday sensory experience. She also observes that in simpler brains, in schizophrenia, or in dreams, such an ability might be diminished. Viewed in this way, mind might be the personalization of the physical brain as it develops and adapts throughout life. More complex brains would have more chance for a more individual, less stereotyped mind.[72] She concludes:

> If mind is seen as the evolving personal aspect of the physical brain, then how might it relate to consciousness? My particular view is that mind can only be realized when we are conscious. After all, we lose consciousness when we sleep, but we do not lose our mind. However, mind is meaningless if we are unconscious. Hence consciousness could be seen as the actual firsthand, first-person experience of a certain mind, a personalized brain. Consciousness brings the mind alive; it is the ultimate puzzle to the neuroscientist. It is your most private place.[73]

For Greenfield the subjective experience of consciousness is the place for a purely scientific survey to end. Jeeves and Berry would agree with this observation, noting that Roger Penrose marvelled at how a material object, the brain, could evoke consciousness. Attempts by physical as well as biological scientists to understand consciousness illustrate how scientific data do not come neatly labelled with interpretation and meaning. They also note that Roger Sperry sees consciousness as a dynamic emergent property of brain activity that is neither identical with, nor reducible to, the neural events of which it is mainly composed.[74] The authors conclude that the scientifically probable view is that

> to do justice to the complexity of the one set of neurochemical brain events occurring during conscious experience, we must give ontological priority to mental life. As Christians we believe that we can be peaceably open-minded about questions such as whether or not consciousness occurs in other animals besides ourselves. The work of primatologists certainly points to the presence of mind-like conscious reflective and deceptive behaviour in the higher non-human primates. There are no problems here for the biblically informed Christian who recognizes that we share many properties with animals, particularly the apes.[75]

### The soul

Human life is embodied life in communities marked by the power of goodness. The Christian view of the soul expressed by Aquinas was based on Aristotle's Forms – the perfect form on which all other material expressions were based. For them the human soul is that which gives human animals the capacity to think abstractly and make moral decisions. Aristotle differed from Plato in insisting that Forms must be expressed in matter and do not have an independent or superior reality. The soul cannot therefore exist without the body.

Modern philosophers speak of the distinctive capacities of the human animal. To speak of human souls is to speak of the intellectual and the moral – and perhaps the emotional – capacities and dispositions of human beings. The key religious concern is the capacity for conscious relationship to an Objective Reality, whether a being or a state, of supreme beauty and goodness. So the view is not of a separate entity but of a materialist version of personhood, whereby the soul enhances our intellectual, imaginative and moral practice.

The profound perception is to see human life as bound by the character of goodness with no reward. This might be criticized as being elitist. If goodness is seen as suffering love in the cross, then resurrection (for Christians) is important because love triumphs – goodness triumphs. If we remove the triumph then it becomes difficult to be a Christian, because a life of suffering love becomes simply a moral stand. However, reductionists such as Richard Dawkins see objective goodness as 'myth-mongering'.

If we speak of self or soul as embodied, can we speak of a continuing self? Conscience may be a relevant factor in the argument, unless this is seen as only moral or spiritual. But then we must ask whether scientific facts are the only facts. We cannot oppose scientific facts but we can move towards the notion of a human person, where objective goodness does in fact exist.

Almost all religions affirm that there is more to human beings than the material body and brain. This is seen as the spiritual dimension. We can define a material object in terms of 3D space and in terms of its composition, all open to analysis; but the spiritual is harder to define – it is not publicly observable nor physically measureable. Keith Ward believes that, more positively, the spiritual 'consists of consciousness (immediate awareness of some object), it has the character of feeling (pleasure in or aversion to the object of awareness), it involves thought (the ability to identify objects and consider possible states as well as actual ones), and it involves goals or purposes (envisioned possible states that would give pleasure)'.[76] For example, a human being can imagine a tropical island.

Ward states that among the world religions the 'dualist view of one continuing and potentially disembodied substantial self is not widely held, though it can be found in Jainism'. The Semitic view places emphasis on the 'vital importance of this earthly, material, embodied existence'.[77]

## Science and the soul

In the twentieth century, there is a clear emphasis on reductive materialism. B. F. Skinner saw humans as nothing more than complex stimulus–response mechanisms. Francis Crick said that 'you, your joys and your sorrows, your memories and your ambitions, your sense of personal identity and free will, are in fact no more than the behaviour of a vast assembly of nerve cells and their associated molecules'.[78] Ward notes that none of these authors suggest what it is that we are nothing more than, yet are agreed that in no way are we spiritual beings.

But, states Ward, 'modern advances in neuroscience and artificial intelligence tend to leave practitioners with a deep suspicion of dualism'.[79] For in studying the brain, scientists are studying consciousness, and brain and consciousness seem to be two aspects of the same thing. So feelings and thoughts are the same events understood from different points of view. PET (positron-emission tomography) scans are able to show that many diverse areas of the brain are activated during one unified mental activity. There was, for example, a difference in the areas active when thinking about faces as opposed to thinking about houses. It is possible to correlate brain states with such phenomenological activities. It is therefore possible to propose that brain-state and phenomenal experiences are two complementary aspects of the same thing, one publicly accessible and measureable, the other private and not measureable in any exact way.

Ward concludes:

Thought becomes rational and responsible when the brain permits it to do so. Thinking rationally depends upon the structure and functioning of a brain of a specific sort. In the absence of such brain functioning, think-ing does not take place. If the brain is damaged, the thought process may well be impaired. This strongly implies that thoughts and feelings develop as the brain makes such developments possible. They do not occur in a quite different nonphysical realm, in some sort of parallel world . . . It looks as though neuroscience has successfully shown the dependence of conscious experience upon the brain. But it has not reduced consciousness to observable states of the brain, and, in fact, it seems to presuppose that there needs to be an independent mode of access to conscious states that is not open to experimental science.[80]

We are left to ask whether we have identified the essence of 'self'/'soul'/ personhood?

### Somewhere to stand

Paul Davies observes:

When it comes to the mental realm, the characteristic qualities are even more distinctive and totally unlike anything else found in nature. Now we are dealing with thoughts, purposes, feelings, beliefs – the inner, subjec-tive world of the observer, who experiences external reality through the senses. These mental entities are clearly not merely 'other sorts of things' – they are in a class apart.[81]

They are not the same as material objects – when you open up the brain you do not see thoughts and feelings, just the complex structure of the cerebrum. We have the problem of how the redness of red differs from the blueness of blue, or the taste of salt. Either these so-called 'qualia' are illusory or they are fundamental emergent properties of nature.

Davies adds to the debate of mind–brain by suggesting two reasons why the mind must be taken seriously. First, a scientific reason: Davies believes that any attempt to bring consciousness within the scope of physics will need to be formulated within the context of quantum mechanics. He states:

the problem of including the observer in our description of physical reality arises most insistently when it comes to the subject of quantum cosmol-ogy – the application of quantum mechanics to the universe as a whole – because by definition 'the universe' must include any observers.

The observer and time become key to our understanding of the universe. We should see the universe as separated into two sub-systems: an observer with a clock; and the rest. 'Then the observer may measure the passage of time relative to the evolution of the rest of the universe.' The observer is vital – in the absence of observers the universe is 'dead'. We cannot ignore consciousness. 'And observers will exist, obviously, only in those "Goldilocks" universes in which the laws and conditions are such as to permit them [consciousness] to emerge.'[82]

Second, a philosophical argument: human minds are much more than mere observers. 'We do much more than just watch the show that nature stages. Human beings have come to *understand* the world, at least in part, through the processes of reasoning and science.' We have come to understand mathematics and through this the hidden cosmic code. 'The weak anthropic principle merely requires observers to observe. It is not necessary for observers to understand. Yet humans do. Why?' Davies concludes

> I am convinced that human understanding of nature through science, rational reasoning and mathematics points to a much deeper connection between life, mind and cosmos than emerges from the crude lottery of multiverse cosmology combined with the weak anthropic principle . . . Somehow, the universe has engineered its own self-awareness.[83]

Davies believes that this cannot be accounted for by the laws of physics. He notes that the genome of a bacterium has millions of bits of information – information that is not encoded in the laws of physics. 'To understand the high information content of life we must recognize that it is the product, not of the laws of physics alone, but the laws of physics *and* the history of the environment together.'[84] This took billions of years and a vast number of processing steps.

Life as we observe it today is 1 per cent physics and 99 per cent history. As we noted in Chapter 3, while Davies denies being crypto-religious, he does believe that

> life and mind are etched deeply into the fabric of the cosmos, perhaps through a shadowy, half-glimpsed life principle, and if I am honest I have to concede that this starting point is something I feel more in my heart than in my head. So maybe that is a religious conviction of sorts.[85]

Added to all this the Christian will want to affirm that human beings are *imago Dei*, created in the image of God, and beneficiaries of God's revelation.

**Key texts**

Susan Greenfield, 1997, *The Human Brain: A Guided Tour*, London: HarperCollins/ Phoenix.

——2008, *id: The Quest for Identity in the 21st Century*, London: Sceptre/Hodder & Stoughton.

Malcolm Jeeves, 1997, *Human Nature at the Millennium: Reflections on the Integration of Psychology and Christianity*, Leicester: InterVarsity Press/Apollos, and Grand Rapids: Baker Books.

**Further reading**

Ian G. Barbour, 1998, *Religion and Science: Historical and Contemporary Issues*, London: SCM Press.

Paul Davies, 2007, *The Goldilocks Enigma: Why is the Universe Just Right for Life?* London: Penguin Books.

Malcolm Jeeves and R. J. Berry, 1998, *Science, Life and Christian Belief*, Leicester: InterVarsity Press/Apollos.

Nancey Murphy, 2002, *Religion and Science: God, Evolution, and the Soul*, Proceedings of the 2001 Goshen Conference on Religion and Science, ed. Carl S. Helrich, Kitchener, Ontario: Pandora Press.

Keith Ward, 2008, *The Big Questions in Science and Religion*, West Conshohocken PA: Templeton Foundation Press.

James Watson, 2003, *DNA: The Secret of Life*, London: Arrow Books.

**Notes**

1 Susan Greenfield, 1997, *The Human Brain: A Guided Tour*, London: HarperCollins/Phoenix, p. 4.

2 Susan Greenfield, 2008, *id: The Quest for Identity in the 21st Century*, London: Sceptre/Hodder & Stoughton, p. 25.

3 Greenfield, *The Human Brain*, p. 18.

4 Greenfield, *The Human Brain*, p. 19.

5 Greenfield, *The Human Brain*, p. 20.

6 Greenfield, *The Human Brain*, p. 23.

7 Greenfield, *The Human Brain*, p. 39.

8 Greenfield, *id: The Quest for Identity*, p. 18.

9 Greenfield, *id: The Quest for Identity*, pp. 31–2.

10 Malcolm Jeeves, 1997, *Human Nature at the Millennium: Reflections on the Integration of Psychology and Christianity*, Leicester: InterVarsity Press/Apollos, and Grand Rapids: Baker Books.

11 Malcolm Jeeves and R. J. Berry, 1998, *Science, Life and Christian Belief*, Leicester: InterVasity Press/Apollos, p. 174.

12 Jeeves and Berry, *Science, Life*, p. 178.

13 Jeeves and Berry, *Science, Life*, pp. 178–9.

14 Robert Winston, 2005, *The Story of God: A Personal Journey into the World of Science and Religion*, London: Bantam Press, p. 11.

15 Winston, *The Story of God*, p. 12.

16 Winston, *The Story of God*, p. 75.

17 Winston, *The Story of God*, p. 77.

18 Jeeves and Berry, *Science, Life*, p. 191.

19 Jeeves and Berry, *Science, Life*, p. 192.

20 Jeeves and Berry, *Science, Life*, p. 196.

21 James Watson, 2003, *DNA: The Secret of Life*, London: Arrow Books, p. 202.

22 Watson, *DNA*, pp. 202–3.

23 Watson, *DNA*, pp. 265–6.

24 Francis Collins, 2007, *The Language of God: A Scientist Presents Evidence for Belief*, London: Simon & Schuster/Pocket Books, pp. 198–9.

25 Ian G. Barbour, 1998, *Religion and Science. Historical and Contemporary Issues*, London: SCM Press, p. 254.

26 Barbour, *Religion and Science*, p. 257.

27 Greenfield, *The Human Brain*, p. 43.

28 Greenfield, *The Human Brain*, p. 44.

29 Greenfield, *The Human Brain*, p. 46.

30 Greenfield, *The Human Brain*, pp. 52–3.

31 Greenfield, *The Human Brain*, p. 68.

32 Greenfield, *The Human Brain*, p. 27.

33 Greenfield, *The Human Brain*, p. 29.

34 Greenfield, *id: The Quest for Identity*, p. 74.

35 Greenfield, *The Human Brain*, p. 114.

36 Greenfield, *id: The Quest for Identity*, p. 76.

37 Greenfield, *The Human Brain*, pp. 108–9.

38 Greenfield, *id: The Quest for Identity*, p. 76.

39 Greenfield, *id: The Quest for Identity*, pp. 57–61.

40 Jeeves and Berry, *Science, Life*, p. 175.

41 Greenfield, *id: The Quest for Identity*, p. 79.

42 Watson, *DNA*, pp. 410–12.

43 Watson, *DNA*, p. 412.

44 Greenfield, *id: The Quest for Identity*, pp. 82–3.

45 Greenfield, *id: The Quest for Identity*, p. 84.

46 Greenfield, *id: The Quest for Identity*, pp. 88–9.

47 Greenfield, *id: The Quest for Identity*, p. 91.

48 Greenfield, *id: The Quest for Identity*, pp. 55–6.

49 Greenfield, *The Human Brain*, p. 106–7.

50 Roger Penrose, 1989, *The Emperor's New Mind*, Oxford: Oxford University Press, p. 526.

51 Greenfield, *id: The Quest for Identity*, p. 115.

52 Greenfield, *id: The Quest for Identity*, p. 116.

53 Greenfield, *id: The Quest for Identity*, p. 123.

54 Greenfield, *id: The Quest for Identity*, p. 127.

55 Greenfield, *id: The Quest for Identity*, pp. 156–7.

56 Greenfield, *id: The Quest for Identity*, p. 160.

57  Greenfield, id: The Quest for Identity, pp. 176–7.

58  Greenfield, id: The Quest for Identity, p. 182.

59  Film AI directed by Steven Spielberg, staring Jude Law, Frances O'Connor, Sam Robards and Haley Joel Osment; distributed by Warner Brothers/DreamWorks; released September 2001; rating 12.

60  Plot summary of the film given on the movie website, http://uk.rottentomatoes.com/m/ai_artificial_intelligence/

61  Nancey Murphy, 2002, Religion and Science: God, Evolution, and the Soul, Proceedings of the 2001 Goshen Conference on Religion and Science, ed. Carl S. Helrich, Kitchener, Ontario: Pandora Press, p. 17.

62  Greenfield, id: The Quest for Identity, p. 213.

63  Greenfield, id: The Quest for Identity, p. 228.

64  Jeeves and Berry, Science, Life, pp. 136–69.

65  Jeeves, Human Nature, p. 125.

66  Barbour, Religion and Science, pp. 258–9.

67  Greenfield, The Human Brain, pp. 121–2.

68  Greenfield, The Human Brain, pp. 139–41.

69  Greenfield, The Human Brain, p. 150.

70  For an exploration of the ways in which children and adults develop in their perception of the world, see: Erik Erikson, 1963, Childhood and Society, New York: Norton; and 1968, Identity, Youth and Crisis, New York: Norton; Lawrence Kohlberg, 'Stage and Sequence: The Cognitive Developmental Approach to Socialization', in David A. Goslin (ed.), 1969, Handbook of Socialization Theory and Research, Chicago: Rand McNally; Jean Piaget, 1967, Six Psychological Studies, New York: Vintage Books; and 1976, The Child and Reality, New York: Penguin Books; James Fowler, 1981, 1995, Stages of Faith, San Francisco: Harper.

71  Greenfield, The Human Brain, p. 157.

72  Greenfield, The Human Brain, pp. 191–2.

73  Greenfield, The Human Brain, p. 192.

74  Jeeves and Berry, Science, Life, pp. 184–5.

75  Jeeves and Berry, Science, Life, p. 186.

76  Keith Ward, 2008, The Big Questions in Science and Religion, West Conshohocken PA: Templeton Foundation Press, p. 134.

77  Ward, The Big Questions, p. 141.

78  Francis Crick, 1994, The Astonishing Hypothesis, New York: Simon & Schuster, p. 3, quoted in Ward, The Big Questions, p. 143.

79  Ward, The Big Questions, p. 145.

80  Ward, The Big Questions, p. 150.

81  Paul Davies, 2007, The Goldilocks Enigma: Why is the Universe Just Right for Life? London: Penguin Books, p. 259.

82  Davies, The Goldilocks Enigma, pp. 260–1.

83  Davies, The Goldilocks Enigma, pp. 261–2.

84  Davies, The Goldilocks Enigma, p. 263.

85  Davies, The Goldilocks Enigma, pp. 302–3.

# 5

## Genes, the Human Genome and Genetic Engineering

### Introduction

There have been amazing advances in biotechnology in the last 20 years. The 1990s saw the planting of millions of acres of genetically modified crops; and Dolly the cloned sheep was subsequently joined by many other domestic animals born asexually by transfer of genetic material. It now is possible to transfer genes from any part of the animal and plant kingdoms to any other. In 2000, the birth of the first 'saviour sibling' occurred, raising the possibility of 'designer babies'. There are a large number of ethical issues to be addressed in these advances in bioscience, which we shall begin to explore in this chapter.

Human genetics has been transformed and the cure for many diseases is now a distinct possibility. Steve Jones observed that no longer does human genetics begin with

> an inherited change (such as a genetic disease) and search for its location. Instead, it uses the opposite strategy, with a logic precisely opposite that of Mendel: from inherited particle to function, rather than the other way around . . . The first breakthrough of this new approach was the success-ful hunt for the cystic fibrosis gene in 1990. It gave a hint as to what was possible and was the introduction to the advances that led to the complete map [human genome] a mere decade or so later.[1]

Possible improvement in global food security has come through various tech-niques of genetic engineering in which agriculture has become much more productive, with the amount of food available per head in the world rising alongside the greatest population explosion in history. However, in the devel-oping world there is still room for progress as half of all crops are lost to weeds, and disease can lead to the loss of entire harvests. Scientists hold out the hope that modern biotechnology can successfully address such problems.

The vitally important 'Green Revolution' has, according to Jones, taken place the Darwinian way with new and productive stocks of rice and wheat being crossed with lines with shorter and stiffer stalks. Just a few genes were involved. Their descendants were crossed with stocks that contained genes for high yield and rapid growth. Genetic recombination did the farmer's job by making new mixtures of genes. 'One simple trick transformed the rural economies of India and China. In fifty years, planned gene exchange gave a six-fold boost in yield, a figure as great as that at the origin of farming ten thousand years before.'[2]

## Genetic engineering

Genetic engineering, recombinant DNA technology, genetic modification/ manipulation (GM) and gene splicing are terms that apply to the direct manipulation of an organism's genes. Genetic engineering is different from traditional breeding, where the organism's genes are manipulated indirectly. Genetic engineering involves the transfer of DNA material from one cell to another. Each living cell contains a nucleus, which controls the activity of the cell. Chromosomes in the nucleus contain the genes which are the carriers of genetic information. Genetic engineering uses the techniques of molecular cloning and transformation to alter the structure and characteristics of genes directly. Genetic engineering techniques have found some successes in numerous applications. Some examples are in improving crop technology, and the manufacture of synthetic human insulin through the use of modified bacteria.

Another example is the use of pig hearts for human transplants. Pig hearts can now be genetically engineered so that they produce human proteins like a coat or film around their heart. This is thought to prevent rejection after transplantation. Genetic engineering of bacteria and plants has been used to create vaccines, antibiotics, blood-clotting factors and therapeutic proteins such as anti-HIV or anti-cancer agents.[3]

Genetic engineering offers the opportunity for greater human intervention in reproduction and evolution of species including humans. The dominant model of nature becomes 'a mechanism to be manipulated for particular ends', and there are important theological and ethical questions here concerning our intervention in God's creation.[4]

## Human genome

The human genome consists of all the DNA of our species, the hereditary code of life. There are 3.1 billion letters of the DNA code arrayed across 24 chromosomes. The letters are written in a 4-letter code and such is the complexity of the information carried within each cell of the human body that a live reading of that code at a rate of one letter per second would take 31 years. Printing them out on A4 sheets of paper in regular font size and binding the sheets of paper together would produce a book that would be a tower nearly 170 metres high.[5]

Human beings at DNA level are 99.9 per cent identical. That similarity applies regardless of ethnicity. This remarkably low genetic diversity distinguishes human beings from most other species. The Human Genome Project completed in 2000 has recognized the complete DNA sequence that makes up human chromosomes.

This library will be useful in the development of both the diagnosis of human genetic diseases and therapies for particular diseases. At present it is illegal in the UK to conduct what is known as germ-line therapy. This is the alteration of the sperm or egg cells that encode the genetic material for the next generation.[6]

## Cloning

Dolly (5 July 1996 to 14 February 2003) was a female domestic sheep remarkable in being the first mammal to be cloned from an adult somatic cell, using the process of somatic cell nuclear transfer (SCNT). She was cloned by Ian Wilmut, Keith Campbell and colleagues at the Roslin Institute in Edinburgh, Scotland. She was born on 5 July 1996 and she lived until the age of six. Her creation aroused worldwide interest and concern because of its scientific and ethical implications.

There are different types of cloning, and cloning technologies can be used for other purposes besides producing the genetic twin of another organism. A basic understanding of the different types of cloning is key to taking an informed stance on current public policy issues and making the best possible personal decisions. In the next section (see pp. 160–5) we will explore the three types of cloning technologies: recombinant DNA technology or DNA cloning, reproductive cloning, and therapeutic cloning.

## Genetically modified crops

Between 1997 and 2005, the total surface area of land cultivated with GM crops increased by a factor of 50, from 17,000 km² (4.2 million acres) to 900,000 km² (222 million acres). Although most GM crops are grown in North America, in recent years there has been rapid growth in the area sown in developing countries. For instance in 2005 the largest increase in crop area planted to GM crops (soya beans) was in Brazil. There has also been rapid and continuing expansion of GM cotton varieties in India since 2002. (Cotton is a major source of vegetable cooking oil and animal feed.) In 2008 –09, some 32,000 km² of GM cotton was harvested in India (up more than 100 per cent from the previous season).

In 2003, countries that grew 99 per cent of the global transgenic crops were the United States (63 per cent), Argentina (21 per cent), Canada (6 per cent), Brazil (4 per cent), China (4 per cent) and South Africa (1 per cent).

The Grocery Manufacturers of America estimate that 75 per cent of all processed foods in the United States contain a GM ingredient. More than 33 per cent of US soya bean crop and 45 per cent of the Canadian oilseed rape crop is genetically modified. Most of these crops have been genetically modified to tolerate herbicide or insecticide, and much of this genetic engineering seems to be for the commercial profit of the producer. Celia Deane-Drummond notes that 'such changes impinge not just on those living in these countries but on all exports as well, including processed food, thus entering the global food supply'.[7]

Various health and environmental risks have been recognized or postulated, for example on human health through allergic reactions and effects on the immune system. For the environment there has been the effect on wildlife, the creation through cross-pollination of super-weeds resistant to herbicides, and a loss of biodiversity. Added to this, patents taken out by biotechnology companies on GM seed are making access expensive, so denying use of this technology to the poorer nations. This raises issues of justice.

## Cloning

### Recombinant DNA technology or DNA cloning

The terms 'recombinant DNA technology', 'DNA cloning', 'molecular cloning' or 'gene cloning' all refer to the same process: the transfer of a DNA fragment of interest from one organism to a self-replicating genetic element such as a bacterial plasmid. (Plasmids are independent, circular, self-replicating DNA molecules that carry only a few genes. They usually occur naturally in bacteria, but are sometimes found in eukaryotic organisms.) The DNA of interest can then be propagated in a foreign host cell.

To clone a gene, a DNA fragment containing the gene of interest is isolated from chromosomal DNA using restriction enzymes and then united with a plasmid that has been cut with the same restriction enzymes. When the fragment of chromosomal DNA is joined with its cloning vector in the lab, it is called a 'recombinant DNA molecule'. Following introduction into suitable host cells, the recombinant DNA can then be reproduced along with the host cell DNA.

### Reproductive cloning

Dolly the sheep and the unexpected discovery that the DNA instruction book could be reprogrammed in cell transfer have opened up many possibilities in the preservation and reproduction of species.

> Over the course of the last decade, discovery after discovery is revealing the remarkable and completely unanticipated plasticity of mammalian cell

types. That in turn has led to the current controversy about the potential benefits and risks of this kind of research, characterized by intense public disagreements that show no sign of lessening.[8]

Dolly's creation was through somatic cell nuclear transfer (SCNT). The nucleus (carrying the complete DNA of the donor sheep) of a single cell removed from the udder of a mature sheep was 'inserted into the rich environment of proteins and signaling molecules found in the cytoplasm of an egg cell'. The egg cell had previously had its nucleus completely removed so that it could provide no genetic instructions, only the environment in which those instructions could be recognized and carried out. 'The udder cell nucleus reverted back to its primitive undifferentiated state. Implanting that cell back into the womb of a sheep gave rise to Dolly, whose nuclear DNA was identical to that of the original sheep.'[9]

### Therapeutic cloning

In November 2001, scientists from Advanced Cell Technologies, a biotechnology company in Massachusetts, announced that they had cloned the first human embryos for the purpose of advancing therapeutic research. To do this, they collected eggs from women's ovaries and then removed the genetic material from these eggs. A skin cell was inserted inside the enucleated egg to serve as a new nucleus. The egg began to divide after it was stimulated with a chemical called ionomycin. The results were limited in success. Although this process was carried out with eight eggs, only three began dividing, and only one was able to divide into six cells before stopping.

Therapeutic cloning, also called 'embryo cloning', is the production of human embryos for use in research. The goal of this process is not to create cloned human beings, but rather to harvest stem cells that can be used to study human development and to treat disease. Stem cells are important to biomedical researchers because they can be used to generate virtually any type of specialized cell in the human body. Stem cells are extracted from the egg after it has divided for five days. The egg at this stage of development is called a blastocyst. The extraction process destroys the embryo, which raises a variety of ethical concerns. Many researchers hope that one day stem cells can be used to serve as replacement cells to treat heart disease, Alzheimer's, cancer and other diseases.

### Use of cloning technologies

Recombinant DNA technology is important for learning about other related technologies, such as gene therapy, genetic engineering of organisms, and sequencing genomes. Gene therapy can be used to treat certain genetic conditions by introducing virus vectors that carry corrected copies of faulty genes into the cells of a host organism. Genes from different organisms that improve taste and nutritional value or provide resistance to particular types of disease can be used to genetically engineer food crops. With genome sequencing, fragments of chromosomal DNA must be inserted into different cloning vectors to generate fragments of an appropriate size for sequencing.

If the low success rates can be improved (Dolly was only 1 success out of 276 attempts), reproductive cloning can be used to develop efficient ways to reliably reproduce animals with special qualities. For example, drug-producing animals or animals that have been genetically altered to serve as models for studying human disease could be mass-produced.

Hundreds of cloned animals exist today, but the number of different species is limited. Some species may be more resistant to somatic cell nuclear transfer than others. The process of stripping the nucleus from an egg cell and replacing it with the nucleus of a donor cell is a traumatic one, and improvements in cloning technologies may be needed before many species can be cloned successfully. There have been clones of sheep, goats, cows, mice, pigs, cats, dogs and rabbits.

Reproductive cloning could also be used to repopulate endangered animals or animals that are difficult to breed. In 2001, the first clone of an endangered wild animal was born, a wild ox called a gaur. The young gaur died from an infection about 48 hours after its birth. In 2001, scientists in Italy reported the successful cloning of a healthy baby mouflon, an endangered wild sheep. The cloned mouflon is living at a wildlife centre in Sardinia. Other endangered species that are potential candidates for cloning include the African bongo antelope, the Sumatran tiger and the giant panda. Cloning extinct animals presents a much greater challenge to scientists because the egg and the surrogate needed to create the cloned embryo would be of a species different from the clone.

The preservation of endangered species is one argument in favour of cloning. Many rare animals, for example giant pandas, are reluctant to breed in captivity. Cloning would be an alternative way of creating new individuals. Cloning could also be used to increase the genetic diversity of a group of animals, particularly when the group includes some individuals who are not breeding and passing on their genes. However, there are two main concerns about using cloning to conserve rare species: cloning might lead people to think of extinction as a temporary state. It might therefore detract from attempts to preserve rare habitats. In addition the mass cloning of a very few individuals in zoos could reduce the worldwide genetic diversity of a species.

In the world of commercial farming, dairy cows are valued for qualities such as good legs, large udders and a high milk yield. The best performing animals can be worth tens of thousands of pounds. In theory cloning could be an ideal way of mass-producing elite farm animals, which may also have other good qualities like resistance to common diseases. In the United States several of the best performing cattle, like Mandy, a prize-winning US Holstein cow, have already been cloned.

It is still extremely expensive to produce cloned animals and, at over £30,000 per copy, it only makes sense for the most valuable stock. However, as cloning becomes more common, the price will drop dramatically. But the general public are not convinced and ask whether milk or meat from cloned animals is safe. The US government has withheld permission to sell cloned produce until various safety studies have been completed. There are also the dangers that widespread cloning could lead to farmers ordering copies of animals cloned from just a handful of individuals, which would considerably reduce genetic diversity, leaving the whole species vulnerable to disease.

In human beings the real excitement comes from the medical benefits of stem cell research in the development of new therapies. For example these therapies may be used in the treatment of type 1 diabetes caused by the premature death of cells that produce insulin in the pancreas; or Parkinson's disease caused by the death of neurons in the substantia nigra resulting in the disruption of those brain circuits that control motor function. Or if we could find a way to regenerate damaged tissue, for example in kidneys or the liver, then transplant surgery would not be needed.[10] Embryonic stem cells, formed at conception, have the potential to turn into any form of complex tissue that makes up the 100 trillion cells of the adult human being. This potential is only in embryonic cells, while the embryo is still a small compact ball of cells. There is great promise here, but also ethical issues that generate strong opinions.

Therapeutic cloning technology may become a realistic option in humans to produce whole organs from single cells or to produce healthy cells that can replace damaged cells in degenerative diseases such as Alzheimer's or Parkinson's. Scientists hope that one day therapeutic cloning can be used to generate tissues and organs for transplants.

To do this, DNA would be extracted from the person in need of a transplant and inserted into an enucleated egg. After the egg containing the patient's DNA starts to divide, embryonic stem cells that can be transformed into any type of tissue would be harvested. The stem cells would be used to generate an organ or tissue that is a genetic match to the recipient. In theory, the cloned organ could then be transplanted into the patient without the risk of tissue rejection. If organs could be generated from cloned human embryos, the need for organ donation could be significantly reduced.

### The risks of cloning technology

In some ways, cloning has proved much easier than expected. However, scientists still don't fully understand the process. For every living clone, there are usually hundreds of failures. A staggering 97 per cent of cloning

attempts don't work. Cloning is an art, not a science. The whole operation is extremely delicate and the embryo can become damaged. It can be
knocked and bumped about during handling in the laboratory. This type of
damage is also thought to be the cause of 'large offspring syndrome' when
cloned animals are born very large. The same problem can occur in calves
born by in vitro fertilization (IVF), a technique that also involves embryos
being handled in the laboratory. They may not develop properly. Embryos
are usually nurtured to the blastocyst stage (about 120 cells) before being
implanted in a surrogate mother. However the chemical 'soup' used to nurture the cloned embryo in the laboratory may not be quite the right mixture
and this remains one major focus of scientific research into cloning.

Before normal reproduction, eggs and sperm are programmed by the
body so that they are ready to create a new individual. However, a cloned
embryo seems to miss out on some of this programming. It is perhaps not
surprising that various mistakes creep in and lead to the death of most clones
before birth. In support of this idea scientists have identified abnormalities
in mouse clones, not with the genetic code itself, but with some of the very
small chemical tags that are attached to the genes. Essential genes might be
'switched off' when they should be on, and others would be on when they
should be off.

Reproductive cloning is expensive and highly inefficient, with most cloning attempts failing to produce viable offspring. In addition to low success
rates, cloned animals tend to have a more compromised immune function
and higher rates of infection, tumour growth and other disorders.

### Human cloning

Due to the inefficiency of animal cloning and the lack of understanding
about reproductive cloning, many scientists and physicians strongly believe
that it would be unethical to attempt to clone humans. Scientists do not
know how cloning could impact mental development. While factors such as
intellect and mood may not be as important for a cow or a mouse, they are
crucial for the development of healthy humans. With so many unknowns
concerning reproductive cloning, the attempt to clone humans at this time is
considered potentially dangerous and ethically irresponsible.

However, therapeutic cloning of human embryos has taken place. In
2005, Professor Ian Wilmut and Kings College London scientists were
granted a licence to clone human embryos for medical research. They have
cloned early stage embryos to study motor neuron disease (MND). Therapeutic cloning for research has been legal in the UK since 2001 but only a
small number of licences have been granted. The Wilmut team was the first
to apply for a therapeutic cloning licence in the UK. The intention of the
technique is not to grow healthy replacement tissue, but the deliberate cloning of embryos that have MND from patients who have the condition. Cells

from these embryos can be used to study how the disease progresses in detail and can be used to try out new drugs to see if they stop the disease from progressing.

Professor Wilmut has stressed that his team has no intention of producing cloned babies, and said the embryos will be destroyed after experimentation. The aim was to generate stem cells purely for research purposes.

## Stem cell research

### Outlining the issues

Every week there are new claims being made about the use of embryonic stem cells and adult stem cells. President George W. Bush and John Kerry fought a US presidential election in 2000 with high-profile campaigns about embryonic stem cell research, and the scientific facts have often been lost in the media debate. The death of the *Superman* actor Christopher Reeves in 2004 also focused attention on stem cell research and the urgent needs of those with spinal cord injury. Scientists believe that stem cells will one day provide effective low-cost treatment for diabetes, some forms of blindness, heart attack, stroke, spinal cord damage and many other health problems. Animal stem cell studies and some clinical trials using stem cells have provided some encouraging results.

Stem cell technology is developing so fast that many stem cell scientists are unaware of important progress by others in their own or closely related fields. Much work is often unpublished, or waiting to be published. Ethical questions arise over the production of embryonic stem cells, which entail the destruction of early stage human embryos.

### Embryonic stem cells

Stem cells are relatively primitive cells that have the ability to divide rapidly to produce more specialized cells. Stem cells in the embryo are capable of huge variation in the kinds of tissues they make, and reproduce rapidly. However, embryonic stem cells are hard to get hold of in humans, and scientists need a supply of human embryos, which requires either breaking the law in some countries or applying for complex licences in others. Embryonic stem cells are also hard to control, and hard to grow in a reliable way. They have 'minds' of their own, and embryonic stem cells are often unstable, producing unexpected results as they divide, or even cancerous growths. Human embryonic stem cells usually cause an immune reaction when transplanted into other people, which means cells used in treatment may be rapidly destroyed unless they are protected, perhaps by giving medication to suppress the immune system, a process that itself carries risks.

This is one reason for intense interest in human cloning technology, therapeutic cloning, which involves combining an adult human cell with a human egg from which the nucleus has been removed. The result is a human embryo which is dividing rapidly to try to become an identical twin of the cloned adult. The resulting stem cells can be used to generate new tissue that is genetically identical to the person cloned. In practice this is a very expensive approach fraught with technical challenges as well as ethical questions and legal challenges.

An alternative is to try to create a vast tissue bank of tens of thousands of embryonic cell lines, by extracting stem cells from so many different human embryos that whoever needs treatment can be closely matched with the tissue type of an existing cell line. But even if this is achieved, problems of control and cancer remain. And again there are many ethical considerations with any science that uses human embryos, each of which is an early developing but complete potential human being, which is why so many countries have banned this work.

### Adult stem cells

Until recently it was thought that cells in the embryo were multipotent – able to give rise to every tissue – but by birth this capacity was permanently lost. That is the reason why almost all research effort focused on embryonic stem cells until the early years of the twenty-first century. However, in 2003 Professor Jonathan Slack at Bath University demonstrated that adult human liver cells can be transformed relatively easily into insulin-producing cells such as those found in the pancreas. Other researchers have used bone marrow cells to repair brain and spinal cord injuries in mice and rats, and some are now doing the same to repair heart muscle in humans.

This should not come as a surprise as almost all cells in our bodies contain our entire genome or book of life: enough information to make an entire copy, which is the basis of cloning technology. So in theory just about every cell can make any tissue. However, the reality is that in most cells almost every gene is turned off – but it now appears that this is not as permanent as first thought. It now seems possible to create cells with a wide range of plasticity, all from adult tissue. The important part of the process is to get the right gene activators into the nucleus.

### Impact of embryonic and adult stem cells on the future of medicine

Let's take an example of how this technology can be used. Suppose you have a heart attack. A cardiothoracic surgeon talks to you about using your own stem cells in an experimental treatment. You agree. A sample of bone marrow is taken from your hips, and processed using standard equipment found in most oncology centres for treating leukaemia. The result is a concentrated number of special bone marrow cells, which are then injected back into your own body – either into a vein in your arm, or perhaps direct into the heart itself.

The surgeon is returning your own unaltered stem cells back to you, to whom these cells legally belong. This is not a new molecule requiring years of animal and clinical tests. Your own adult stem cells are available right now. No factory is involved, nor any pharmaceutical company sales team. What is more, there are no ethical questions (unlike embryonic stem cells), no risk of tissue rejection, and no risk of cancer. Between 2006 and 2009 several cases of such treatment were reported in Australia, the United States and the UK. We understand why research funds are moving to adult stem cell technology and away from embryonic stem cell programmes.

In April 2009 it was reported that British scientists had developed the world's first stem cell therapy to cure the most common cause of blindness.[11] Surgeons predict it will become a routine, one-hour procedure that will be generally available by 2015. The treatment involves replacing a layer of degenerated cells with new ones created from embryonic stem cells. It was pioneered by scientists and surgeons from the Institute of Ophthalmology at University College London and Moorfields eye hospital. The treatment will tackle age-related macular degeneration (AMD), the most common cause of blindness. It affects more than 500,000 Britons and the number is forecast to increase significantly as people live longer.

However, at the Harvard Medical School progress has been made in treating AMD with adult stem cells. Trials have shown partially restored sight in animals with retinal damage. Clinical trials are expected by 2012, using adult stem cells. By 2015, it is hoped that people will be able to be treated routinely with their own stem cells.

## Human genome

### *Outlining the issues*

Francis Collins begins his discussion with the account of a family with a defective gene that led to breast cancer.[12] A dangerous mutation in a gene (now known as BRCA1) on chromosome 17 was found to be present in 35 members of one family. Its identification meant that carriers could be checked through regular mammograms. In the future he believes that it will be possible for all of us to discover if we have any dangerous mutations in our genes and seek remedial action. Nevertheless, the way such knowledge, coming from the mapping of the human genome, is applied will carry an ethical dimension. Personal readouts of our genetic make-up will allow the recognition of risk of illness and also which drugs are likely to be most effective for us. But they may also, if made more widely available, affect employment and life assurance cover.

Barbour agrees with Jeeves and Berry that we are not captive of our genes.

He states that we don't know what most of our DNA segments do and, more importantly, human identity and behaviour are the product of experience as well as genes. He also recognizes freedom as self-determinism at the level of the individual person, whereby motives, intentions and choices are not coerced.

He notes that the theological and ethical issues posed by genetic modification include: social justice – who profits or benefits; human dignity – vanity or manipulation; and unconditional love – an individual's worth is not in the absence of defect or disease. He concludes:

> we can acknowledge the power of genes in evolutionary history and in present human behaviour. But as we look to the future, our choices – including our decisions about genetic modification – are not determined by our genes; they are influenced by our values and ideals upheld in our religious tradition.[13]

### Saviour siblings: a case study[14]

In October 2000, great concern was expressed over the ethics of creating 'designer babies'. In the USA, the Nash family were involved in the 'engineering' of baby Adam as an exact tissue match for his sister Molly, to act as a donor to save her from the genetic disease *Fanconi anaemia*. In the UK, dozens of couples have already opted for pre-implantation genetic diagnosis (PGD) to avoid giving birth to children with serious genetic disorders such as cystic fibrosis and haemophilia. In June 2003, this issue was raised again. Michelle and Jayson Whitaker's baby, Jamie, was genetically selected while he was still an embryo to be a near perfect match for four-year-old Charlie. The couple went to an American clinic for test tube baby treatment because the selection procedure is not allowed in the UK.

New techniques offer great hopes but also raise ethical dilemmas, particularly in the emotive field of fertility. Is it right to bring a child into the world with a predetermined genetic make-up to offer a lifesaving cure for an existing child? And if so, is it also right for would-be parents to choose characteristics – blue eyes, for example – of an unborn child, the so-called 'designer baby'? If we just follow common sense, we might welcome the first but oppose the second. We might reason that in seeking to avoid the trap of 'designer babies' we may prevent giving humanitarian aid to those parents who wish to save their children.

On Radio 5 Live (23 June 2003), Professor Robert Winston expressed his view that the central issue is that such a child has effectively been brought into the world as a kind of commodity, and will know this. He posed the question of how this child will feel as it grows up, always knowing that it is the perfect organ donor for any problem that its sibling may have, and he expressed his fear that the child would be obliged to give other stem cells to a sibling later in life. He suggested that doctors should be focusing on find-ing realistic cures rather than a solution that he felt had little chance of working. To Professor Winston's questions we may add the following:

- For the scientist who has developed the technique the dilemma is summed up in the question, 'We can, but should we?'
- Doctors and clinicians find themselves wrestling with surprising non-scientific questions, such as, 'How do I feel when I can play God?'
- For parents, family and medical staff in a situation where one child is produced as a source of 'spare parts' for a sibling – even as just one reason for being born – the question arises, 'Is this child being treated as second class?'
- The wider scientific question concerns the human gene pool. If we move into the area of designer babies, where only the perfect are born, are we limiting the possibility of the unique, the genius, the 'abnormal'? Will we risk denying society of the inventive, the artistic, the creative and the eccentric?
- From a theological point of view, we will want to stress that we are not captives of our genes. We have freedom of will, and we are all open to the transformation of the Holy Spirit.
- From a sociological perspective, the question is, 'Are we in danger of moving into eugenics?' Is this a return to the kind of medical experiment conducted by the Nazi party in Germany in 1930s and 1940s?

Figure 5.1 may help to focus our reflection.

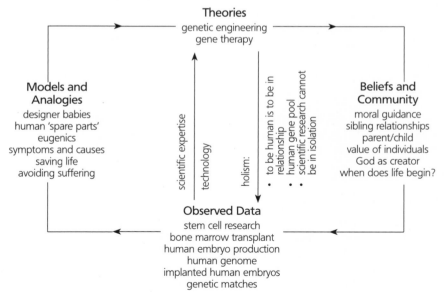

**Figure 5.1**[15]

We start with the observed data:

- Medical science is able to treat certain life-threatening disorders through bone marrow transplants and stem cell implants.
- Medical science has perfected the production of embryos in the laboratory.
- Medical science is able to identify and isolate individual genes in human embryos.
- It is possible for embryos of a specific genetic make-up to be implanted in a mother's womb.
- It is possible to produce a child who has the exact genetic match to be the perfect donor for a sibling with a life-threatening disorder.

If we follow the vertical upward arrow on the diagram, that is, of scientific materialism – asserting 'we have the technology' – we find ourselves in the position of being able to provide a potential cure for certain genetic diseases. This is the theory, at least. But we note the misgivings of Robert Winston, and his concern over possible success rates for the procedure.

We see the relevance of considering the left-hand pathway on the diagram, where the observed data passes through the sharing of models and analogies, which evoke understanding and response. This is the area of imagination and leaps of sympathy. We will want to consider the following:

- Designer babies may be an ultimate end point of this process.
- One child might be reduced to being produced as 'spare parts' for another, and so a mere 'commodity'.
- There is an analogy with the 1930s experiments in eugenics.
- There is a trap in treating symptoms rather than seeking the cause and so a possible cure.
- But, positively, there is the possibility of saving life and avoiding suffering.

Beyond this, it will be useful to explore the right-hand side of the diagram and consider the influence of beliefs in both scientific and religious communities. Some of the issues we may identify as:

- The help sought by doctors in ethical and moral guidance for the techniques that they are researching and perfecting.
- Inherited values about the relationship of siblings to each other, and of children to parents, which might be changed where it is known that one child has been produced for a particular reason.
- Belief about the value of each human life to God.
- Understandings of God as the author and creator of life.
- Differing convictions about when human life begins: fertilization, implantation, 'quickening', or viable existence outside the womb?

Finally, we can consider the vertical downward arrow in the diagram, testing a theory or a practice through understanding persons and the world as a whole. First, what makes a human being human is relationships – with each other, with the whole created world, and with God. One must ask whether these relationships are in danger of being destroyed by genetic manipulation. There is, second, the state of the natural gene pool of which each individual is a part. When we restrict human reproduction, will we prevent novelty and diversity, which can result in genius? Theologically, too, we may be restricting God's grace in creation. Third, scientific research on human beings cannot act in isolation, as environmental science is helping us to understand the holistic nature of the whole of creation.

## Genetically modified crops

### Outlining the issues

Genetic modification is simple in its basic concept. Desirable genes are snipped out of one organism and transferred to another with the aim of improving some characteristic of the latter. In 2007 some 99 per cent of all transgenic crops worldwide were either herbicide-resistant crops or *Bt* crops: '*Bt* plants have been transformed to produce a natural insecticide from the bacterium, *Bacillus thuringiensis*, in their tissues. This makes the plants toxic and unpalatable to a whole range of insects.'[16]

A second generation of crops has been genetically engineered to produce more vitamins or essential minerals. The best known example is 'Golden Rice' developed as a source of vitamin A in the developing world. A third generation of GM crops is being developed to produce medicines such as vaccines. There is also interest in producing crops that will be able to deal with extreme conditions such as cold, heat, drought or salinity. However, plants that survive in such conditions tend to be slow growing with low yields, and Hodson notes that the problem with salt tolerance is that, unlike herbicide resistance, it is controlled by many genes and is very complex.

### The positive and negative aspects of GM technology

Steve Jones observes that one of the successes was the new crop triticale, a hybrid between wheat and rye, which can grow in dry places and is of benefit to agriculture in places such as the American Great Plains, where there is low rainfall. Modern molecular biology allows genes, once alien to each other, to be moved into interaction in one organism.[17]

There are aspects of such genetic engineering that are wrong. In the 1930s, new hybrids of corn were produced, the seed of which was controlled by the companies that purchased the crop. There was a further control as 'no longer could the producer use his own seed for the following year because a hybrid plant produces new and unfavourable mixtures amongst its off-spring'. More recently, the new 'terminator technology' has gone a step further in preventing engineered plants from setting seed and forcing farmers to buy new seed for every harvest.[18]

The 12,000-year-old practice in which farm families save their best seed from one year's harvest for the next season's planting may be coming to an end since the year 2000. Some biotechnology companies in the United States are patenting seeds. The patented technology enables a seed company to genetically alter seed so that the plants that grow from it are sterile; farmers cannot use their seeds. The patent is broad, applying to plants and seeds of all species including both transgenic (genetically engineered) and conventionally bred seeds.

Up to 1.4 billion resource-poor farmers in the developing world depend on farm-saved seed and seeds exchanged with neighbours as their primary seed source. A technology that restricts farmer expertise in selecting seed and developing locally adapted strains is a threat to food security and agricultural biodiversity, especially for the poor. If the so-called 'terminator technology' is widely licensed, it could mean that the commercial seed industry will enter entirely new sectors of the seed market – especially in self-pollinating seeds such as wheat, rice, cotton, soya beans, oats and sorghum.

With the patent announcement, the world's two most critical food crops – rice and wheat, staple crops for three-quarters of the world's poor – potentially enter the realm of private monopoly. Monsanto, the world's third-largest seed corporation and second-largest agrochemical corporation, has acquired this new technology which provides a genetic mechanism to prevent farmers from germinating a second generation of seed. In this way seed companies will gain the biological control over seeds. Monsanto had agreed not to release the controversial genetically modified plants commercially, and the UN had imposed a 'de facto' ban on the technology. But the victories gained by environmental and agricultural activists may be short lived, as pressure is placed on the United Nations Convention on Biological Diversity (UNCBD) to allow companies to control such technology.[19]

Jones states that 'thirty million hectares of land were planted with GM crops in 1998; and a million Chinese farmers used engineered cotton. So alarmed is the public (and so over-priced the seeds) that in the West at least, the acreage has been reduced since then.' But such concerns should not let us lose sight of the positives:

Some of the technology aims to increase the range of places in which particular crops can live, with genes that make them tolerant to salty soil, or higher temperature, or shortage of water, or allow growth for a larger portion of the year.[20]

Some genes fight the organism's biological enemies, producing natural pesticides. It is possible to transfer such genes from one species into another, to cut down the use of chemical sprays. A pesticide much used by organic farmers is taken from a bacterium, *Bacillus thuringiensis*, which is lethal to many insects. The toxin genes have now been introduced into cotton, reducing the chemicals used on the fields.

A related trick inserts a gene that makes the plant resistant to artificial weedkillers. 'Round-Up' is much used by soya bean farmers. 'Round-Up Ready' plants (which represent about three-quarters of all genetically modified crops) have a gene that breaks down the chemical, so that the field can be sprayed to kill the weeds but leave the harvest untouched.[21]

People in many developing countries have little meat in their diets. A vegetarian diet tends to be short of certain amino acids. Hence the enthusiasm for Golden Rice which has a new gene within it for vitamin A, whose deficiency causes half a million children in the developing world to become blind each year.

Many other such genetic modifications are being trialled, but they cost a great deal of money, which results in patents being taken out by the companies that develop them. The West has also taken native materials from the Third World and patented them for itself, for example vincristine and vinblastine, developed in the 1960s as a treatment for leukaemia, came from the Madagascan periwinkle.[22]

## Some observed dangers of GM technology

One fear is that herbicide-resistant genes might get from crop plants to their weedy relatives. This could be a problem for oilseed rape and sugar beet in Britain, and sunflowers in the United States, which have plenty of local relatives with which they could hybridize. There is a risk of playing with the unknown in much of this technology. Yet, as Watson points out, in the 1960s pest control was mainly through chemical insecticides, which were poisoning the ground and the people. In the twenty-first century genetic engineering has produced crop plants with built-in pest resistance. To Watson it seems ironic that the green protestors, who were against poisoning the land with chemicals, are also the most vociferous against genetic modification.[23]

The real promise for farming comes through inserting genes from one species into another, but public alarm was raised through the 'Frankenstein Food' label, voiced by people who claimed with no evidence that such foods were harmful. The word 'engineering' didn't help the perception of the public, who are suspicious of technical fixes by science. For example, one project used genes from Brazil nuts put into soya beans to provide a certain amino acid. As this is in short supply in the developing world it might have saved thousands of children. Instead, the project was abandoned as a small number of people are allergic to nuts. The risks were low and the benefits high, but the project was still abandoned.

Watson discusses the effects of GM crops on the ecological environment, which were perceived to be harmful by some. He cites the case in 1999 of the Monarch butterfly caterpillars, which were being killed by the pollen from *Bt* corn. He notes that it is true that the *Bt* gene is intentionally lethal to insects, but the test case context was far more extreme than a natural situation, and also no comparison was made with the indiscriminate damage that alternative chemical insecticides would produce. He observes that at least the *Bt* toxin only affected those insects seeking to eat the corn.[24] Another worry concerned 'super-weeds' where herbicide resistance migrated into the weed population by interspecies hybridization. Watson believes this to be unlikely as the hybrids would tend to be weaker species. While we should be cautious we must accept that where GM crops are nutritionally and environmentally safe they should be used. For example, the Chinese attitude is entirely pragmatic: with 23 per cent of the world's population but only 7 per cent of its arable land, China needs the increased yields and added nutritional value of GM crops if it is to feed its population. And with global warming leading to increasingly large areas of the earth's surface subject to drought, there will be an ever-increasing emphasis on food security, as we will discuss in Chapter 6.

## Theological discussion

### Outlining the issues

A variety of ethical issues arise, for example should tests for BRCA1, discussed earlier, be carried out on children, for whom no appropriate treatment is possible? It has been agreed that an age of over 18 years would be appropriate in this case. Then there is also the question of whether or not third parties should be aware of the genetic information. This would clearly have a significant impact in the area of life assurance and, in the United States, for health insurance. There is also the question of whether or not employers or prospective employers should have access to such information as it may have a detrimental effect on employment potential.

Collins rightly observes that many bioethical issues are complicated. Across the world people come from vastly different cultural backgrounds and religious traditions. In a secular and pluralistic society, is it realistic that any group could agree on the right course of action in difficult circumstances? Collins quotes the work of T. L. Beauchamp and J. F. Childress,[25] who recognize four almost universal ethical principles:

1 Respect for autonomy – a rational human being should have the freedom to choose.

2 Justice – the requirement for fair, moral and impartial treatment of all persons.
3 Beneficence – the mandate to treat others in their best interest.
4 Nonmaleficence – first do no harm (Hippocratic oath).[26]

Such principles are also to be found in the sacred texts of various religious faiths, but conflicts often arise over the ways in which these principles are balanced. Society often has to reach a consensus, which by its very nature may not have universal agreement.

## Therapeutic cloning and embryo research

Much of the argument goes along the lines of the traditional pro-life, pro-choice debate. The Roman Catholic Church has said that 'every possible act of cloning humans is intrinsically evil' and can never be justified. Other faith communities are more divided in their views, and it is here that the ethical dilemma is located. When a human sperm and egg come together there is the potential for human life, and taking cells from the embryo leads to the destruction of that embryo and thus of that potential human life. This leads to some significant questions, the central one being: when does human life begin?

This debate, which has been ongoing for centuries, is not helped by our greater knowledge of the development of the human embryo. Collins maintains:

from a biologist's perspective, the steps that follow the union of sperm and egg occur in a highly predictable order, leading to increasing complexity, and with no sharp boundaries between phases. There is therefore no convenient biological dividing line between a human being and an embryonic form that might be called 'not quite there yet'.[27]

He notes the arguments about development of a nervous system, but concludes by noting that the division of the embryo to form identical twins takes place at the 'two-cell stage', resulting in two distinct embryos with identical DNA sequences. Thus it becomes difficult not to accept that the spiritual nature of a person is defined at conception.

However, Jeeves and Berry make a significant point when they note that the survival of a foetus to birth is not the norm (only 31 per cent survive, and many naturally aborted foetuses are found to be recognizably abnormal in their genetic complement). They then courageously argue that we can only speak of God being involved with us from conception as the retrospective view of a rational being (Jer. 1.5). They maintain that a young foetus is biologically alive, but there can be no firm certainty that it is spiritually alive, although lack of certainty must mean protection of all foetuses.[28]

So can we ever justify deriving stem cells from human embryos? It is widely accepted that infertile couples might use IVF, where eggs are fertilized in a Petri dish, observed for three to six days to assess development, after which a small number (usually one or two) are implanted in the mother. The remaining embryos are frozen, but will inevitably be later discarded. Collins observes that many of those who object to embryonic research in stem cell treatments accept the production of embryos by IVF for parents desperate to have a child.[29]

We can list the main objections to any form of embryo research as:

- people shouldn't play God
- cloning violates human dignity and makes people into products that can be replaced
- cloning makes people in human image, not God's
- cloning involves destroying embryos
- cloning amounts to unethical experimentation on people
- clones will be considered inferior to 'real people'
- cloning will change family relationships
- cloning will change human relationships and the nature of society
- it's one step short of a Brave New World.

However, the problem of using human stem cells in therapeutic treatments may be overcome by the same technique that produced Dolly the sheep, namely somatic cell nuclear transfer (SCNT). This involves no sperm-and-egg fusion. The DNA is derived from something like a skin cell, which everyone would agree has no moral value, as we shed millions every day. 'Similarly,' notes Collins, 'the enucleated egg cell, having lost all of its own DNA, has *no* potential of ever becoming a living organism, and therefore also does not seem deserving of moral status.' Taking us even further away from a moral problem, Collins predicts that in the near future we will be able to take a skin cell and place it in a cocktail of signalling molecules which will allow stem cells to develop.[30] Collins believes that SCNT of skin cell and enucleated egg is not part of God's plan to create a human being and is therefore not morally objectionable, whereas embryonic stem cell research may be seen as morally wrong. To oppose all research in this area including SCNT would mean that an ethical mandate to alleviate suffering is trumped by other perceived moral obligations. So are we playing God? Clearly the concern would be lessened if we could count on human beings to play God as God does, with infinite love and benevolence. Our track record is not so good. Difficult decisions occur when a conflict arises between the mandate to heal and the moral obligation to do no harm. But, says Collins, 'we have no alternative but to face those dilemmas head-on, attempt to understand all of the nuances, include the perspectives of all the stakeholders, and try to reach a consensus'.[31]

## Genetically modified crops

In like manner, we can ask whether or not GM technology is wrong because it means 'playing God' in moving genes from one plant to another? We could argue that this has always been done in plant breeding of closely related species. But the difference today is that we are moving genes from organisms that are not closely related.

It is unlikely that GM crops are a health risk, as some GM crops have been grown for over ten years in the United States with no problems for food. It is true that there are some environmental risks in the destruction of non-target organisms, but there is very little evidence of this happening. GM genes have escaped into related weeds or crops. This has happened with herbicide-resistant genes from oilseed rape escaping into related weeds, with the resulting concern over 'super-weeds'. This raises the possibility of target organisms becoming herbicide resistant so that stronger and stronger herbicides are used on herbicide-resistant crops.

Perhaps the greater concern is over global corporations taking a stranglehold on worldwide food production. In the 1990s, large multinationals began to buy up seed companies so that now GM crop technology is controlled by a few companies interested in profit rather than in feeding the world. But fears over such control have receded with the consumer rejection of GM foods. In the UK the Government held a public consultation on GM crops and food in 2003. The results showed widespread opposition, mostly over political issues as to who was taking the decisions and their intentions, especially those of government and multinationals. So while GM crops are being grown in increasing amounts in more and more countries, there remain concerns over safeguarding the interests of economically weaker nations and the biodiversity of the planet, while also allowing scientific progress to be made.[32]

Heap et al. note the importance of food security in this debate. The World Food Summits held in Rome in 1996 and 2002, called by the Food and Agriculture Organization, renewed a global commitment to the fight against hunger. In 2008, 850 million people were chronically hungry and up to 2 billion lacked food security intermittently. The causes included drought in Africa and Australasia, flooding in SE Asia, consumer demand in China and India, and the conversion of land for the growing of biofuels. Consumption of food is now increasing faster than population growth as more people adopt a lifestyle and diet once limited to the rich nations.[33]

Heap et al. maintain:

In terms of food security, current agricultural practices in many countries are unsustainable. The amount of cultivated land supporting food production was 0.44 hectares (ha) per capita (person) in 1961; today it is about 0.26 ha; by 2050 it will be in the vicinity of 0.15 ha per capita.

Modern agricultural techniques have damaged land productivity by enabling erosion, causing waterlogging and compaction of soil, and producing overgrazing, salination and pollution.[34]

And all the time the population is increasing.

Heap et al. question whether or not the future lies in new technologies that bring about positive effects for food security through reduced pesticide use and better carbon balances. The International Assessment of Agricultural Knowledge, Science and Technology for Development (IAASTD) report in 2008 had reservations particularly about the genetic modification of plants as a way forward in helping to feed Africa's poor: 'However, genetic modification can increase the range of options for the improvement of crop yields, disease resistance, storage properties of products, and the protection of farmers from exposure to large amounts of pesticides and herbicides.' An IAASTD report in 2009 stated that the way in which the world grows its food would have to change radically to better serve the poor and hungry if the world was to cope with a growing population and climate change while avoiding social breakdown and environmental collapse.[35]

## Somewhere to stand

A World Council of Churches (WCC) report in 1989 dealt with genetic engineering, reproductive technologies, patents, environmental effects and military applications, together with the impact on the developing world, in which strict regulations and bans were recommended. In contrast, Celia Deane-Drummond notes the positive response of the Anglican Church's Board for Social Responsibility towards both the Human Genome Project and GM crops in 1998, which she believes was in part an oversimplification of the issues.[36]

The Roman Catholic Church has given a great deal of attention to human genetic engineering and is against all forms of germ-line therapy and IVF-style treatments, but is more positive in its attitude to genetic manipulation of animals and plants.

The Church of Scotland's Technology Project took a firm anti position on cloning, believing that as science does not know any boundaries there should be a global ban. A spokesperson for Comment on Reproductive Ethics (CORE) said, 'Human cloning remains dangerous, undesirable and unnecessary.' This view has been echoed on numerous occasions by spokespersons for the ProLife Alliance, who state that the creation of cloned human embryos destined for experimentation and subsequent destruction is particularly abhorrent.

Overall, Deane-Drummond concludes that the Church is ambivalent towards all forms of genetic engineering, although the WCC were more aware of the global issues and the effects on the poorer nations of the world.

In a helpful discussion of 'wisdom' in the Bible, Deane-Drummond notes that belief in God as creator is taken as read and that faith and reason are indistinguishable from each other. Thus observation of the natural world is not about seeking evidence for God's existence, but rather emphasizes the celebration of God's creativity. She finds Wisdom's place in creation is outlined in Proverbs 8.22–31.[37]

She notes the place of humility in regard to creation and the sense in which human beings do not have an autonomous mandate to rule, and draws attention to God's declarations to Job in Job 38—41. Wisdom is portrayed in three ways: human, social and cosmic. Human wisdom is aware of its limitations; social wisdom deals with societies, nations and issues of justice. She notes that 'a broad approach that takes into account *both* the *goodness* of creation and the particular human social and environmental *consequences* of human action is in continuity with the biblical Wisdom tradition'. In addition she notes that 'the cosmic scope of Wisdom refers to the emphasis on the human and natural environment considered as a whole rather than in any dualistic sense'.[38] In the New Testament, the Prologue to the Gospel of John (John 1.1–18) and Colossians 1.15–20 express the relationship between Christ and creation.

In looking at genetic engineering Deane-Drummond asks:

How far should we be allowed to become co-creators with God in engineering crops and animals for our own benefit? How far should we take transgenic experimentation, especially that relating to human beings? Should there be a moratorium on all human cloning? How do we distinguish one research project from another in terms of its likely risk and benefit for humanity and the earth?

She notes:

unlike the creation spiritualities that have flourished in much contemporary theology, a theology of Wisdom serves to unite themes of creation and redemption by identifying Christ the Redeemer and the divine Logos with Sophia, the Wisdom of God involved in the creation of the world.[39]

The concepts of stewardship and redemption will be addressed in Chapter 6, where we consider human beings as both co-creators in the image of God and co-redeemers in union with Christ. Key to the argument that Deane-Drummond rehearses is the wisdom to recognize the presence of God in the new technologies. There are key questions to which we need answers. Are we achieving God's purposes? Do we know what God intends? Are we excluding God from our discussions?[40]

Deane-Drummond quotes the positive views of Ted Peters[41] who, she says, 'believes that our fear of genetic engineering is based on a false sense of genetic determinism. He argues that giving humans more freedom does not take away God's freedom', and that 'if genetic engineering can be used for good, then it becomes a sin not to use it'. But this raises ethical issues of what is good in the economy, politics and production of food.

Deane-Drummond concludes:

> it would be naïve to suggest that we can go back to an agrarian culture in ignorance of modern technology. However, I suggest that too great a focus on human achievement and human freedom obscures other theological principles, such as the mandate to give proper respect to the animal world.[42]

She believes that cloning animals does not affirm the goodness of the creature, but merely places them as instruments of human manipulation. The only activity that she considers in a positive light is cloning to prevent extinction, but even this simply covers over human responsibility for extinction of species. She does not recognize technological manipulation as an activity of stewardship.

The support or rejection by theologians of genetic technologies depends on their presumptions about anthropology. An optimistic anthropology sees humans as co-creators and agents of evolution. A pessimistic anthropology sees human sinfulness usurping God's place as creator. Deane-Drummond helpfully concludes:

> Wisdom, on the one hand, affirms the special dignity of the human race, but the idea of Wisdom as agent of creation of the world shows that it is also cosmic in scope. Wisdom would, however, encourage caution on the part of humans rather than impulsive action.[43]

The major tensions that face the world are:

- the desire for long healthy lives versus the integrity and humanity of the foetus
- the desire for research in biotechnology versus a just share of that technology for the poorest people of the world
- the need to feed the world versus the need to protect biodiversity.

Deane-Drummond rightly remarks that 'Wisdom is helpful in that it does not deny reason or deny science its place, but it puts it in a wider context of social justice, prudence and temperance', which are much needed in what is often a heated debate.[44] I believe that the exploration of human beings as both co-creators and co-redeemers, in the next chapter, will help to address these issues.

## Key texts

Francis Collins, 2007, *The Language of God: A Scientist Presents Evidence for Belief*, London: Simon & Schuster/Pocket Books.
Celia E. Deane-Drummond, 2001, *Biology and Theology Today: Exploring the Boundaries*, London: SCM Press.
Steve Jones, 2000, *The Language of the Genes: Biology, History and the Evolutionary Future*, London: Flamingo/HarperCollins.

## Further reading

Ian Barbour, 2002, *Nature, Human Nature, and God*, London: SPCK.
Martin J. Hodson and Margot R. Hodson, 2008, *Cherishing the Earth: How to Care for God's Creation*, Oxford: Monarch.
Malcolm Jeeves and R. J. Berry, 1998, *Science, Life and Christian Belief: A Survey and Assessment*, Leicester: InterVarsity Press/Apollos.
James Watson, 2003, *DNA: The Secret of Life*, London: Arrow Books.
Robert S. White (ed.), 2009, *Creation in Crisis: Christian Perspectives on Sustainability*, London: SPCK.

## Notes

1 Steve Jones, 2000, *The Language of the Genes: Biology, History and the Evolutionary Future*, London: Flamingo/HarperCollins, p. 66.

2 Jones, *The Language of the Genes*, p. 269.

3 Celia E. Deane-Drummond, 2001, *Biology and Theology Today: Exploring the Boundaries*, London: SCM Press, pp. 58–9.

4 Deane-Drummond, *Biology and Theology*, p. 71.

5 Francis Collins, 2007, *The Language of God: A Scientist Presents Evidence for Belief*, London: Simon & Schuster/Pocket Books, pp. 1–2.

6 Deane-Drummond, *Biology and Theology*, p. 55.

7 Deane-Drummond, *Biology and Theology*, p. 63.

8 Collins, *The Language of God*, p. 245.

9 Collins, *The Language of God*, pp. 246–7.

10 Collins, *The Language of God*, pp. 246–8.

11 http://www.timesonline.co.uk/tol/news/uk/health/article6122757.ece

12 Collins, *The Language of God*, pp. 236–41.

13 Ian Barbour, 2002, *Nature, Human Nature, and God*, London: SPCK, p. 70; see also Malcolm Jeeves and R. J. Berry, 1998, *Science, Life and Christian Belief: A Survey and Assessment*, Leicester: InterVarsity Press/Apollos, pp. 160–1.

14 Based on case study in John Weaver, 2006, *Outside-In: Theological Reflections on Life*, Oxford: Regent's Park College/Macon: Smyth & Helwys, pp. 149–55.

15 This is based on a diagram that integrates scientific methods, and that I offered in John Weaver, 1994, *In the Beginning God*, Oxford: Regent's Park College/Macon:

Smyth & Helwys, p. 16. This in turn was a modification of two models of the structures of scientific and religious thinking proposed by Ian G. Barbour, 1990, *Religion in an Age of Science*, London: SCM Press, pp. 32–6.

16  Martin J. Hodson and Margot R. Hodson, 2008, *Cherishing the Earth: How to Care for God's Creation*, Oxford: Monarch, p. 183.

17  Jones, *The Language of the Genes*, p. 270.

18  Jones, *The Language of the Genes*, p. 275.

19  Hope Shand and Pat Mooney, 'Terminator Seeds Threaten an End to Farming', *Earth Island Journal*, Fall 1998. Google 'terminator seeds' and follow link to http://www.thirdworldtraveler.com/Transnational_corps/TerminatorSeeds_Monsanto.htm

20  Jones, *The Language of the Genes*, p. 275.

21  Jones, *The Language of the Genes*, p. 276.

22  Jones, *The Language of the Genes*, p. 278.

23  James Watson, 2003, *DNA: The Secret of Life*, London: Arrow Books, pp. 135–6.

24  Watson, *DNA*, p. 160.

25  T. L. Beauchamp and J. F. Childress, 1994, *Principles of Biomedical Ethics*, New York: Oxford University Press.

26  Collins, *The Language of God*, pp. 243–4.

27  Collins, *The Language of God*, p. 250.

28  Jeeves and Berry, *Science, Life*, pp. 161–6.

29  Collins, *The Language of God*, pp. 251–2.

30  Collins, *The Language of God*, p. 253.

31  Collins, *The Language of God*, p. 272.

32  Hodson and Hodson, *Cherishing the Earth*, pp. 184–8.

33  Brian Heap, Flavio Comim and George Wilkes, 'International Governance and Root Causes of Unsustainability', in Robert S. White (ed.), 2009, *Creation in Crisis: Christian Perspectives on Sustainability*, London: SPCK, p. 73.

34  Heap, Comim and Wilkes, 'International Governance', p. 74.

35  Heap, Comim and Wilkes, 'International Governance', pp. 75–6.

36  Deane-Drummond, *Biology and Theology*, pp. 77–80.

37  Deane-Drummond, *Biology and Theology*, p. 88.

38  Deane-Drummond, *Biology and Theology*, p. 91.

39  Deane-Drummond, *Biology and Theology*, pp. 94–5.

40  Deane-Drummond, *Biology and Theology*, pp. 98–9.

41  Ted Peters, 1997, *Playing God: Genetic Determinism and Human Freedom*, London: Routledge, pp. 157–78.

42  Deane-Drummond, *Biology and Theology*, p. 111.

43  Deane-Drummond, *Biology and Theology*, p. 117.

44  Deane-Drummond, *Biology and Theology*, p. 143.

# 6

## The Environment and Care for Creation[1]

### Introduction

#### The issues

In the West we live in a throwaway society. So much of what we use for our daily lives, be it milk cartons or cars, electrical goods or felt-tip pens, is disposable, designed to wear out or be put in the rubbish bin. This extends sadly even to our natural resources: coal, oil, natural gas, forests and fish. Worse still, our society has a similar attitude to people and their needs or skills. So much of the way in which we live is controlled by short-term economics. In suggesting that we need to move away from a materialistic lifestyle, Gregg Easterbrook is right to point out that 'men and women cannot reform nature unless they first reform themselves'. He goes on to challenge:

> If the human soul is to be saved, the materialist age must be overcome: Green thinking, now focused on opposition to industry and development, will eventually focus on the more subtle and telling question of the harm materialism does to humanity, not nature.[2]

Lynn White was right to point out that 'what we do about ecology depends on our ideas of the man–nature relationship'.[3] For White the problem in large part was down to one Christian view of creation, which suggested that every part of creation was there to serve the purposes of human beings. He did however concede other Christian views, in that St Francis can be seen as the patron saint of ecologists.

Richard Foltz suggests that the greatest obstacle to meaningful discussion of the environmental crisis is the lack of a strong public conviction that it actually exists. Western consumerism and advertising are not channels of the truth about the situation. For example, advertising encourages North Americans to buy SUVs (four-wheel-drive sport utility vehicles) to enjoy the world of nature, which through their use we are helping to destroy.[4] There is often a failure on the part of the media to link the effects of global climate change with the causes. For example, hurricanes in the Caribbean and mud slides in the Philippines are presented as effects of global warming, but no mention is made of their connection with our global use of fossil fuels through increased road and air travel.

In 1989 there was a great outcry about the destruction of the Amazon rainforest. Viewed from the UK, it made good sense to call for a moratorium – the destruction of the rainforest was causing environmental change, not only in Brazil but also to the global climate, which meant that we in the West would also suffer through the effects of global warming. However, in Brazil it looked a little different – I remember the newspaper headline in one of the leading newspapers, which I read in Brasilia: 'Has anyone asked the British and other Europeans where their forests have gone?' There is a self-centred paternalism or, worse, hypocrisy, when rich Western nations want to prevent the poorer developing nations from doing what they have already done, in using natural resources to further their economic development. The just answer would be for the rich nations of the world to share their resources with the poorer nations to enable them to develop without further destruction of the environment.

The human-centred model of control and exploitation of creation has been challenged by modern ecology, which recognizes that we are intimately involved with creation. We are challenged by the recognition that the human impact on the world may be triggering irreversible and catastrophic changes in the environment.[5] Sarah Tillett notes that the decline in biodiversity affects the capacity of the earth to sustain human needs and reduces the resources of plant and animal species. 'The environment is an issue of justice, and when the environment is damaged it is often the poor who suffer most.'[6] These are important questions for the Christian Church to address – conservation, pollution, ecology, stewardship and justice – as we seek for a theology for earthkeeping.

### Theological basis

We start with a model of God, who is both transcendent creator and immanent sustainer of the whole universe. This is the God who has created and is creating (Gen. 1.1—2.3), and whose character is 'creativity', as Kaufman interprets the description of God in John 1.1–5.[7] This is the God who declared that the created world was good (Gen. 1.31), and beyond the initial human rebellion and destruction, made a covenant with the renewed world after the Noah Flood (Gen. 9.9–11).

Human beings are created *imago Dei*, in the image of God, sharing God's creativity and God's care of the planet (Gen. 2.15). But the Fall (Gen. 3) and the Tower of Babel (Gen. 11) demonstrate that there are always the problems of human selfishness and wanting to play God that get in the way; they still do. The result is that God had to redeem human beings and the planet. God has done this in Christ (Col. 1.20); and redeemed human beings, *in Christ*, are to be channels of God's redeeming love for all creation (Rom. 8.19–21). This is summarized in Figure 6.1:

| imago Dei | in Christ |
|---|---|
| co-creators | co-redeemers |
| channels of creativity and care | channels of redemption and reconciliation |
| marked by stewardship | marked by restoration and transformation |
| Genesis 1 and 2 | Romans 8.18–22 |

Figure 6.1

## An approach to exploring the issues

In exploring the nature of global environmental issues we begin with a review of the current situation before moving on to an analysis of the facts, a consideration of biblical and theological perspectives, and concluding with some thoughts and proposals about Christian responses. But, as we seek to communicate the vital importance of this situation, we need to hear a caveat from David R. Loy, who laments that a few hours in the classroom is useless against 'the proselytizing influences that assail them [his students] outside the class – the attractive (often hypnotic) advertising messages on television and radio and in magazines and buses that constantly urge them to "buy *me* if you want to be happy"'.[8] An opinion poll of 3000 young people (aged 15–17 years) worldwide, conducted by the BBC in October 2006,[9] bears this out, for while 51 per cent understood climate change, only 17 per cent had done anything to change their lifestyle, and a mere 5 per cent rated it as the most important issue facing the world.

But it is not only young people who fail to understand the urgency of the crisis. Under the headline 'Psychological barriers hobble climate action', Reuters reported the conclusions of a 2009 meeting of a task force of the American Psychological Association, which noted that while most Americans, 75–80 per cent in a Pew Research Centre poll, said climate change is an important issue, it still ranked last in a list of 20 compelling issues such as the economy or terrorism. Despite warnings from scientists that humans need to make changes now if they want to avoid the worst effects of climate change, most people did not feel a sense of urgency. They believe that numerous psychological barriers are to blame, including: uncertainty over climate change, mistrust of the messages about risk from scientists or government officials, denial that climate change is occurring or that it is related to human activity, and undervaluing the risk.[10]

I share my version of the pastoral cycle as a framework for exploration in Figure 6.2.

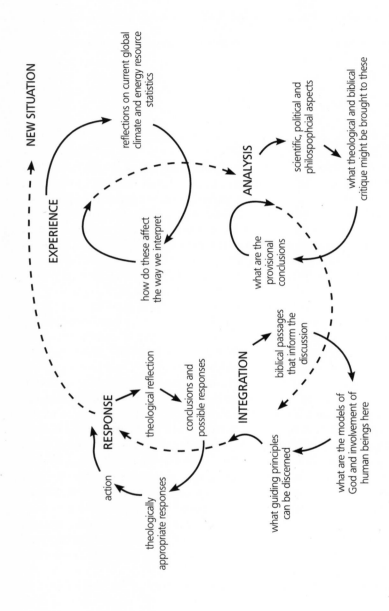

Figure 6.2

## The current situation

### *World population*

Delicate checks and balances in the natural world have kept the population of most species at a constant level – the one exception is human beings, where 300,000 years BP there were 1 million; 10,000 BP, 5 million; 2000 BP (1 CE), 250 million; 1800 CE, 1000 million; 1900 CE, 2000 million; 1980 CE, 4000 million, 2000 CE, 6000 million, 2009 CE, 6800 million, and projected to grow to 9000 million by 2040 CE. Better nutrition, control of disease through immunization and improved sanitation have led to lower infant mortality and a resulting rise of population in a geometric progression. In 1980, one-fifth of the population were destitute, but Marvin Soroos[11] asks how the environment will survive if we achieve the promise of global prosperity for the Four-Fifths world. 'The bottom line', says Sean McDonagh, 'is that in most Third World countries the populations will be controlled. There is a limit to the carrying capacity of particular bioregions, and famine, starvation and death can take over.'[12] The question for the world is whether we will control population in a caring humane way or do nothing and watch the more violent control of population unfold before our eyes.

### *Atmosphere*

Global warming is natural and is vital for the survival of life on planet Earth. Without an atmosphere the Earth's surface temperature would be $-18°C$, whereas with our atmospheric mantle it is $+15°C$. Instability in the greenhouse effect is the result of human activity such as the burning of fossil fuels creating build-up of $CO_2$ gas in the atmosphere. $CO_2$ concentration has risen from 290,000 parts per billion by volume (ppbv) in 1900 to 360,000 ppbv in 1990, with a further 30 per cent increase expected by 2050. Over the same period methane has risen from 900 to 1700 ppbv, and nitrous oxide, which causes acid rain and smog, has risen from 285 to 310 ppbv. There has been a depletion of the ozone layer mainly caused by chlorofluorocarbons (CFCs) used in fridges and air-conditioners, which react with ozone to produce chlorine monoxide. In addition, $SO_2$, produced in large quantities by power stations and other industry in which coal and oil is burnt, combines with water in the atmosphere to become the main source of acid rain. The responsibility for these increases in harmful emissions is largely that of Western nations. For example, 83.7 per cent of the increase of atmospheric $CO_2$ in the period 1800–1988 was the result of industrial and technological activity in the USA, Europe, Japan and Australia.[13]

The rising levels of $CO_2$ and other greenhouse gases since 1800 have led to global warming. Slight increases in global temperatures have led to shrinking glaciers and ice-caps, and sea-level rises. Between 1890 and 1990 the Earth's surface temperature has risen by 0.3–0.6°C, with the 1990s being the hottest decade since the fourteenth century, and 2006 the hottest year for over 300 years. The Intergovernmental Panel on Climate Change noted in a report in 2007 that the warmest 12 years since records began were: 1990, 1995, 1997, 1998, 1999, 2000, 2001, 2002, 2003, 2004, 2005 and 2006. 'Whatever the causes, the prospect for the twenty-first century is dramatic, as scientists predict an increase in global warming [mean earth surface temperature] of between 1 and 5°C, or even higher.'[14]

The results are being and will be seen in sea-level changes, river flow and groundwater levels. Melting of the ice sheets will give a sea-level rise of 20–50 cm by 2050. In low-lying countries such a rise would be devastating, for example, some 10 million people in Bangladesh live below the one metre contour. A rise in sea temperature will lead to more frequent and more violent hurricanes and tropical storms, and as rainfall patterns change desertification is likely in many subtropical regions.[15]

Former Vice President of the USA Al Gore's film *An Inconvenient Truth*[16] ultimately presents a persuasive argument that we can no longer afford to view global warming as a political issue, but rather need to see it as the biggest moral challenge facing our global civilization. Nevertheless, there are other views which suggest that global warming should not be linked to $CO_2$ emissions.[17] But we might question the motive of these alternative voices. Nick Davies notes that in spectacular fashion the oil companies PR machine rolled into action in the face of Kyoto. 'Within months of the UN producing its first report endorsing the idea of man-made climate change in 1989, Exxon and other big corporations started setting up pseudo groups, the first and biggest was the Global Climate Coalition.'[18] The PR groups focused, as the tobacco companies had done some 40 years earlier, on doubt and lack of certainty in the scientific reports. Al Gore notes that over a period of 14 years of 928 scientific articles that were examined none doubted the fact that global warming was related to carbon emissions, while 53 per cent of 636 news articles cast doubt on the view that human beings played a role in global warming. The media gave the impression that the scientific community was divided, whereas in actual fact it was not and is not.[19]

## Biosphere

Previous generations have depended on the dilution of toxins and human waste pumped into the rivers and oceans. Now these are reaching dangerous levels, especially in lakes and partially enclosed seas: for example the Black Sea, where the Danube is dumping 60,000 tons of phosphorus and 340,000 tons of inorganic nitrogen into its waters every year, is now 90 per cent sterile. The pulp mills of Sweden and Finland dump 400,000 tons of chloride compounds into the Baltic Sea every year.[20] Destructive pressures on the oceans do not only come in the form of pollution, there are also fishing methods, which are causing dramatic decreases in fish stocks. For example, fish catches have increased from 3 million metric tons per year in 1900 to 90 million metric tons in 1989. A United Nations report in 2009 stated that nearly 80 per cent of the world's marine fish stocks were either fully to heavily exploited, over exploited, depleted or slowly recovering.[21]

On the land we are moving in excess of 42 billion tons of rock and soil per annum, mostly through various forms of mining.[22] Draining wetlands and removing trees is leading to changes in water table levels and the stability of mountain sides, as evidenced in the landslide on the island of Leyte in the Philippines on 17 February 2006, when 200 cm of rain fell in ten days.

We are doing serious damage to the rainforests of the world, where as many as 80 per cent of animal and plant species are to be found. The rainforests also stabilize the world's climate as 60 per cent of the rainfall is held and transpired back to the atmosphere. The forests also lock up billions of tons of carbon. We are losing one of the earth's greatest biological resources. Rainforests once covered 14 per cent of the earth's land surface; now they cover a mere 6 per cent, and experts estimate that the last remaining rainforests could be consumed in less than 40 years. One and one-half acres of rainforest are lost every second with tragic consequences for both developing and industrial countries. It is estimated that nearly half of the world's species of plants, animals and microorganisms will be destroyed or severely threatened over the next quarter century due to rainforest deforestation.

In the study of ecosystems scientists are emphasizing the delicate balance of nature. Ecology is not a chain of cause and effect but a web of interconnectedness. 'Once we learn that the lives of snails and sparrows are linked to our own in a dozen ways, the meaning of ecology gradually expands to include every other aspect of human life and well-being.'[23]

## Energy resources and the nuclear power option

We are using ever-increasing amounts of fossil fuels through industrial development, power generation, the ubiquitous motor car, and cheap global air travel. The technological/silicon chip revolution is also greedy for energy.

Under the Kyoto Protocol there are internationally agreed targets for carbon emissions covering the period up to 2012, targets that were revised at the United Nations Conference on Climate Change at Copenhagen in December 2009. Any strategy to reduce $CO_2$ emissions will require large changes in the energy system and for society: efficiency, electricity produced without carbon emissions, and the reduction of fossil fuels in powering vehicles. Therefore there is a need for new options in renewable sources of energy and for new technologies.

The United Kingdom might be taken as representative of the use of power in Western nations. The report compiled by Sir Nicholas Stern for the UK Government, published in November 2006, dealt with the economics of climate change.[24] According to the report, a rise of 4°C would put between 7 million and 300 million more people at risk of coastal flooding each year, there would be a 30–50 per cent reduction in water availability in southern Africa and the Mediterranean, agricultural yields would decline by 15–35 per cent in Africa, and 20–50 per cent of animal and plant species would face extinction. At the Copenhagen climate change conference in February 2009 Stern stated that a 6°C rise in global surface temperature was likely, and that governments should prepare for a 4°C rise. Scientists announced at the conference that a 4°C rise would lead to the loss of 85 per cent of the Amazon rainforest.

In the UK, 95 per cent of $CO_2$ emissions result directly from fuel combustion, and the energy system will be key to any action to reduce such emissions. The main sources of these emissions in the UK are power stations (28 per cent), industry and business (32 per cent), transport (25 per cent), and domestic heating (17 per cent). It is hoped that renewable electricity from wind, wave, tidal, biomass and solar sources may have a major role in power generation by 2050. Some like hydro have been established for many years. The UK is very well endowed with renewable resources, yet uses less renewable energy than most EU countries.

A role for nuclear power in the UK cannot yet be defined, since concerns about radioactive waste and low probability but high consequence hazards may limit or preclude its use. Costs of production could fall substantially if new modular designs are effective. However, nuclear power generation is unlikely to compete with fossil fuels on cost alone, but might have a significant role as sources of oil and natural gas run low and if low carbon emissions are required.

In 2009, nuclear power produced 25 per cent of UK electricity, but in the period up to 2025 all but one of the power stations will have reached their expected lifespan. Radical new technologies could produce a new generation of smaller, modular and inherently safer reactors, which might be significantly more competitive than those available today. But environmental risks remain a concern. The recommendation of the Energy Futures Task Group in 2001 was that there should be a full re-examination of the nuclear power issue. If a nuclear power component was required over the long term, then the UK should maintain and develop its expertise, to keep the option of designing, building, running and eventually decommissioning new plant, along with addressing issues of waste disposal and public confidence in safety.[25]

However, the *Energy Review*, in the autumn of 2006, took a more pragmatic view, seeing nuclear power as a solution to both the reduction of carbon emissions and for securing an energy supply as North Sea natural gas resources diminished. In 2009, 11 sites for new nuclear power stations were announced – at Dungeness in Kent, Sizewell in Suffolk, Hartlepool in Cleveland, Heysham in Lancashire, Wylfa Peninsula in Anglesey, Oldbury in Gloucestershire, Hinkley Point in Somerset, Bradwell in Essex, and Sellafield, Braystones and Kirksanton in Cumbria.

At this juncture it is important to point out that renewable sources of energy are not entirely problem-free. For example, wind farms are pollution-free but are not completely environmentally friendly. The harnessing of wave power requires the development of barrages, which will have a considerable effect on the environment and the habitat of various species, especially shellfish, birds, algae and plankton life. The construction of barrages on coastal margins can lead to the shifting of sand and gravel banks, coastal erosion, and the permanent flooding of tidal flats, with the resulting loss of habitats. However, it could also be argued that some new environments and habitats are created.

The two sources of natural energy that do not result in substantial environmental 'pollution' are solar and volcanic, but these are restricted to particular parts of the world. Iceland leads the way in tapping into volcanic heat sources, although there are places even in the UK where this is possible. Solar energy is most reliable where weather conditions produce continuous sunshine all year round. However, even in northern European countries there is a growing use of solar power.

## Economics

In the developing world we should be aware that there can be a lethal spiral as a result of poverty: population growth → ecological crisis → social conflict. Shortages of water, forests and especially fertile land, coupled with rapidly expanding populations are the cause of great hardship. People pressure on land → destruction of environment → famine and migration → ethnic and religious tension → and as society breaks down population growth takes place – it is a lethal spiral.

## A case study

### Context

The Intergovernmental Panel on Climate Change (IPCC)[26] meeting in Nairobi, February 2007, reported that warming of the climate system is unequivocal. They report that at continental, regional and ocean basin scales, numerous long-term changes in climate have been observed. An IPCC report released in April 2007 provided a summary of the effects of global climate change, which included the recognition of rising Arctic sea temperatures and reduction in the size and thickness of the ice sheets; rising sea levels forcing the displacement of millions of people from coastal areas; and falling agricultural yields, particularly in the developing world, forcing many people to migrate into other areas of the world (if current climate trends continue). It is expected that there will be widespread changes in precipitation patterns and amounts, with extreme weather events including droughts, flash flooding, heat waves, and the intensifying and increased frequency of tropical storms, hurricanes and cyclones.

The meeting of the IPCC in Bangkok in May 2007 presented a dire picture with a predicted 6°C increase in global surface temperature by 2100 (if current trends of increasing greenhouse gas emissions continue), but noting that a 2°C rise would see water shortages for 2 billion people by 2050; the extinction of 20–30 per cent of species; and between 140 million and 1 billion people suffering from extreme food shortages as a result of droughts and floods. There will also be increases in malaria, dengue fever and diarrhoea. But the assessment of the facts at the end of 2008 suggested that the situation was worse than had hitherto been suspected. Jonathon Porritt writing in the *Guardian* newspaper stated:

A lot has been going on out there in the natural world since 2005. There is three years' worth of published peer-reviewed evidence, a lot of it from the frontline of the eco-systems most directly affected by climate change. The vast majority of those studies tell us incontrovertibly that the impact of climate change is more severe and materializing much more rapidly than anything reflected in the fourth assessment report (IPCC 2007). It's much worse out there, and it's getting even worse even faster.[27]

This presented a challenge for the national delegations who met in Poznań.[28] For, even if they had wanted to draw on that new evidence to justify a more progressive policy position, they would have to break previously agreed protocols. Porritt continued:

This is particularly surreal in terms of all the evidence coming in from the Arctic, which has seen a 4°C rise in average temperatures over the past few decades. Arctic sea ice reached an all-time low in 2007, the Greenland ice cap is undergoing accelerated melting, and there are growing worries about the melting of the Siberian permafrost, which has the potential to release huge volumes of extra greenhouse gases into the atmosphere.

It's this kind of evidence that has persuaded Nick Stern that his own 2006 report[29] on the economics of climate change got it wrong ('We underestimated the damage associated with temperature increases, and we underestimated the probability of temperature increases'), and has led Jim Hansen, the US's pre-eminent climatologist, to warn that the current target for stabilization of $CO_2$ at 450 parts per million (ppm) in the atmosphere is woefully inadequate. There is a growing school of thought that 350ppm represents a far more realistic safe upper limit – which is more than a little problematic, given that the concentration is already 384ppm.

The IPCC meeting in Budapest, 9–10 April 2008, discussed, among other issues, the impact of global warming on the hydrological cycle.[30] Observational records and climate projections provide abundant evidence that freshwater resources are vulnerable and have the potential to be strongly impacted by climate change, with wide-ranging consequences on human societies and ecosystems. Observed warming over several decades has been linked to changes in the large-scale hydrological cycle such as: increasing atmospheric water vapour content; changing precipitation patterns, intensity and extremes; reduced snow cover and widespread melting of ice; and changes in soil moisture and runoff.

The snow-covered area of the world has decreased by 10 per cent since the 1960s. Some 97 per cent of the world's water is salt water in the oceans. Of the available fresh water, 77 per cent is held in the glaciers and ice caps, and therefore the melting of the glaciers is a threat to the earth's freshwater reserves.

### The impacts of climate change on water resources in Nepal

At the beginning of 2008 I had the opportunity to visit Nepal and observe a project tackling environmental issues. One of the staff of PEEDA (People, Energy, Environment and Development Association) had undertaken analysis of long-term hydrological, meteorological and glaciological data from the Nepal Himalayas. The picture in Nepal is one snapshot of a world in crisis.

Global warming has led to changes in precipitation patterns with longer periods of drought and periods of more intense precipitation, which give rise to increased frequency of floods and landslides. Warmer temperatures increase the water-holding capacity of the air, which results in increased evapotranspiration, reduction in soil moisture, decrease in ground water reserves, and a reduction in river flow.[31] In addition, increased temperatures reduce the growing season, and therefore productivity, and reduced river flow affects hydropower generation and the aquatic ecosystem. Reduced water resources may also lead to conflict between users.

Water supply is crucial to livelihoods, power generation and the economy of Nepal: 63 per cent of agricultural land depends on rainfall; 93 per cent of Nepal's workforce is in agriculture; and 91 per cent of Nepal's electricity comes from hydropower plants. Agriculture throughout tropical Asia is vulnerable to the frequent floods, severe droughts, cyclones and storm surges that result from climate change. Floods remove soil, and water scarcity reduces production. Increased temperatures are reducing the growing season for rice, and therefore productivity. For example, a 1°C rise in global surface temperature would see a 6 per cent decline in rice production in the southern India state of Kerala, and each 0.5°C rise would reduce wheat production in north-west India by 10 per cent. A 4°C rise would see a reduction of 60 per cent in the wheat yield of Nepal.[32]

As temperatures rise the volume of glaciers will reduce, with a decreased storage of fresh water, which is vital for domestic use, irrigation, and hydropower for people in the mountains and the cities. This is demonstrated by the presence of dry water courses and daily power cuts (in the winter months). It is estimated that 86 per cent of the glaciers and 58 per cent of the ice reserves will be gone by 2050 with no further increase in global surface temperature, and a warming of 0.06°C per year will see no glaciers left in the Nepal Himalayas by 2070.[33]

The overall temperature range is widening with maximum temperatures increasing and minimum temperatures decreasing. There is also a change in overall precipitation with increasing high-intensity rainy days in the monsoon and decreasing low-rain days in the winter. The result is winter droughts and summer floods. This, with the reduction in the glacier ice reserve, means increasing water demands along with decreasing water supply. The resulting reduction in levels of agricultural production is leading to increases in poverty, famine and starvation.[34] This may lead to a large percentage of the 29 million population of Nepal becoming environmental refugees.

### Addressing the situation

Faced with these predictions we need to consider how such changes of crisis proportion should be addressed. Chaulagain recommends that there be both adaptation to water shortages and adaptation to extreme events. There should be a holistic and integrated development approach for water resources development, the management of water resources, the promotion of indigenous and sustainable water efficiency technologies, rainwater harvesting, and regional and international co-operation. Alongside these there should be a recognition of risk areas, the relocation and settlement of populations in areas of high risk, flood prevention measures, early warning systems, and the implementation of water resources projects including hydropower.[35]

The impact of global climate change is greatest in the developing world. Observations show that the fraction of the planet's land surface in drought has risen sharply since the start of the 1980s. It is estimated that at the beginning of the twenty-first century 2–3 per cent of the world's land area was under drought; by 2050 this could rise to 12 per cent, with all the associated poverty and extreme food shortages. Researchers at the Hadley Centre[36] project that by 2100, if significant mitigation does not take place, around half of the planet's land surface will be liable to drought. Some less developed countries are likely to be severely affected, with Africa, South America and parts of South East Asia likely to see worsening conditions.

## Analysis – Changing Views and Emphases

### In the field of science

Modern cosmology has discovered a finely tuned universe, in which human beings appear to have been woven into the fabric since its beginning. An expanding universe with a beginning and an end, exhibiting design and apparent purpose, supports the concept of a creator God. A universe that includes natural disasters, suffering and human-generated pollution accords with being the creation of a self-limiting God who gives choice to creation. Here is our understanding of God who accompanies and suffers with creation. A universe that moves from Big Bang to Big Crunch or Heat Death, and in which there is a delicate balance both to produce and destroy life, forces us to consider carefully both our own future and our care of the planet. Here is our understanding of the place of humanity in creation, as both *imago Dei* and stewards of creation.

Ecology has brought to light the unforeseen effects that human interference with natural processes often has; and this is why we can no longer plead inadvertence as the excuse for technological excess. As we noted in the Introduction, Ruth Conway observes that 'we are part of a world frantically pushing at technological frontiers . . . we are also part of a world whose technologies are threatening the very basis of life'.[37] She believes that our human-centred culture is in the grip of a technological power that is out of control.[38] We need to recognize that technological fixes are not the answer, and that even while shoring up Western lifestyles may have deleterious effects on people in the developing world.

### In philosophy

We have seen the emergence of ecological mysticism, with an appeal, by some, to Eastern religions or to Gaia, a personification of nature. There is a desire for a closer, more wholesome relationship with nature.

Marvin Soroos notes that McKibben, in *The End of Nature*, maintains that we can no longer see nature as separate from human society.[39] In the 1980s, scientists coined the phrase 'global change' to demonstrate their conclusion that the human impact on the environment is neither temporary nor benign, as we are altering the basic functioning of the earth's systems. The view that democratic governments will preserve the environment is misplaced as the 'environmental footprint' of the richer nations is greater than the poor in both consumption and pollution.

Robin Attfield recognizes that the effects of global warming raise new ethical issues of equity between peoples and generations.[40] He identifies the tension between the human needs of present peoples and the land needs of future generations. Neglect of these issues now may lead to dire consequences for future generations. But he then goes on to discuss the equity issues that exist today between countries. He says, 'the control of anthropogenic carbon emissions requires an international solution; but the issue of which countries should limit or reduce their emissions is not an easy one'.[41] For example, developing countries need to increase their emissions to develop, and so developed countries are morally obliged to limit their emissions.

But sadly, as David R. Loy notes, we are dominated by the philosophy of the market. He states that 'in contrast to the cyclic time of pre-modern societies, with their seasonal rituals of atonement, our economic time is linear and future-directed, since it reaches for an atonement that can no longer be achieved'[42] – an ever-expanding surplus of economic expansion. He concludes that 'the market is not just an economic system but a religion – yet not a very good one, for it can thrive only by promising a secular salvation that it never quite supplies'.[43]

### In politics

The 1989 G7 Economic Summit set up a conference on environmental ethics, which advocated the practice of responsible stewardship. A significant watershed was reached with the United Nations Conference on Environment and Development in Rio de Janeiro in 1992, which was attended by over 25,000 people, resulting in the Framework Convention on climate change, which was signed by 160 countries. The first principle of the 27 in the Rio Declaration reads: 'Human beings are at the centre of concerns for sustainable development. They are entitled to a healthy productive life in harmony with nature.' However, notes Houghton, 'despite such statements of principle from a body such as the United Nations, many of the attitudes which we commonly have to the Earth are neither balanced, harmonious nor sustainable'.[44]

The Rio summit has been followed by two further Earth Summits in Kyoto (1997), and Johannesburg (2002). The Kyoto summit produced the Kyoto Protocol, which is an international agreement setting targets for industrialized countries to cut their greenhouse gas emissions. The protocol established in 1997 was based on the principles set out in the framework agreement signed in 1992 at Rio de Janeiro. Targets were set, for example EU countries are committed to cutting their 1990 levels of emissions by 8 per cent by 2012. Although 55 countries signed up to this agreement, three of the largest polluters – Australia, Russia and USA – did not, although Russia subsequently signed in November 2004. George W. Bush said that the Kyoto Protocol would gravely damage the US economy. However, on coming into office, Barack Obama pledged the United States' commitment to a revised treaty at Copenhagen in 2009. Depressingly, the UN has predicted that global emissions will rise by 10 per cent by 2010, and that only four EU countries are on track to meet their targets.[45]

Robin Attfield notes that the Kyoto Protocol agreed quotas based on emissions in 1990, which, although favouring the biggest polluters, was the only feasible basis for agreement. This is not ethically defensible but was based on pragmatism in the face of the intransigence of Northern countries.[46] Equality and redistribution in terms of the use of resources, reduction in pollution, development of technology and quality of life will be difficult for the developed countries to accept. Any answer will need to include the replacement of carbon-based energy sources by renewable sources of energy.

The third Earth Summit was held in Johannesburg (August 2002), entitled 'World Summit on Sustainable Development'. Little of substance was achieved. Issues of energy, along with water and sanitation, global warming, natural resources and biodiversity, trade, and human rights were all addressed. However, the only issue on which some modest progress was made was the commitment to halve the number of people lacking clean drinking water and basic sanitation by 2015. Andrew Hewett of Oxfam International said, 'Most of them lacked the guts and will to achieve a brave and far-reaching agreement that might have effectively tackled the problems of poverty and the decaying environment.'[47]

Although the UN Climate Change Conference at Copenhagen in December 2009 tackled the worsening global climate crisis, a change of heart is still needed. The important issue of justice has to be addressed, where we recognize that God's world is created for the benefit of all human beings.

## In theology

Lynn White suggested that Christians thought themselves superior to nature, contemptuous of it, and willing to use it for every whim. As Berry notes, the religious answer that White himself recognized is to be seen as redemption and repentance.[48] However, Sam Berry reminds us that we should also note that stewardship has been a major theme of Christian relationship to nature throughout the Church's history. For example, the Fathers of the Church, Justin Martyr, Theophilus of Antioch and Tatian, developed a theology of creation. Celtic spirituality was much aware of the presence of the divine in the world of nature. Among others we might note Francis of Assisi (1182–1226) and Hildegard of Bingen (1098–1178), who saw in the world the presence of God. Doctrinally, these people considered that God's image was to be seen in the trustworthiness and responsibility of human beings; and emphasized that the Hebrews saw kingship as servanthood.[49]

The World Council of Churches' study paper *Accelerated Climate Change: Sign of Peril, Test of Faith*[50] outlined the following points for action by the Church:

• evaluate the scientific evidence

- present a theological and ethical framework based on God's love, sovereignty and justice
- present responses and targets
- to reduce the threat of global warning will require a new vision of what constitutes a 'good life'
- defining the Church's role in global justice and creation spirituality.

Looking towards this new millennium, Sean McDonagh stated that there is no New Testament support for 'an exploitative, throwaway consumer society which in the last four decades has destroyed the natural world in so many parts of the globe and produced mountains of non-biodegradable and toxic waste which will plague the people and creatures of planet earth for centuries'.[51] He rightly maintains that the problem stems from our emphasis on wealth, profit, possessions and power, and that our materialistic approach to defying death through consumerism is in reality destroying life.

## Biblical foundations

### The basis

We can explore Genesis 1—11 as a basis for our concern for the environment. Genesis chapters 1 and 2 present a picture of the beginnings of the universe and this world. We find the theological declaration that God created it, God ordered it, God loved it and God was pleased with it. With such affirmation of God's purposes, we, who claim to worship God, should be concerned about creation.

But then tragedy strikes in the form of human beings with God-given free will. Human beings decided that they wanted to be like God and know all the answers. They became jealous and violent and the killing started. They believed that they had no need of God and God's wisdom as creator at all. This is recounted in Genesis 3—5. In our modern technological world we should be warned that we, who play God and think we know all the answers, should be concerned about the outcomes of our actions.

The story progresses through the account of the Noah Flood in Genesis 6—9. God was disappointed with creation, God regretted what he had done, and God destroyed all but Noah, his family and the animals God ordered him to preserve. When the Flood receded at God's command, God made a covenant with Noah and the whole of the created world. If God cares in this way, if God is concerned, and if God has declared this covenant of faithful love with creation, then we too should covenant with God in our care of the planet.

But sadly the story of human power play returns in Genesis 11, where human beings seek to scale the heights of God by building their Tower of Babel, only to become scattered and confused. We have built our 'tower' of industrial development, committing the sin of idolatry as we did so. We seek to become 'world-creators', claiming for ourselves that which belongs to God. The result has been a trail of violation, failure and destruction.

We recognize the counterpart of this tragic story at Pentecost, the birth of the Church as a restored and redeemed community, modelling to the world the possibility of a new humanity in Christ.

### The value that God places on all life

It is important to avoid compartmentalizing ecological reflection, separating human concerns from those of the whole of nature. We not only understand the loss of rainforests and their unique floras and faunas, we also recognize that tribal cultures are being destroyed. It is not only that finite resources are being consumed at an alarming pace, but also that people's lives are being exhausted, their needs and their dreams ignored. So Christians should have solidarity with the poor and should oppose poverty. Jesus expressed his mission as: 'I have come that they may have life, and have it to the full' (John 10.10).

Out of his community's experience of God expressed in the life and ministry of Jesus Christ, John proclaims that the creation of the universe is brought about by the Word of God (John 1.1–5). And John tells us that God sent his son to the world because he loved it (John 3.16). From this we can assume that the creator of this world loves the world and human beings so much as to give himself to the world, offering a restored and new creation, and eternal life through his son. In love God rescues and restores what might otherwise be condemned.

In Christ there is a new creation, but as ever in the New Testament, there is a now but not-yet aspect. There are the first fruits of the Spirit, but still creation groans as it waits for God's human creatures to reach their perfect humanity (Rom. 8.18–23). To believe in Christ in this world is to believe against reality – Christ is risen, but we live in a world of suffering, pain and destruction. It is hope, because now salvation for all creation is only seen in outline. But this cannot be a cheap hope, human beings must act in hope – the Spirit gives us the possibility to be what we are to become, the children of God. The same message is found in Colossians 1.15–20; note verses 19–20:

> For God was pleased to have all his fullness dwell in him, and through him to reconcile to himself all things, whether things on earth or things in heaven, by making peace through his blood, shed on the cross.

The whole of creation is brought back into relationship with God through the cross. This takes place as human beings find their restored relationship with the Creator, through the cross. God is deeply and passionately involved in the world; God is no absentee landlord, but indwelling, accompanying, incarnate, and present as Holy Spirit. There are important implications in this understanding for relationships both with the Creator and with creation.

It is in Christ that creation is redeemed. The universe is created and then blessed and sanctified, as celebrated in the seventh day, the Sabbath. 'The Sabbath reflects on faith in the creator-redeemer, who is Alpha and Omega, the beginning and the end. As he consummates his work in creation, so he will complete his purposes in redemption as the incarnate Lord.'[52] Jesus declared the Sabbath principle at the beginning of his ministry (Luke 4.18–19) and Christians are called to live as Sabbath-keepers (Rom. 8.18–21).

### Sharing and giving

We note that the Old Testament concept of *shalom* involves a creative relationship with God, with other human beings and with the whole of creation. There must be a oneness, a sharing in love with all, for us who celebrate the new covenant in bread and wine. In the words of the 1974 Lausanne Covenant:

> We affirm that God is both the Creator and the Judge and that we therefore should share his concern for justice and reconciliation throughout human society and for the liberation of people from every kind of oppression. We recognize that in living under the authority of scripture, we cannot be selective. [53]

The cancelling of debts owed by the developing world should find an important place in this discussion. McDonagh has identified that these debts have also led to severe environmental damage.[54] He noted that loans from the World Bank have financed ecologically destructive projects, the Bank ignoring the environmental considerations of dams and hydroelectric and irrigation projects. Debt repayment has increased the destruction of the tropical rainforests in Brazil and South East Asia, where, for example, in the Amazon region the forest has been burnt to provide land for beef production to supply the global fast-food market.[55]

### Stewardship

Stewardship implies caring management, not selfish exploitation; it involves a concern for the present and the future as well as self, and recognition that the world we manage has an interest in its own survival and well-being independent of its value to us. It has been noted that both Christian and secular agencies have latched on to the concept of stewardship in examining the way in which humans should relate to the rest of the natural world. 'But we can use the concept of stewardship as an easy retreat to a comfortable concept which avoids coming to terms with deeper theological issues of the environmental crisis.'[56] We can fall into the danger of God as the absentee landlord, who leaves human beings in charge. A theology that separates God from the natural world is less likely to respect it than one which sees God as indwelling creation.

Stewardship is not only a matter of how wealth is distributed, but also how it is acquired. Wealth is acquired from the finite resources of the planet, so stewardship must be concerned with issues of ecological and political exploitation, respecting the integrity of creation. The biblical word 'dominion' must no longer be misunderstood as domination. 'As awareness of the consequences of consuming non-renewable resources or of permanently affecting the ecological balance increases, so does our accountability, both to God and to our neighbour, of this and of future generations.'[57]

We are created as co-creators with a freedom to participate in God's purposes. Our purpose is linked to our capacity for responsibility. The idea of the natural world as a resource belongs to a human-constructed financial model – the idea that everything is there for the good of humanity. This leads us to consider justice. There is a danger that as long as we can justify something as benefiting humanity, it will be acceptable under our stewardship ethic. We justify the destruction of woodland, wilderness and wetlands for agriculture to feed humans, and the flooding of river valleys for hydroelectric power. Such a view is entirely anthropocentric.

## Justice

There are clear questions of justice when we consider pollution, exhaustion of natural resources and the inequality of the availability of creation's gifts. Gustavo Gutiérrez distinguishes three meanings of poverty:

- material poverty – the lack of economic goods which are necessary for life
- spiritual poverty
- a biblical understanding that recognizes that poverty contradicts the meaning of the Mosaic religion and the Christian faith, which is to give people dignity.[58]

There must be the elimination of exploitation and poverty that prevents the poor from being fully human. So Christians should have solidarity with the poor and should oppose poverty. A key text is the Jubilee manifesto of Luke 4.18–19.

Leonardo Boff believes that the present socio-economic system is oppressive. He says that 'experience shows that within the dependent liberal-capitalist system . . . there is no salvation for the poor, no respect for basic rights, and no satisfaction of basic needs'.[59] This is because capitalism works on the logic of the greatest profit in the shortest time. He maintains that liberal thinking that sees global biotechnology as the providential solution for the world is in error. He says that 'it is an agenda for guaranteeing survival (by providing food), but not for promoting life (by creating conditions for people to produce their food)'.[60] We might draw a comparison with Satan's temptation of Jesus to turn stones into bread (Matt. 4.2–4). Boff says that human beings are not simply hungry animals in need of food – satisfied through 'technological messianism' – they must be able to participate through creativity, to feed themselves. For Boff, science, technology and power are part of a programme of redemption, construction, consolidation and expansion of human life and freedom, which starts with those who have the least life and freedom.[61]

Development that pollutes and undermines life-support systems is a contradiction in terms. It is here that we will want to note the responsibility of richer nations in terms of justice. Mere economic growth is not an indication of development – injustice prevails where people's basic needs are left unmet. The uneven distribution, control and use of natural resources are serious justice issues: for example, the average USA citizen uses the natural resources used by 200–300 citizens of Asian countries. The rapid depletion of non-renewable natural resources raises the question of our responsibility to future generations. Poverty can frequently be a source of ecological destruction, but 'unless the poor have alternate sources of food and basic needs like fuel, they too will wantonly destroy whatever natural environment is around them'.[62] It is unjust to leave them with no alternative.

Peter Carruthers suggests that Sabbath and Jubilee give three principles for farming and food production: sharing – with the poor; caring – for the earth; and restraint – of power and wealth. But he warns that there are huge disparities in the world between the overfed and the hungry; there are imbalances in the world food system, there is unfair trading, and a growing industrialization of agriculture, which is destroying the environment. Instead of keeping the Sabbath we have a 'Sabbath-less society'.[63]

We need a theology for earthkeeping that is holistic and not dualistic (separating out human beings as above the rest of the world); that recognizes God's immanence as well as God's transcendence; that is relational, recognizing the trinitarian relatedness of the God of creation; and that recognizes sin as the main factor in environmental destruction. Sin alienates us from God, from our fellow human beings and from the natural world.

We can address this through our celebration of the Sabbath. The Sabbath breaks us free from the chains of ownership and consumerism. 'The Sabbath is an occasion of thanksgiving, a feast of contentment and enoughness . . . The fallow season constrains human activity and limits human exploitation of both the natural order and of the poor . . . Sabbath requires letting go.'[64]

### Anticipated eschatology[65]

Tom Wright argues that 'the whole point of New Testament Christianity is that the End came forward into the present in Jesus the Messiah.'[66] Worship is the Church's only possible response to Jesus, because Jesus is the only option for human reconciliation, both with God and within humanity. We might consider Tom Wright's view that

> Jesus' offer of forgiveness, then, was in itself a way of saying that the Kingdom was dawning in and through his work. Equally . . . his *demand* of mutual forgiveness among his followers is not to be seen merely as part of an abstract ethical agenda. It is part of what we might call the eschatological torah . . . Not to forgive one another would be a way of denying that the great, long awaited event was taking place; in other words, it would be to cut off the branch on which they were sitting.[67]

Anticipated eschatology rejects indifference to suffering and the repeated tendency to 'overlook present injustices culminating from other factors, such as colonialism, neo-colonialism and globalization, and to look forward to future heavenly bliss'.[68]

It rejects the world-view that believes that all nations and people have a place in the world that they should gratefully accept without practical hope for change in their present sufferings. Instead it offers to bring real hope for change and freedom. When the Church demonstrates the concept of anticipated eschatology it will seek to act as a vehicle of freedom and justice for those enslaved. In encouragement of anticipated eschatology, Wright states: 'You are following Jesus and shaping our world, in the power of the Spirit; and when the final consummation comes the work that you have done . . . will stand, will last.'[69]

Anticipated eschatology hopes that the gospel will influence lives by the activity of the Spirit of God; that it will transform the lifestyles of Christians and guide them to live sacrificially cross-shaped lives, which look to the needs of others. Christians live as those who know that the current reality of the world challenges the God-given responsibility to neighbours both local and global.

The Christian call is to behave as: *prophets* – helping people to see the world of creation as it is; as *priests* – 'living sacramentally, receiving all creation as a gift, transforming it and returning it to God';[70] and as *kings* – defending the rights of the poor and disadvantaged, accountable stewards before God.

## Theological reflection

### *Co-creators and co-redeemers*

Human beings are created *imago Dei*. They share God's creativity, which is demonstrated in human skills, research and technological development. But sin, injustice and the destruction of creation are the trade marks of human activity, our greed and selfishness demonstrated in the exhaustion of Earth's resources and a lack of desire to share God's good gifts with the whole world.

As we have said, stewardship needs to be understood in terms of God working through us, rather than of God as an absentee landlord. Stewardship can be expressed in terms of human beings created *imago Dei*, in the image of God; invited to be in Christ; and in Christ to become children of God. We recognize that Christians are involved in the *missio Dei* – God's mission in the world. God the creator, who is love, creates a world with freedom, lives with the pain of human rebellion, and seeks to redeem a broken world.

The natural world is not people's complete environment; God and God's grace also form the human environment. We cannot reduce environment to a biological chain of vital processes. 'An adequate theology of the environment therefore involves God, the human person and nature; thus problems concerning the environment cannot be resolved in purely socio-political terms.'[71] There is often a danger of the ecology label being used by people to promote their own materialistic ideologies, for example the nuclear lobby, or the development of some biofuels.

It is helpful to consider Moltmann's trinitarian view of creation, which is his basis for understanding the relationship of God with creation. Moltmann explains the character of the triune God in terms of *perichoresis* – 'mutually indwelling as a perichoretic community of Father, Son and Holy Spirit. Likewise, God's relationship with his creation is one of mutual indwelling.'[72] Moltmann sees evolution as creative but not as redemptive, and so we should not confuse evolution with redemption nor teleology with eschatology. We will therefore want to stress the transformative contribution of Christian discipleship.

We are helped in this understanding of Christian discipleship through Paul Fiddes' exploration of the Trinity and pastoral practice.[73] For Fiddes our participation in the life of God affects the way we do theology, we are not observers but are involved in the energy and patterns of the divine life. When we ask how we live and move and have our being in God, Fiddes' image of dance helps us to move away from rational doctrines to a participation in movement (*perichoresis*), which I would express as being in the Spirit. Such participation has freedom to respond and is the outworking of God, who in love allows us to be. However, God always seeks to encourage us in God's desire for our life. I agree with Fiddes that the whole world is a place to encounter God. It is in the universe that we see God's creativity continuously at work. We have a sacramental universe that displays God's grace, love and faithfulness, and which in this sense can be described as expressing the body of the trinitarian God,[74] as Christ expresses what it is to be truly human.

It can be argued that if God is love and created all things in love, then it is more helpful to think of creation carried out by the Word of God, who became incarnate in human form (John 1.1–14). God assumes human form in space and time. Our true humanity is to be located in Christ, and when we locate ourselves outside Christ we find ourselves in disharmony with God's purpose for the well-being of creation.[75]

In the Bible we recognize that the Creator is the Covenant God and Redeemer God, who became incarnate in Jesus Christ. In union with Christ, Christians are invited into fellowship and partnership in God's mission in and for the world. It is in this role that Christians may become co-creators and co-redeemers with God. It is not that human beings are able to create or to redeem, but in co-operation with God, the Holy Spirit works through human beings. The following is a useful summation of this argument:

> We should envisage sacraments drawing us deeper into the heart of the interweaving flow of relationships in God. The key is participation, so that God is always open to make room for the world, while remaining an event of relationship in God's own self. God has a body, in so far as finite bodies are in God, and so movements of love and justice in God are expressed through bodies.[76]

Bringing creation and redemption together, Michael Northcott maintains that a Christian environmental ethic requires as its source and guide the knowledge of God as creator and redeemer of all life, which is definitively revealed in the life, death and resurrection of Jesus Christ, the incarnate Word,[77] and stresses:

> The cosmic Christ is not only Lord of the lives and bodies of Christians but Lord of the whole created order, and the implications of the resurrection extend beyond the lives of Christians to reveal God's intention to restore the righteous peace, or *shalom*, of the whole of creation.

So we affirm that it is in the original purpose of material life, and creation's original relatedness to God that we find ourselves in the rest of the natural order. Without this affirmation our human response to the event of resurrection, even though enabled by the indwelling Spirit of Christ, would find no echo or correspondence with our life as embodied and reasoning humans, and this would leave us in the Gnostic position. It would leave us with a

Christian ethical project that was dangerously detached from the location of the Christian life in the time and space and bodies of this material world.[78]

Northcott notes that the prophets saw Israel's exile and the ecological degradation of the land as consequences of their failure to keep the covenant which God had made with them, and on which the care and fertility of the land depended (Isa. 5.8–10; 24.1–6). Here we see a connection between human injustice in terms of the equal sharing of creation's gifts, especially in the exclusion of the poor and through environmental degradation. God's character of righteousness and justice are also writ large in the material and moral framework of the creation which God has made, and with which God remains in continuing relationship. Here we see the ecological nature of God and God's created justice.[79]

Our duty of respect for the natural order arises, then, from the 'original recognition that the world is not ours but God's, and that in its design and order it displays not an independent order of being from human being, available for human remaking at will, but a shared realm of *created* being'.[80] Sabbath worship and Christian worship joins with the praise that all creation consciously or unconsciously offers to the Creator. Northcott maintains that we cannot limit the implications of Jesus' command to love our neighbour as ourselves to other human persons. We are called to love creation, to love nature, because we share with nature in the restoration which is promised in the resurrection of Jesus Christ.

### Celebrating the Eucharist as participation in the redemption of creation

Theology and worship give the prophetic words to proclaim. Obedience to God can be summed up in the words of the prophet Micah, who says in answer to the question, 'With what shall I come before the Lord?' 'He has shown all you people what is good. And what does the Lord require of you? To act justly and to love mercy and to walk humbly with your God' (Mic. 6.6–8).

Following this prophetic command Christians bring the life of the world into the worship of the Church. The celebration of the Lord's Supper brings the Sunday and Monday worlds together. It is thanksgiving to God for everything that God has accomplished in creation, redemption and sanctification, and for God's work of bringing the Kingdom to fulfilment in spite of human sin. As William Lazareth states: 'The very celebration of the Eucharist is an instance of the Church's participation in *God's mission* to the world. This participation takes everyday form in the proclamation of the Gospel, service of neighbour and faithful presence in the world.'[81]

The incarnation in history demonstrates God's clear identification with the created world of space and time. The celebration of the Lord's Supper with its backward look to the life, death and resurrection of Christ, and its forward look to the hope of the consummation of the world in God's eternal Kingdom, celebrated in the physical elements of bread and wine, embrace the whole of life and human existence. Lazareth rightly concludes:

> Solidarity in the Eucharistic communion of the body of Christ and *responsible care* of Christians for one another and the world find specific expression in the liturgies: in mutual forgiveness of sins; the sign of peace; intercession for all; the eating and drinking together; the taking of the elements to the sick and those in prison or the celebration of the Eucharist with them.[82]

Christians recognize that the Lord's Supper extends beyond the church congregation to the whole world. They understand God to be present in all human life and beyond this to God's work in sustaining the whole environment. They understand that God is immanent in the whole of creation, and that the incarnation declares God's solidarity with the whole of the created order. Christians recognize that redemption and restoration of the poor, weak and vulnerable includes the atmosphere, biosphere and ecosystems of the world we inhabit. This is the love and ministry of the servant Christ in which Christians share and in whose mission they are invited to participate.

### Repentance and restoration

Sallie McFague, in her essay 'An Ecological Christology',[83] urges the Church to answer the question 'How have you been committed to the reign of God?' She believes that the natural world might be envisaged as 'the new poor', believing that justice, rights, care and concern should be extended to the whole of creation. She challenges us to recognize that Jesus' ministry to God's oppressed creatures must include our deteriorating planet. For McFague, sacramental Christology is the embodiment of God in creation, as well as the hope of new creation.

Christians have a contribution to make. God created and entrusted the earth, and will redeem the whole of creation (Rom. 8.19–22). The challenge is to learn to think and act ecologically. There is a need to be reawakened to the gospel ethic, and recognize that human greed is at the root of the environmental crisis. Understanding and perceiving the situation and moving to a change of heart or mind is *metanoia* – repentance. There are steps to be taken in sustainable consumption, which involve ethical choices in purchases and in lifestyle. There is a need to recognize our ecological footprints on the earth – our impact on our local and global environment. Environmental audits can be taken of churches and communities, and eco-congregations established.

For Western Christians there is a need to develop a global perspective that recognizes the impact of their lifestyle choices, and their economic, trade and industrial decisions on the rest of humanity. In accepting their relationship with the developing world, Western Christians must actively seek to address the issues of justice and poverty, which are an integral part of global environmental concerns. We identify the links of the increased consumption of fossil fuels, global warming and climate change, with starvation and water shortages in the developing world. We also recognize the unfair distribution of resources and restrictive practices in international trade that are a factor in increasing environmental destruction in parts of the developing world.

## Responses

### *An urgent situation*

In environmental terms we recognize that the world has a window of as little as 20 years in which to think and act globally. The world may face a global eco-crisis in the next 50 years. Scientists have become surer about just what human activities are doing to the climate, but there are many uncertainties in our predictions, particularly with regard to the timing, magnitude and regional patterns of climate change, due to our incomplete understanding of, for example, sources and sinks of greenhouse gases, which affect predictions of future concentrations.

There is a need to take action to stabilize the situation. Some actions have already been taken which affect the emissions of greenhouse gases, for example the Kyoto (1997) and Montreal (1987) Protocols regarding emissions of $CO_2$ and CFCs. Other actions that can be taken are, a reduction of deforestation and an increase in afforestation, reductions in methane emissions, and an aggressive increase in energy-saving and conservation measures.

The path to follow is neither too difficult nor too costly, but requires a clear political resolve. There is a need to provide incentives for energy-saving; a need to develop renewable energy sources; a need to provide developing countries with the necessary technology; and investment should take note of long-term environmental requirements. The demand of consumers can have far-reaching effects. It is a matter of what we want and are prepared to pay in both costs and consequences. The future is therefore, to some extent, in our own hands.

### *The Earth Charter*[84]

A clear universal response can be summed up under the following principles, presented under the 'Earth Charter' in Richard Foltz's *Global Anthology*:

- respect Earth and life in all its diversity
- care for the community of life with understanding, compassion and love
- build democratic societies that are just, participatory, sustainable and peaceful
- secure Earth's bounty and beauty for present and future generations
- protect and restore the integrity of Earth's ecological systems – biodiversity and natural processes
- prevent harm as the best method of environmental protection – if in doubt – precaution
- adopt patterns of production, consumption and reproduction that safeguard Earth's regenerative capacities, human rights and community well-being
- advance the study of ecological sustainability
- eradicate poverty as an ethical, social and environmental imperative
- ensure that economic activities and institutions at all levels promote human development in an equitable and sustainable manner
- affirm gender equality and equity as prerequisites to sustainable development
- uphold the right of *all* to human dignity, health and spiritual well-being
- strengthen democratic institutions – accountable government
- integrate into formal education and lifelong learning the knowledge, values and skills needed for a sustainable way of life
- treat all living beings with respect and consideration
- promote a culture of tolerance, non-violence and peace.

## A Gospel ethic

Christians face the task of articulating the gospel with relevance, to speak prophetically and relevantly to the environmental and social issues of our day. Sadly often the Church misses the opportunity and others take on the task – this is particularly the case with the environment. The growth of the Green Movement is the clear example, where there has been little Christian involvement.

The Church should be at the forefront in campaigning for sustainable development, addressing social and economic injustice in the world. There needs to be a holistic response that looks to the interests of all who share God's world. Examples are seen through the advocacy and capacity-building activities of Christian Aid, CAFOD, and Tearfund in the developing world, and the conservation projects of A Rocha.

Sallie McFague asks if there can be an ecological answer to Jesus' question: 'Who do you say that I am?' (Mark 8.29).[85] She believes that eschatological Christologies that look to renewal and a resurrected creation address the despair of a deteriorating world, and that Jesus' ministry to the oppressed can be extended to nature, which she sees as the 'new poor'. She maintains that 'If the Redeemer is the Creator, then surely God cares also for the other 99 per cent of creation, not just the 1 per cent (actually, less than 1 per cent) that humans constitute.'[86] She says that 'our consumer culture defines the "dominant life" as one in which "natural resources" are sacrificed for human profit and pleasure and "human resources" are the employees who will work for the lowest wages'.[87] But God with us suggests the range and promise of divine concern. Sacramental Christology is the embodiment of God in creation, as well as the hope of new creation. Therefore justice, rights, care and concern should be extended to the natural world.

## Living with climate change

Paula Clifford, who is Christian Aid's head of theology, explores the current environmental crisis through the letters to the seven churches in the book of Revelation.[88] She draws upon examples of the impact of global climate change on the poor, taken from Christian Aid's work with the disadvantaged and vulnerable peoples of the developing world. She urges the Church to express its prophetic voice, to be repentant of its part in ecological violence, and to act together to bring about redemption. Among her parallels with the seven churches she sees the Church in the West as being lukewarm on climate change (see the letter to the church at Laodicea, Rev. 3.14–22), and failing to recognize the resultant injustice for the poor who are unable to protect themselves against climate change.

She draws attention to the horror of environmental destruction portrayed in Revelation 16, echoed in Simon Woodman's exploration of Revelation. Woodman observes that empires that take dominion over the earth frequently engage in ecological violence. He notes that the environmental judgements of Revelation are not personally targeted punishments aimed at those who deny the lordship of Christ, but rather are images evoking the inevitable end results of the human capacity for empire and exploitation. He expresses the same thoughts as Paula Clifford, that the environmental call of Revelation is therefore for the Church to discover its vocation as witness to an alternative, non-exploitative expression of humanity, focused around the lordship of the one on the heavenly throne. However, any such activity will always be perceived as a direct challenge to the idolatrous claims exercised by the satanic empire of Babylon in all its forms, something that inevitably places the Church at odds with the dominant powers of the creation-destroying empires of earth.[89]

Paula Clifford believes that it is important to move away from a problem-solving approach to global climate change and recognize that we have to live with climate change. Understanding that this is a global problem necessitates a global approach. The Christian Church is a worldwide community making up some one-third of the world's population and as such is in a unique position to take up the challenge of restoring and renewing creation.

Hope comes through a change of lifestyle as a mark of Christian discipleship.[90]

## Co-redeemers

God's covenant with Noah marks a new beginning after the Flood. Bernard W. Anderson points out that this is 'fundamentally an ecological covenant that includes not only human beings everywhere but all animals – "every living being [*nepeš hayyâ*]" . . . [and] the earth itself'.[91] He also emphasizes that this is an 'everlasting covenant' or a 'covenant in perpetuity', which shows 'God's absolute commitment to the creation'.[92] This is a covenant that neither sets restrictions to the species nor limits on time. It is inclusive for all time.

Non-human creation, as depicted in the Bible, has a role in giving glory to God and in teaching human beings about God's ways (Ps. 19.1; Prov. 6.6; Ps. 104.10–1). The apostle Paul tells us how the whole creation is groaning and waiting to be set free to share the 'freedom of the glory of the children of God' (Rom. 8.21). Paul Fiddes argues that although these are poetic images they bear testimony to some kind of response which the natural world can make or fail to make to the purposes of God, a response which in some way is connected to the human response.[93] The call of Christ is expressed as 'Whoever wants to be my disciple must deny themselves and take up their cross and follow me' (Mark 8.34).

This is a different sort of life, a Christlike life, a life that is in Christ. It is to deny self – to move away from a selfish materialistic lifestyle; to take up the cross-shaped life of sacrificial love, sharing God's good gifts of creation with all; and to follow Jesus, in his compassion for others and for the world. The call is to join in Christ's redemptive mission. So to be co-redeemers – for Christ's redeeming love to flow through us, in the power of the Spirit – we must:

- *Deny self:* live more simply, use less of the world's resources; treat the created order with care.
- *Take up the cross:* live sacrificially for the sake of others; give up our greed; sacrifice our wants.
- *Follow Jesus:* see the created world as an expression of God's order and love; see everyone as equally valued by God; take special care of the poor and the outcast; and love our neighbour as ourselves.

Northcott concludes:

Envisaging the human relation to nature in terms of love has profound implications for the modern social form; for the cost-benefit calculus which insures that billions of animals every year are imprisoned in cruel and valueless life to provide cheap proteins for humans; the corporate and inter-governmental calculus which sets as a price on international debt repayment the systematic clear-cutting of ancient forests and the environmental exclusion of peasant farmers and tribal peoples from their ancestral lands; the market ideology which sets the putative good of 'private' transport above safe space for children and walkers and wild things to play and relate and make community.[94]

Humans must make connections between the love of God which sustains them, the call of God to love neighbour, the care of the environment, and the worship of God.

Helle Liht notes that Moltmann brings together the creation, God's act in the past, and the redeemed created order, God's future that was inaugurated by Christ's resurrection. He argues that according to the understanding of the New Testament, Christ's death and resurrection carry historic, eschatological and cosmic dimension. Moltmann says:

> There can be no redemption for human beings without the redemption of the whole of perishable nature. So it is not enough to see Christ's resurrection merely as 'God's eschatological act in history'. We also have to understand it as *the first act in the new creation of the world*. Christ's resurrection is not just a historical event. It is a cosmic event too.[95]

Paul places the redemption of human beings in the context of the redemption of the whole creation, which is powerfully expressed in his letter to the Romans (8.18–25).

## Somewhere to stand

The land and its resources belong to God and not to human beings. God is revealed as a God of order, power and faithfulness, and God is involved in creation. Human beings are invited by the Creator to be co-creators, taking part with God in the care and sharing out of the riches of the world. Covenant, with its themes of relationship, justice and sin, becomes the key underlying principle for our thinking. God, the creator, draws us into a covenant relationship with Godself, which involves us in the responsible and accountable stewardship of creation. Here we recognize the need to address pollution and the related issues of ozone layer damage and adverse climate change. We are also challenged to be just in our dealings with all other human beings. Understanding God's justice and God's desire and care for every human life leads us to ask questions about our use of the earth's resources as well as our pollution of the earth's surface and atmosphere. Recognizing human sin becomes a vital element in controlling our use and abuse of energy sources. It is so easy for greed, the desire for power and selfishness to control the way we behave.

Christians must learn to think and act ecologically, to repent of extravagance, pollution and wanton destruction, and to recognize that human beings find it easier to subdue the earth than they do to subdue themselves. Christians face the task of articulating the gospel with relevance; of speaking prophetically and relevantly to the environmental and social issues of our day; and of rediscovering a holistic doctrine of creation. The native American Cree people have a saying: 'Only when the last tree has been cut, the last river poisoned, and the last fish caught, only then you will realize that one cannot eat money.'[96]

## Key texts

Richard Foltz (ed.), 2003, *Worldviews, Religion, and the Environment: A Global Anthology*, Belmont CA: Wadsworth/Thomson Learning.

John Houghton, 2009, *Global Warming: The Complete Briefing*, Cambridge: Cambridge University Press.

John Weaver and Margot Hodson (eds), 2007, *The Place of Environmental Theology: A Guide for Seminaries, Colleges and Universities*, Oxford: Whitley Publications/Prague: IBTS.

Robert White (ed.), 2009, *Creation in Crisis: Christian Perspectives on Sustainability*, London: SPCK.

## Further reading

K. C. Abraham, 'A Theological Response to the Ecological Crisis', in David Hallman (ed.), 1994, *Ecotheology: Voices from South and North*, Geneva: WCC/Maryknoll NY: Orbis Books.

Ian Ball, Margaret Goodall, Clare Palmer and John Reader (eds), 1992, *The Earth Beneath: A Critical Guide to Green Theology*, London: SPCK.

R. J. Berry (ed.), 2006, *Environmental Stewardship*, London: T&T Clark.

Dave Bookless, 2008, *Planetwise: Dare to Care for God's World*, Leicester: Inter-Varsity Press.

Paula Clifford, 2009, *Angels with Trumpets: The Church in a Time of Global Warming*, London: Darton, Longman & Todd and Christian Aid.

Ruth Conway, 1999, *Choices at the Heart of Technology: A Christian Perspective*, Harrisburg PA: Trinity Press.

Martin Hodson and Margot Hodson, 2008, *Cherishing the Earth: How to Care for God's Creation*, Oxford: Monarch.

Sean McDonagh, 1999, *Greening the Christian Millennium*, Dublin: Dominican Publications.

Michael Northcott, 2007, *A Moral Climate: The Ethics of Global Warming*, London: Darton, Longman & Todd and Christian Aid.

Nick Spencer and Robert White, 2007, *Christianity, Climate Change and Sustainable Living*, London: SPCK.

Sarah Tillett (ed.), 2005, *Caring for Creation. Biblical and Theological Perspectives*, Oxford: Bible Reading Fellowship.

## Notes

1 Some of the material in this chapter first appeared in my previous work, John Weaver and Margot Hodson (eds), 2007, *The Place of Environmental Theology: A Guide for Seminaries, Colleges and Universities*, Oxford: Whitley Publications/ Prague: IBTS, and John Weaver, 2009, 'Co-Redeemers: A Theological Basis for Creation Care', *Perspectives in Religious Studies*, vol.36, no. 2, National Association of Baptist Professors of Religion, Georgia: Mercer Press.

2 Gregg Easterbrook, 'The New Nature', in Richard Foltz (ed.), 2003, *Worldviews, Religion, and the Environment: A Global Anthology*, Belmont CA: Wadsworth/ Thomson Learning, pp. 54–5.

3 Lynn White, 1967, 'The Historical Roots of our Ecological Crisis', *Science* 155, pp. 1203–7.

4 Foltz, *Worldviews*, p. 4.

5 Church of England's Mission and Public Affairs Council, 2005, *Sharing God's Planet*, London: Church House Publishing, p. 3.

6 Sarah Tillett (ed.), 2005, *Caring for Creation: Biblical and Theological Perspectives*, Oxford: Bible Reading Fellowship, p. 14. Much of this book is based on the work of A Rocha, whose five core commitments are: Christian, Conservation, Community, Cross-cultural and Co-operation. Two of their objectives are: 'To encourage the Church to undertake the biblical responsibility to act as good stewards of God's world, and to provide practical advice on how to go about this . . . to advocate and resource action locally, nationally and internationally, in pursuit of environmental protection and sustainable development' (p. 18).

7 Gordon D. Kaufman, 2004, *In the Beginning . . . Creativity*, Minneapolis MN: Fortress Press.

8 David R. Loy, 'The Religion of the Market', in Foltz, *Worldviews*, p. 68.

9 http://www.bbc.co.uk/pressoffice/pressreleases/stories/2006/12_december/04/poll.shtml

10 http://www.reuters.com/article/environmentNews/idUSTRE57462A20090805

11 Marvin S. Soroos, 'From the End of History to the End of Nature', in Harto Hakovirta (ed.), 2003, *Six Essays on Global Order and Governance*, Finland: Figare/Safir, p. 40.

12 Sean McDonagh, 1990, *The Greening of the Church*, London: Geoffrey Chapman, p. 73.

13 Sean McDonagh, 1999, *Greening the Christian Millennium*, Dublin: Dominican Publications, p. 66.

14 Bill McGuire, 2004, *Climate Change 2004*, Benfield Hazard Research Centre, p. 1, referenced in *Sharing God's Planet*, p. 7.

15 McDonagh, *Greening the Christian Millennium*, pp. 64–5.

16 Film *An Inconvenient Truth*, directed by Davis Guggenheim, released 15.09.06. A documentary film which won 18 awards including 2 Oscars (March 2007) for Best Documentary Features and Best Achievement in Music Written for Motion Pictures, Original Song – 'I need to wake up' by Melissa Etheridge.

17 In a controversial documentary, film-maker Martin Durkin argues that the theory of man-made global warming has become such a powerful political force that other explanations for climate change are not being properly aired. See further details on the Channel 4 website: http://www.channel4.com/science/microsites/G/great_global_warming_swindle/index.html

18 Nick Davies, 2008, *Flat Earth News*, London: Chatto & Windus, p. 187.

19 See Sir John Houghton's letter to the *Baptist Times* (14 August 2008), who states: 'As any climate scientist familiar with the whole range of scientific literature will testify, the overwhelming message from new, recent scientific papers is that the consequences of climate change are likely to be more serious and severe than we have been predicting so far.' Houghton was co-chair of IPCC scientific assessments 1988–2002.

20 McDonagh, *Greening the Christian Millennium*, pp. 85–6.

21 UN Food and Agriculture Organization, http://www.fao.org/

22 Church of England, *Sharing God's Planet*, p. 11.

23 Howard Snyder, 1995, *Earth Currents: The Struggle for the World's Soul*, Nashville TN: Abingdon Press, p. 242.

24 http://www.guardian.co.uk/politics/2006/oct/30/economy.uk

25 Energy Futures Task Force, 2001, *Energy for Tomorrow: Powering the 21st Century*, London: DTI, p. 7.

26 Google IPCC Nairobi 2007 and follow link to www.ipcc.ch

27 http://www.guardian.co.uk/commentisfree/2008/dec/10/comment-porritt-poznan-copenhagen-environment

28 http://unfccc.int/meetings/cop_14/items/4481.php The United Nations Climate Change Conference in Poznań on Saturday 13 December 2008 ended with a clear commitment from governments to shift into full negotiating mode the following year in order to shape an ambitious and effective international response to climate change, to be agreed in Copenhagen at the end of 2009. Parties agreed that the first draft of a concrete negotiating text would be available at a UNFCCC gathering in Bonn in June of 2009. At Poznań, the finishing touches were put to the Kyoto Protocol's Adaptation Fund, with parties agreeing that the Fund would be a legal entity granting direct access to developing countries. Progress was also made on a number of important ongoing issues that are particularly important for developing countries, including adaptation, finance, technology, reducing emissions from deforestation and forest degradation, and disaster management. A key event at the conference was a ministerial round table on a shared vision on long-term co-operative action on climate change. Ministers gave a resounding commitment to achieving an ambitious and comprehensive deal in Copenhagen that can be ratified by all.

29 http://www.hm-treasury.gov.uk/sternreview_index.htm The United Kingdom Government commissioned Sir Nicholas Stern to make an economic assessment of climate change. The report published in November 2006 presented the following key points among others: carbon emissions have pushed up global temperatures by 0.5°C; if no action is taken on emissions, there is more than a 75 per cent chance of global temperatures rising between 2–3°C over the next 50 years, and a 50 per cent chance that average global temperatures could rise by 5°C; melting glaciers will increase flood risk; crop yields will decline, particularly in Africa; rising sea levels could leave 200 million people permanently displaced; up to 40 per cent of species could face extinction; extreme weather and rising temperatures could reduce global

output by 10 per cent with the poorest countries losing the most.

30 Intergovernmental Panel on Climate Change, 28th Session, Budapest 9–10 April 2008, IPCC-XXVIII/Doc. 13 Technical Paper on Climate Change and Water, Executive Summary.

31 Narayan Prasad Chaulagain, 2007, *Impacts of Climate Change on Water Resources of Nepal*, Aachen: Shaker Verlag, p. 2. Narayan is a member of the PEEDA team and this publication presents the results of his doctoral research in the Nepal Himalayas, carried out at the University of Flensburg, Germany.

32 Chaulagain, *Impacts of Climate Change*, p. 22.

33 Chaulagain, *Impacts of Climate Change*, p. 83.

34 Chaulagain, *Impacts of Climate Change*, pp. 117–18.

35 Chaulagain, *Impacts of Climate Change*, p. 120.

36 The Met Office Hadley Centre provides a focus in the UK for the scientific issues associated with climate change. See http://www.metoffice.gov.uk/climate change

37 Ruth Conway, 1999, *Choices at the Heart of Technology: A Christian Perspective*, Harrisburg PA: Trinity Press, p. 2.

38 Conway, *Choices*, p. 4.

39 B. McKibben, 1989, *The End of Nature*, New York: Anchor Books, quoted in Soroos, 'From the End of History', in Hakovirta, *Six Essays*, pp. 25–46.

40 Robin Attfield, 'Global Warming, Justice and Future Generations', in Hakovirta, *Six Essays*, pp. 71–86.

41 Attfield, 'Global Warming', p. 75.

42 Loy, 'The Religion of the Market', in Foltz, *Worldviews*, p. 69.

43 Loy, 'The Religion of the Market' in Foltz, p. 73.

44 John Houghton, 1994, *Global Warming*, Oxford: Lion, p. 117.

45 Google 'European $CO_2$ emissions' for the latest figures.

46 Attfield, 'Global Warming', p. 76.

47 Reported by Anthony Browne in *The Times* (London), 31 August 2002. See also Andrew Hewett's Oxfam Press Release, 3 September 2002.

48 R. J. Berry, 'Rejection of the Creator', in Tillett, *Caring for Creation*, p. 44.

49 R. J. Berry, 'Green Religion and Green Science', in David Atkinson, 1994, *Pastoral Ethics*, Oxford: Lynx, p. 124.

50 WCC Study Paper, 1994, *Accelerated Climate Change: Sign of Peril, Test of Faith*, Geneva, summarized in McDonagh, *Greening the Christian Millennium*, pp. 80–4.

51 McDonagh, *Greening the Christian Millennium*, p. 15.

52 James Houston, 'Creation and Incarnation', in Tillett, *Caring for Creation*, p. 95.

53 See: www.lausanne.org

54 McDonagh, *Greening the Christian Millennium*, p. 39.

55 McDonagh, *Greening the Christian Millennium*, p. 40.

56 Clare Palmer, 'Stewardship: A Case Study in Environmental Ethics', in Ian Ball, Margaret Goodall, Clare Palmer and John Reader (eds), 1992, *The Earth Beneath: A Critical Guide to Green Theology*, London: SPCK, p. 68.

57 P. N. Hillyer, 'Stewardship', in David Atkinson and David Field (eds), 1995, *New Dictionary of Christian Ethics and Pastoral Theology*, London: SPCK, p. 814.

58 Robert McAfee Brown, 1990, *Gustavo Gutiérrez: An Introduction to Liberation Theology*, Maryknoll NY: Orbis Books, pp. 56–7.

59 Leonardo Boff, 'Science, Technology, Power and Liberation Theology', in Foltz, *Worldviews*, p. 500.

60 Boff, 'Science, Technology', p. 501.

61 Boff 'Science, Technology', p. 503.

62 K. C. Abraham, in David Hallman (ed.), 1994, *Ecotheology: Voices from South and North*, Geneva: WCC/Maryknoll NY: Orbis Books, pp. 68–9.

63 Peter Carruthers, 'Creation and the Gospels', in Tillett (ed.), *Caring for Creation*, p. 74.

64 Church of England, *Sharing God's Planet*, p. 28.

65 I am indebted to Ken Franklin (an MTh student at Cardiff University 2006–8) for the thoughts developed in this section.

66 N. T. Wright, 2000, *The Challenge of Jesus*, London: SPCK, p. 137; see also: F. F. Bruce, 'Eschatology', in Walter Elwell (ed.), 1991, *The Concise Evangelical Dictionary of Theology*, London: Marshall Pickering, p. 199.

67 Wright, *The Challenge of Jesus*, p. 48.

68 Mary Getui, 'Eschatology', in Virginia Fabella and R. S. Sugirtharajah (eds), 2003, *The SCM Dictionary of Third World Theologies*, London: SCM Press, p. 85.

69 Wright, *The Challenge of Jesus*, p. 139.

70 Church of England, *Sharing God's Planet*, p. 24.

71 Paul Haffner, 'A Christian Ecology', in Robert Whelan, Joseph Kirwan and Paul Haffner, 1996, *The Cross and the Rain Forest: A Critique of Radical Green Spirituality*, Grand Rapids MI: Eerdmans, p. 126.

72 James Houston, 'Creation and Incarnation', in Tillett, *Caring for Creation*, p. 91.

73 Paul Fiddes, 2000, *Participating in God: A Pastoral Doctrine of the Trinity*, London: Darton, Longman & Todd. We can suggest that it is spirituality that Fiddes describes as 'participating in God', which he explores through community, power, intercessory prayer, suffering, forgiveness, death and spiritual gifts. This discussion is strengthened through a complementary exploration of God's vulnerability, love, life, Spirit and incarnation. My own view is that participating in God is a participation in God's mission in the world. It is recognizing our own stories, our fellow travellers in the faith, the holistic nature of the gospel, the community outside the Church, and the natural world of which we are a part. The needs of a broken world lead us towards a spirituality that has depth and integrity. We celebrate this through broken bread and poured-out wine, where we enter into God's story of salvation, forgiveness and new life in Christ.

74 Fiddes, *Participating in God*, p. 299.

75 Houston, 'Creation and Incarnation', pp. 88–9.

76 Fiddes, *Participating in God*, p. 300.

77 Michael S. Northcott, 'Ecology and Christian Ethics', in Robin Gill (ed.), 2001, *The Cambridge Companion to Christian Ethics*, Cambridge: Cambridge University Press, pp. 213–5.

78 Northcott, 'Ecology' in Gill, *The Cambridge Companion*, p. 216.

79 Northcott, 'Ecology', pp. 221–2.

80 Northcott, 'Ecology', p. 224.

81 William H. Lazareth, 1983, *Growing Together in Baptism, Eucharist and*

*Ministry: A Study Guide*, Geneva: WCC, p. 51.

82  Lazareth, *Growing Together*, p. 73.

83  Sallie McFague, 'An Ecological Christology. Does Christianity have it?' in Foltz, *Worldviews*, pp. 336–8.

84  Included as an appendix in Foltz, *Worldviews*, pp. 591–6.

85  McFague, 'An Ecological Christology', p. 334.

86  McFague, 'An Ecological Christology', p. 337.

87  McFague, 'An Ecological Christology', p. 337.

88  Paula Clifford, 2009, *Angels with Trumpets: The Church in a Time of Global Warming*, London: Darton, Longman & Todd and Christian Aid.

89  Simon Woodman, 2008, *SCM Core Text: The Book of Revelation*, London: SCM Press, pp. 209–12.

90  Clifford, *Angels with Trumpets*, pp. 112–31.

91  Bernhard W. Anderson, 1994, *From Creation to New Creation: Old Testament Perspectives*, Minneapolis MN: Fortress Press, p. 156, quoted in Helle Liht, 2008, 'Restoring Relationships: Towards Ecologically Responsible Baptist Communities in Estonia', unpublished MTh thesis, IBTS, Prague.

92  Anderson, *From Creation to New Creation*, pp. 156–8.

93  Paul S. Fiddes, 2003, *Tracks and Traces: Baptist Identity in Church and Theology*, Carlisle: Paternoster Press, p. 56.

94  Northcott, 'Ecology', p. 225.

95  Jürgen Moltmann, 1995, *Jesus Christ for Today's World*, London: SCM Press, p. 83, quoted in Liht, 'Restoring Relationships', pp. 38–41.

96  Margot Käßmann, 'Covenant, Praise and Justice in Creation', in Hallman, *Ecotheology*, p. 49.

# 7

## Models of God – Bringing Science and Faith Together

### Introduction

#### Outlining the issues

We noted in the Introduction that Steven Weinberg commented in his book *The First Three Minutes* that the more the universe seems comprehensible, the more it seems pointless. Weinberg believes that doing science gives human beings some sense of grace in the midst of being trapped in a hostile world.[1] Another hope-less observation was made by Jacques Monod who, commenting on life based on the findings of molecular biology, concluded that 'the ancient covenant is in pieces; man at last knows that he is alone in the unfeeling immensity of the universe, out of which he emerged only by chance'.[2] Richard Dawkins likewise points to the ruthless nature of evolution in dispensing with species that are ineffective:

> Unrelentingly and unceasingly, as Darwin explained, 'natural selection is daily and hourly scrutinizing, throughout the world, every variation, even the slightest; rejecting that which is bad, preserving and adding up all that is good; silently and insensibly working, whenever and wherever opportunity offers, at the improvement of each organic being'. If a wild animal habitually performs some useless activity, natural selection will favour rival individuals who devote the time and energy, instead, to surviving and reproducing. Nature cannot afford frivolous *jeux d'esprit*. Ruthless utilitarianism trumps, even if it doesn't always seem that way.[3]

We add to these views those of ordinary people who question the extreme suffering of the people of Darfur, Rwanda, or in the Holocaust, or the suffering caused by natural events such as earthquakes and tsunami. What sort of model of God do we have? Can there be a God in such a world as this? Yet Paul Davies is able to say of human existence in the vast expanses of the universe:

> What is man that we might be party to such a privilege? I cannot believe

that our existence in this universe is a mere quirk of fate, an accident of history, an incidental blip in the great cosmic drama. Our involvement is too intimate . . . We are truly meant to be here.[4]

Jerry Coyne reflects that evolution does not leave us in a barren naturalistic and materialistic world. He observes that 'there is no reason . . . to see ourselves as marionettes dancing on the strings of evolution'. 'Genetic' does not mean 'unchangeable'. He recognizes that while the world is full of selfishness, immorality and injustice, we also find kindness and altruism.[5]

And in commenting on the 26 December 2004 South East Asian tsunami, Matthew Parris (award-winning columnist and confessed atheist), writing in *The Times* (1 January 2005), states that he believes that we would not want a world without the 'thrill' of cataclysms. A world without any risk would be a dull world. A world that was predictable and controllable would not be Utopia. He believes that it is important for human beings to be humbled in the face of their frailty.

In this final chapter we will explore the models of God that may be proposed in the light of our experience and scientific understanding of the world.

## Models of God seen in the natural world

Any understanding of the nature of God based upon scientific discovery of the natural world is equally capable of leading towards a position of no belief as to belief, because they are not proofs. Realizing this, from Calvin to Barth there have been Christian thinkers who have stressed the need for revelation, as opposed to reason. Their criticism is not just that rational arguments do not work; they make the theological point that our knowledge of a God who is other than us must come from God's own initiative, whereas with natural theology the movement seems to be from us to God.

However, natural theology takes on a different aspect if we begin from the initiative God takes in coming to meet us in the world. God does not stand outside creation; God is involved with it, sustaining it by God's power.[6] God continues with this work; in the imagery of Genesis 1—2, the seventh day of Genesis 2.1–3 has not brought creation to an end but runs out into history.

The biblical picture is of God's continuous involvement with creation described in terms of the 'covenant' agreement that God initiates and offers. Israel understood the world as God's good creation in the light of her experience of the exodus from Egypt, the covenant made at Sinai, and entry into the Promised Land. It was from its experience of the life, crucifixion and resurrection of Christ, and the establishment of the new covenantal community in the power of the Holy Spirit, that the New Testament Church understood God's intention to perfect and complete creation. Thus the natural world is given a place in the whole story of God's purpose to make covenantal fellowship, a process with an eschatological goal. In contrast to a theist view, biblical natural theology looks to a biblical God, the God of Israel, the Father of Jesus Christ, who is personal and opens Godself to all the hazards of love for others. It places God in an immanent, intimate relationship with creation.

A natural theology that builds a concept of God totally outside the experience of revelation and the community of faith belongs to Greek philosophy rather than to Hebrew concepts of the world.

### Where have the discoveries of science led us?

The quest of modern cosmology for a 'theory of everything' may be understood as a search for the cause behind the Big Bang or the quantum explanation of multiverse. There is a wistful belief that if only one could find the equation that brought all the factors together, the law by which the other laws work, one would be able to explain how the Big Bang happened. John Barrow helps us with the central theological issue. He considers the three basic factors of God, the universe and the laws of nature, and then draws up three groups of parallel propositions:

1 Either the laws of nature existed before the universe (a 'first cause'); or the laws are dependent on the universe; or the laws are to be equated with the universe.
2 A similar set of propositions can be made with regard to God: either the universe is part of God ('panentheism' – everything in God); or God is part of the universe (a creation of the human mind); or God is the same as the universe ('pantheism').
3 Again, a third set of propositions might be: either the laws of nature are part of God; or God is part of the laws of nature; or the laws of nature are the same as God.[7]

There is, of course, no logical necessity for coming to the conclusion that the universe points to the God of the Christian Scriptures, but there is an interesting affinity between the first of these propositions in each set, and a potential here for a 'suggestive' natural theology. It makes sense then, as we consider the 'fine-tuning' of the universe, to think of a creative divine Mind behind the universe. Yet having reached such a point in the argument, Bertrand Russell's conclusion is still open to us as a logical possibility: namely, there is the explanation of brute fact, that the universe is just there and that is all.

## How does theology approach these issues?

Theology takes a broader overview of the whole of human experience, bringing together the physical, mental, emotional and spiritual aspects of being to produce a holistic view of the universe in which we exist. Theology explores the nature of the creator God, who makes sense of all that science is uncovering in the universe.

The Bible presents us with God's ordering of creation. It shows us God's covenantal relationship with creation. The human side is through a relationship with God in worship, and a caring relationship with nature. But, we find that paradise is lost; creation is broken, constantly in need of restoration. The Bible also expresses the hope of redemption. It is not only human beings who suffer in such a 'fallen world'; the biosphere, which is becoming increasingly polluted and exhausted, also suffers. As Paul wrote to the church at Rome:

> The creation waits in eager expectation for the children of God to be revealed ... We know that the whole creation has been groaning as in the pains of childbirth right up to the present time. Not only so, but we ourselves, who have the first-fruits of the Spirit, groan inwardly as we wait eagerly for our adoption, the redemption of our bodies. (Rom. 8.19, 22–23)

We live in a world of suffering, pain, pollution and exploitation, but the Christian hope is in transformation of individuals and through them of creation, in Christ crucified, resurrected and ascended.

The theological view of the world is a holistic view (physical and spiritual) and so there must be an agreement between science and theology, if both pictures of the universe are correct. Understanding the world in which we live is a quest that unites science and theology, and such a quest will require an openness to God, Scripture and scientific research. The world is not a neutral place and, if it is the creation of God, we should expect a study of the universe to be a starting point for recognizing the creator.

Both theology and science are seeking to make sense of the world that they experience, and their methodologies are not totally different. In each case the search for a rational understanding is motivated by belief and a desire for truth. As such there must be a common ground for dialogue. Science is able to investigate the universe because human beings have a measure of transcendence over the world, and theology is able to bring a greater degree of understanding because it recognizes the transcendence of God, who reveals God's purposes to humankind.

# Suffering in a world created by a God of love

## The issues

The 'problem' of suffering arises when we postulate an omnipotent, loving God as the creator of a world in which there is disorder, destruction, pain and suffering. This leads to questions. What sort of God do we believe in? What sort of God is the creator of this world? The presence of pain and suffering has led to accusations or conclusions that God is fallible, powerless, capricious and bad. But then we are left to ask, what would the creator of a perfect world be like? A world in which there was no pain or suffering, in which no one did anything bad, a world in which there were no earthquakes, volcanoes, cyclones or hurricanes, in which nothing ever went wrong, would be predictable, absolutely controlled, lacking any choice or free will. Such a world would be boring, frustrating and prison-like.

A God who gives choice and free will allows creation to develop, to explore, to discover good and bad, to experience pain and pleasure, to know love and hate. We should ask: what sort of God can we find in the Scriptures? What sort of God could be described as a loving parent?

## Suffering in the natural world

Hearing the scientific stories challenges us to recognize that any theological reflection on creation today, if it is to remain relevant, must not lose sight of the pain of the earth, or forget the forces that are destroying it, by flying off into an abstract discussion on creation and creaturehood. At the same time, a discussion of scientific models of creation would be the poorer if it did not place a discussion of our current experience within a broader philosophical context.

The important question that will underlie our reflection is, what sort of God do we believe in? There are a variety of myths in ancient cultures, some of which are nature-denying and some of which emphasize its importance in the scheme of things. Enlightenment science has led to views that are at best deist (God winding up the clockwork motor of a world that runs according to physical laws) and at worst reductionist, with no place for the divine. The reductionist view leads us to the conclusion of meaninglessness. A universe without hope would be a desperate place in which to exist.

In the natural world there are disastrous effects of geotectonics and of extreme weather systems. These pose theological questions about the nature of God. We now know the structure of the Earth's crust; we can predict where earthquakes are likely to occur; and we know that the evolving structure of the crust is necessary for the development of the rocks and minerals, on which much of our industrial development is based. What will we say when a major earthquake occurs along the San Andreas Fault in California?

It surely could not be used as an objection to belief in a God who is intimately involved with creation, and who has provided humanity with the materials for an industrialized society through such structures in the Earth's crust.

When we consider the world's weather we see hurricanes, tornadoes and cyclones. These cause a great deal of damage, hardship and death. There are parts of Bangladesh, for example, where cyclones cause flooding and death on a large scale every year. We know what causes climatic systems and we can predict weather patterns. Beyond such knowledge we also recognize the need of a dynamic climate system in producing the variety of world climates and the resulting natural produce of fruit, vegetables and the life of rainforests that is the natural resource of most of our important medicines. Therefore we might say that the storms are a natural part of the fruitful creation that we enjoy.

Before we quickly blame God for death and destruction we realize that our knowledge of the working of the world brings with it the responsibility of sharing our knowledge, resources and living space with those who are poor and who suffer through the climate of their location.

An understanding of God's involvement with creation is fundamentally important. Central to our understanding is to recognize that God in freedom chose to create a universe that is contingent in itself. The picture of evolution presents us with God's risk in such a creation, with mutations, extinctions and fortunate survivors an integral part of the process. The same genes that give rise to human development can also lead to disease and death. There are abnormal cells that produce cancer, the altered or missing chromosomes that cause genetic diseases, and the intrusion of microbes that lead to illness and death. God-given skill and knowledge allows us to develop treatments for many of these. We are back to the question of what kind of God.

The God who is immanent within creation is not insulated from the risks that God asks others to bear, but will suffer along with creation. In creating human beings at a distance from Godself and with free will, God risks the pain of rebellion, while longing for the response of obedient love.

### The Tsunami on 26 December 2004: a case study

A large tsunami struck South East Asia in the early morning of 26 December 2004 bringing destruction and death to the coastal margins of Thailand, Indonesia, Malaysia, Burma, Sri Lanka, India, the Andaman and Nicobar Islands, the Maldives and East Africa.

Rowan Williams wrote, 'The question "How can you believe in a God who permits suffering on this scale?" is therefore very much around at the moment and it would be surprising if it weren't – indeed it would be wrong if it weren't' (*Sunday Telegraph*, 2 January 2005). He is also quoted as saying: 'Every single random accidental death is something that should upset a faith bound up with comfort and ready answers. Faced with the paralysing magnitude of a disaster like this, we naturally feel more deeply outraged and also more deeply helpless' (*The Times*, 3 January 2005). The Bishop of Norwich, the Rt Revd Graham James said: 'God has given us an Earth that lives and moves. It is not inert, it is alive – that is why we can live. A living and moving Earth has its dangers. Christianity never avoids the darker side of human existence.'

The US Geological Survey reported that the movement that took place was in the order of 30–40 metres. Pressure had built up over 200 years – no major earthquakes have occurred on this plate margin since 1797 and 1833. Some of the smaller islands off the south-west coast of Sumatra may have moved to the south-west by about 20 metres. The north-west tip of Sumatra may have moved 36 metres south-west, and sea-level changes of + or − 2 feet have been recorded. The earthquake measured 9 on the Richter scale, the equivalent of 190 million tons of TNT (or 9500 Hiroshima bombs). In terms of plate tectonics (discussed in Chapter 3) the Indian Plate is being subducted beneath the Burma Plate along the line of the Sundra Trench. This is where the epicentre of the earthquake was located.

There is an important theological issue to be addressed here. In 1755, an earthquake off the coast of Portugal caused a tidal wave that destroyed much of the port of Lisbon and thousands of people lost their lives. The Lisbon earthquake is cited by many people as a turning point for belief in a loving, sovereign God. But we now know the structure of the Earth's crust; we can predict where earthquakes are likely to occur; and we know that the evolving structure of the crust is necessary for the development of the rocks and minerals on which much of our industrial development is based.

Concerning the Indonesian earthquake of 26 December 2004, Jonathan Sacks (the Chief Rabbi) asked in *The Times* (1 January 2005) why God allows terrible things to happen to his people. He reflected on the 1755 Lisbon earthquake, which occurred on All Souls Day, and in which 60,000 died. There were religious believers at the time who saw this disaster as God's judgement on a sinful Lisbon. But why Lisbon rather than other cities, and why the young, the frail and the saintly? Such a suggestion is unacceptable as it blames the victims for their fate. Sacks observed that what distinguished the biblical prophets from their pagan predecessors was their refusal to see natural catastrophe as an independent force of evil, proof that at least some of the gods are hostile to humankind. Essential to monotheism is that conflict is not written into the fabric of the universe. That is what redeems tragedy and creates hope.

So we can affirm that we live as physical beings in a physical world with all its dynamic activity, a world in which earthquakes occur and people die. If it were not so we would not know pleasure, desire, achievement, freedom, virtue, creativity, vulnerability and love. We would be robots programmed to sing God's praise.

Philip Stott (Emeritus Professor of Biogeography, University of London) writing in *The Times* (29 December 2004), believes that it is human failings that allow natural disasters to wreak havoc. This earthquake had calamity written all over it. But he notes that what was more galling was that geologists would have been fully aware of that seismic event hours before the waves struck land. Lamentably, nobody knew who to warn. By contrast, in the Pacific Ocean there are sophisticated seismic and satellite early warning systems, but not in the Indian Ocean. The technology is available, and could be made available to these countries, but its use depends on effective regional and local government. Civil wars and political corruption make such governmental warning systems difficult. He advocates action to give data and establish local warning structures.

But such problems also exist in the developed world. Local government in Naples has allowed the development of houses, villas and settlements on the slopes of Vesuvius, a volcano due for an eruption on the scale of the one that buried Pompeii and Herculaneum under a pyroclastic flow. Such a high-temperature (1000°C), fast-moving (up to 750km/hr) cloud of volcanic ash and gas destroys everything in its path.

We can conclude that those of us who inhabit the quieter geological regions of the planet have a particular moral responsibility to assist those who do not. But how do we fit our understanding of God into this natural disaster? Descriptions of God as all-powerful, all-loving, all-knowing and ready to intervene can be unhelpful. How can God be both good and almighty when there are disasters such as this in the world? However, the New Testament reveals a God who is self-emptying, one who gives freedom, is powerless, crucified and suffering.

## A theological perspective

We have little problem in identifying where human sinfulness in such a free creation is the cause of the suffering of the innocent ('moral evil'), but cases of disease and the tragedy of natural disasters will be far more difficult. We cannot begin to deal with these problems without asking serious questions about how we believe that God acts in the world, and this also involves a scientific perspective. The transcendent God has the power to intervene in human affairs, and the immanent God is in the position where God is able to intervene. But if we propose that God does intervene on occasions, we are left with the difficult theological question of why God does not do so more often, and hence have to ask what kind of a God would behave like this. I suggest that we might keep the notion of 'intervention' for rare, defining moments of revelation. Otherwise, the model of 'intervention' is not a helpful one in considering the continual action of God; it is too one-sided, and I suggest that we should be cautious in employing it. It would be better to think of a God who does new things on the inside of creation and in co-operation with it in a way that does not infringe its freedom, though I acknowledge a mystery about the way that this happens.

Within the contingency of nature suggested by science, there is room for the emergence of 'natural' evil due to the distortion of living organisms at microscopic levels. Science demonstrates that the same processes that gave rise to the evolution of human life, namely the mutation of genes, also lead to disease and death. This is to be understood in theological terms as the risk God takes in endowing creation with freedom. In individual cases of suffering we will still of course have to wrestle with the questions of healing and wholeness, alongside pain and grief. There is no simple rational formula that can be applied to dissolve the mystery. In the mystery of suffering we will need to hold on to the model of suffering love that we see displayed in the cross of Christ, where we find the Creator suffering with and on behalf of the world.

Theodicy meaning 'justice of God' was coined by Gottfried von Leibniz (1646–1716) to refer to this very work of defending the idea of a just God in the face of what seems contrary evidence. Traditionally Christian theology has tried to hold together that God is almighty and all-loving and that we, as human beings, can have some measure of understanding of God's nature.[8] But one of these three aspects has always been lost or necessarily redefined. Nigel Wright, in exploring the nature of evil and the character of God in his book *The Fair Face of Evil*,[9] recognizes the challenge of Auschwitz and addresses this central question: if God is so loving and powerful, why does he not prevent suffering, or why does he allow suffering in the first place? Wright suggests that the horrors of history and of our current world context might lead us to ask whether God is either a loving Father, who is impotent, or a cosmic sadist, who lacks love.

In the light of the violence and injustice revealed in events such as Auschwitz, Ronaldo Munoz likewise suggests that there are three possible philosophical positions: God wills or at least allows it; God is above all such things and is not concerned about them; or God is unable to prevent such things.[10] The first suggestion presents the picture of a punishing God. The second image is of a God who is indifferent to the sufferings of the world. It is this third alternative, that God cannot prevent injustice and violence, that Munoz insists takes us closer to the experience of the suffering peoples of the world. He believes that the two statements – 'God is almighty' and 'God cannot prevent suffering' – are only contradictory if God is placed outside the world. But when we posit an immanent God, who in love is involved with the oppressed, through love, combating evil, then the contradiction and scandal are turned into mystery.

Munoz also alerts us to the fact that the theoretical expression of the theodicy question may not be the most helpful way of wrestling with such a fundamental aspect of human experience. There will always be the sense that any such rational answer will be unsatisfactory as we face such a mystery. But if we were to ask fundamentally the same question, but from a personal and existential perspective, we might ask, 'Where was God in the Holocaust?' or 'Where was God on 26 December 2004?'

As Christians it is our understanding of the cross that will help us to locate God in the midst of evil and suffering. Paul Fiddes also acknowledges that no theological argument can justify the mountain of misery represented by Auschwitz, but notes that the *Shema* of Israel and the Lord's Prayer were prayed in Auschwitz, indicating something of God's presence there. The same was seen to be true in the midst of the tsunami disaster. Fiddes argues that we can affirm that God is present in such extreme experiences as Auschwitz, present as the one who suffers. This conviction that God suffers will also prevent the construction of any argument that God directly causes suffering, although God may allow suffering. This is part of an understanding that God freely accepts self-limitation for the sake of the freedom given to creation,[11] and impinges upon our whole concept of God. For 'the question of theodicy is deeply bound up with the notion of the passibility (capable of feeling suffering) of God'.[12]

In his book *Love's Endeavour, Love's Expense*, W. H. Vanstone offers a graphic portrayal of this, daring to take as a paradigm the tragedy at Aberfan in South Wales on 21 October 1966, when a coal tip slid down on to a school and caused the deaths of over 100 children. Here God's step of creative risk was a step of disaster. Science and technology enabled coal to be mined; human greed seen in the demand for profit led to the siting of spoil heaps where they were; and the result, following freak weather conditions, was the suffering of the innocent. But our faith, affirms Vanstone, is not in a creator who permits disaster from the top of the mountain, but rather in one who is at the foot of the mountain receiving the impact. God's limitless love is evidenced in not abandoning people in their suffering but suffering with them.[13] With such a belief in the self-emptying of God, Christianity should have no hesitation in attributing to God that authenticity of love that it recognizes in Jesus Christ.[14] Limitless love is not incompatible with the existence of evil and suffering in the world, since this is the consequence of the freedom that is given by such loving creativity.

In our attempt to offer a response to the concerns of theodicy we must necessarily consider our understanding of the power of God. We have already noted how Paul Fiddes combines an insistence on the suffering of God with an understanding of God's self-limitation. In his work *Past Event and Present Salvation*, he returns to this theme and asks again, 'Can there be any theology after Auschwitz?' No theology which speaks of the goodness of God in creation will entirely satisfy in these circumstances. But Fiddes says that we may

*begin* a theodicy by affirming that God has passed over to his creation a radical freedom to be itself, and that he has limited himself in this way because he wants to make and enjoy fellowship with personalities who have, like himself, the ability to create. With their freedom to respond to God's purpose and to make their own contribution to his project, there also comes the risk that such personalities may slip away from the Good. Evil and suffering have thus emerged from creation as things strange to God, a disruption which he has not designed.[15]

Keith Ward appears to favour the view partly held by Augustine, and in recent times by theologians such as John Hick, that the worst kinds of suffering are the result of the free choice of human beings rejecting God and choosing self-centredness; natural evil poses a different question. To assert that God truly and radically shares our suffering asks questions about our understanding of God as the 'Almighty'. To proclaim that God is all-powerful means that God is the one who gives life, and the more God gives life to others the more God limits Godself.

Following on from this, locating God in Indonesia among those who suffer points us to a God, to use Vanstone's image, in the pile of debris on the beach rather than at the top of the wave. Fiddes maintains that the cross of Jesus 'assures us that God himself never directly inflicts suffering: a suffering God is to be counted among the victims and not the torturers'.[16] While suffering can sometimes enrich the character of the one who suffers and lead others to acts of compassion, 'confronted by an Auschwitz (or the South East Asian tsunami) even these benefits fall short of convincing us that the risk of creating a free universe was justifiable'. Fiddes continues by suggesting that

the affirmation that God himself shares the consequences of the risk he took is the most satisfactory theodicy we can achieve, and enables us to think of God and Auschwitz together, as long as we can speak of his transforming the effects of evil and suffering.[17]

When we consider the global environmental crisis we are helped by the views of liberation theology. Jon Sobrino, in attempting to explore the suffering of oppressed peoples in the developing world, speaks of the general agreement among theologians about the reality of suffering, its negativity, the fact that it is unwanted by God, and that in one way or another it is the consequence of sin.[18] But Sobrino states that for liberation theology 'the major form of suffering in today's world is historical suffering – suffering unjustly inflicted on some by others'. He goes on to say:

Historical suffering is massive, affecting the majority of humanity, making it practically impossible for people to direct their own lives, causing a poverty that brings death slowly and violently. In the presence of such suffering, theology must understand itself as an intellectual exercise whose primary purpose is to eliminate this kind of suffering. Briefly stated, suffering in today's world means primarily the sufferings of people who are being crucified, and the purpose of theology is to take these people down from the cross.[19]

He believes that in a world of suffering it is the humanity of human beings and the faith of believers that is at stake, and along with these the relevance and credibility of theology.[20] Sobrino tightly binds together theology and human suffering, the purpose being to find here some redemption. He concludes:

> The most truth-filled place for any Christian theology to carry out its task is always the suffering of our world, and in the crucified people of our world, theology finds, as part of the Christian paradox, its own salvation, its proper direction, and the courage to carry out its task.[21]

Sobrino believes that rich Western Christians find their salvation in their response to the suffering poor. In searching for God in the tsunami disaster we have wanted to affirm that we find God among those who suffer, seeking to bring about transformation and redemption.

With the help of modern science we are able to predict where and when natural disasters are likely to take place. So countries that are rich in resources and technology could counter such anticipated problems and avoid the worst effects if they had the willpower to accept the economic costs; for example, houses need not be built in an earthquake zone, and farmers need not farm on the side of Mount Etna. Poorer countries cannot themselves take evasive action; unless developed countries are willing to share their wealth, living space and expertise with others less advantaged, large populations will go on living – for example – on the coastal flood plains of Bangladesh. Thus, raising the moral question of the goodness of God also involves a moral issue for us.

Suffering will always have a dimension of mystery, and no explanation, even one that finds God sharing the risk and pain of creation in the cross, seems to be sufficient. But, like Job, 'all believers in God will finally bow before the utter mystery of the divine being, from which all things arise, and to which all things must finally return' (Job 42.1–6). For David Atkinson, the book of Job 'confronts us with failure, and with suffering for which there is no explanation'.[22] He maintains that we have to rethink our theology in the face of suffering and injustice. The book of Job calls us to see things from a divine rather than a human perspective.

There are searching questions for Christians in the face of 'natural evil'. Why did God allow this? Where was God in all this? Can there ever be belief in God after 26 December 2004? Atkinson notes that Job's friends were uncomfortable when face to face with that which defied their theology:

'They insisted on treating suffering only as a problem to be solved, rather than being willing to cope with the uncertainty of facing its mystery.'[23]

As we move towards the close of the book of Job, we find God speaking. We recognize that the Wisdom writer wants to tell us that divine wisdom is greater than human wisdom. In chapters 38 and 39 God asks Job a series of questions. Did you know this? Did you know that? Do you understand everything? Job is silenced by his ignorance and inability. In Job 41.11 God says that everything under heaven belongs to God. There may be some value in considering Romans 8.28–39 alongside this – nothing can separate us from the love of God – that God is able to hold on to us through suffering, pain, torture and death.

In the end (Job 42.1–6), Job is humbled in God's presence. He has been caught up into the purposes of God, of which he knows nothing. He has to trust in the Creator. Christians trust God, who loves and suffers with and for the world. Looking to the death of Christ, the lengths to which God's love will go is demonstrated. There is no promise of freedom from suffering, nor is the mystery of God explained, but there is the promise of grace and hope (Rev. 21.1–4).

## Bringing science and theology together

### A tentative model

From the beginning, the biblical picture is of God's continuous risky involvement with creation described in terms of the freedom God grants, and 'covenant' agreement God initiates and offers. John Hick has suggested that the risk God takes in creation can be understood as his creating human persons at a 'distance' from Godself, to give room for genuine response rather than being overwhelmed by God's glory.[24] Paul Fiddes takes up this idea, extending it to all levels of nature, and suggesting that God thereby freely exposes Godself to whatever new things, alien to God's purposes, might emerge from the choices of an unresponsive creation.[25] He further proposes that this risk can be pictured in the symbol of 'non-being'. The making of creatures 'from nothing' (ex nihilo) means that as finite beings they will always be limited by non-being, as a boundary to life, which is typified by death. While this 'non-being' is neutral in itself, the freedom that God has granted to creation leads to an environment in which a lapsing towards hostile non-being is practically inevitable. That is, the human 'no' to God (sin) results in an aggressive and alienating power that wants to reduce personal life and relationships to nothingness.[26]

In creation 'from nothing' therefore, God exposes Godself to a 'non-being' which begins as a natural boundary to life and which becomes increasingly hostile and alien to God. It is possible to represent this diagrammatically, as shown in Figure 7.1. Alongside this theological statement, and interacting with it, we can place the Big Bang of cosmology through which God creates our universe (which may or may not be part of a multiverse) with its fine-tuning, and through whose evolution we see the development of self-conscious human beings. We have a whole series of arrows, all of which are pointing in the direction of the space–time arrow, but which represent the contrasting movements of development and disorder.

There is the arrow of evolution, giving an increasing complexity and variety of life forms within an 'open system'; but paired with this arrow of development is that of disorder as entropy increases and the cosmos heads towards the Big Crunch or Heat Death. Parallel to these cosmic movements is the arrow of sin leading towards hostile non-being, paired with the arrow of redemption as God continuously participates in creation to seek to draw it back to God.

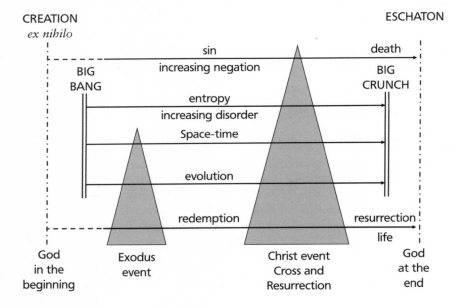

Figure 7.1

We should notice that the 'theological' and 'scientific' beginnings are not exactly simultaneous, as we cannot know whether God's initial act of creation is identical with the creation of this universe. So also the end points are not co-terminus, as God's consummation of the universe is God's initiative and not a matter of scientific prediction. We also need to recognize that from a theological standpoint all these arrow-lines are transfigured by one defining moment, when God participates in creation in the deepest possible way through the incarnation of Christ. As Eberhard Jüngel says, 'In the death of Jesus Christ God's "Yes" which constitutes all being, exposed itself to the "No" of the nothing . . . and in the Resurrection, this "Yes" prevailed over the "No".'[27] So there is the possibility of humans being taken out of the descent to hostile non-being and being caught up in the Being of God who is on the way to God's goal of new creation. Through cross and resurrection the arrow of redemption ends in resurrection and renewal for the whole cosmos.

Figure 7.1 puts in picture form the mutual witness of science and faith that I have been exploring in this section. It also expresses the complex relation between evolutionary progress and entropic decline in a scientific cosmology, which parallels the complex relation between fallenness and redemption in a Christian view of the world. It is not possible in a scientific perspective to make the neat distinction between entropy at a level of individual systems and openness at the level of the whole system of the universe. Nor are the arrow-lines of movement according to science and theology simply analogous; there is a real interaction between them, which we have only begun to explore here.

Another feature of complexity belongs to God's goal in creation and redemption. On the one hand, according to the New Testament, God is sure to bring about a perfected creation, which celebrates God's glory, and brings forth joy and thanksgiving and praise from every living thing. This is seen as the ultimate deliverance of creation from frustration and suffering into the freedom and bliss of God (Rev. 21). It is the final working out of the goal of creation set out in Genesis 2.1–3, and can be seen as the fulfilment of the fine-tuning and anthropic principle suggested by modern cosmology. But at the same time, the arrow-line of human development allows for real freedom in making choices and selecting possibilities; so we must ask whether the end is fixed or a risk.

Here I think that Fiddes is right to draw our attention to the nature of God's project in making persons. He suggests that when we are dealing with persons, we cannot separate the road from the destination.[28] He proposes, then, that the risk upon which God has embarked is real and serious, though not a total one. God has a certain hope in the fact of the end, which shifts creation on to an altogether new level of existence; but there is a genuine openness about the route and therefore the content of the end, which is the nature of the persons who are being reconciled. So there is room for tragedy as well as for triumph in God's victory over suffering. In the final vision of God the worshippers will not be disappointed, but God knows that they may not have reached their full potential.

There are moments of special definition within the experience of God's people, which were and are looked back upon as exceptional; these are represented by shaded segments in the diagram. It is reasonable to claim that some historical events happened at the time of Israel's leaving slavery in Egypt that were understood as exceptional by those who participated in them. Faith can perceive God's special revelation occurring in the normal events of the physical world; for example, there was the strong wind blowing back the waters of the Sea of Reeds,[29] and the resulting destruction as the tide swept back in. The miracle is seen with the eye of faith; it is belief and faith in God who acts for deliverance. It is possible that here we have an instance of divine intervention, bringing about a combination of tides and winds at just the right time in a way that may have broken through the regularity of natural laws. But the point of the event is revelation – through it the people discover who God is, and they also discover who they are in his creation. God is the God who saves, and they are the people whom he saves. For Christians, the supreme moment of definition and revelation is found on a cross on a hillside outside Jerusalem, and an empty tomb a couple of days later. Here we can discover the God who saves, and that we are people whom God wills to save.

But these events are not proof; they must be apprehended by faith. This salvation is a process, and as such includes our vulnerability as well as God's risk. In Exodus 14.19–20, we find the vulnerability of the 'cloud', where God places Godself between the Israelites and the Egyptians, which is followed by the power of the parting of the sea. In the Passion narratives we see the vulnerability of the cross, where God places Godself between us and hostile non-being, which is followed by the power of the resurrection.

## Making sense of the world

God reveals divine transcendence and immanence in creation. Cosmology is helping us to understand the magnitude, majesty and careful purpose that is to be found in the universe, and so helps us to understand more about the power and care of God. Geology and biology help us to see the evolutionary path that has culminated in the presence of conscious human beings, and help us to recognize the God who has journeyed with his creation. In the 'disasters' of exploding stars, earthquakes, volcanoes, storms and mutated plants and animals we have seen something of the suffering that is involved.

Nancey Murphy seeks to reconcile theology with the sciences, drawing on the works of John Howard Yoder and James McClendon, to support the view that Scripture finds its authority in the context of its being read and applied by a community of believing people. She notes that McClendon emphasizes God's faithful, costly and redemptive love in nature and the whole human story. This allows her to draw her higher level of explanation model to a helpful conclusion. She believes that the late modern world offers the scholar three sealed compartments: the sciences, the moral sphere and the religious sphere. She claims that these three should be related to each other: 'Without God's revelation in Jesus, we have no way of knowing what is the ultimate purpose of human life, or what are the highest goods human beings can reasonably strive to attain.'[30] Each of the sciences has its own boundary questions, which require an answer at a higher level. Murphy is able to demonstrate that such boundary questions might reasonably be answered through the Christian understanding of the loving creator God, who suffers with his creation, and who has revealed himself to us in Jesus Christ.

Both theology and science are seeking to make sense of the world that they experience, and their methodologies are not totally different. In each case, the search for a rational understanding is motivated by belief and a desire for truth. As such there must be a common ground for dialogue. Science is able to investigate the universe because human beings have a measure of transcendence over the world, and theology is able to bring a greater degree of understanding because it recognizes the transcendence of God, who reveals his purposes to humankind. Understanding the world in which we live is an undertaking that unites science and theology, and the search for truth will not succeed without a commitment to belief and a readiness for testing, confirmation and correction.

## Models of God

### Biblical belief

In our examination of the background to the Old Testament declarations concerning creation and belief in the Creator, we have discovered that the people reflected upon their experiences and redefined their faith. Through the defeat and despair of exile in Babylonia, they reflected upon their own traditions, the religious mythologies of their captors, and upon their own experience of life and the world they inhabited. In the face of the religious beliefs of their conquerors, and in spite of the destruction of their homeland and religious centre of worship, they were able to declare that Yahweh, the covenant God of Israel and her history, was also the unique creator of the universe, and Lord of the nations. The creation struggle motif of Canaanite and Babylonian mythology is taken and used in portraying Yahweh's conquest of Israel's enemies, where the chaos god Leviathan is identified with Egypt and Babylon. In the creation story itself, Israel's God is the creator of all the monsters, they are not rival deities. The astral deities are denied their power, they too are Yahweh's creation, signs of God's faithfulness, marking times and seasons. Human beings are important to Israel's God, they possess God's character, they have a special relationship with God, and they are given the responsibility of caring for creation. From their place in Yahweh's creation, and their relationship with God, the creation narrative flows out into the people's history, where God accompanies them.

We see God portrayed as transcendent creator, yet immanent in the history of the people; God shares a covenant relationship, characterized by grace, with the people, through which the trinitarian nature of God is expressed. All of creation is the place of God's activity and presence, but God's relationship is never coercive. God gives freedom to creation and as a result lives with the risk that such freedom poses. The story of God's people is one of self-centred rebellion, yet God's promise is the hope of redemption for the whole of creation. In the light of creation, covenant, freedom and redemptive hope, people are called to worship. Worship is the climax of the creation story, of the covenant with Noah, and the response of the people to each experience of God in their history.

The New Testament reflection on creation, and of the role of Christ in the creation of the universe, was in the light of the birth, life, death and resurrection of Jesus. The apostle John was able to take the Greek concept of *logos* and see Jesus as the Word, through whom God had created the universe and all of life (John 1.1–5). In the letter to the church at Colossae, the apostle Paul recalls a hymn of the Church that expresses the place of Christ in creation, and in the redemption of the Church and the world (Col. 1.15–20). Here we find the reflection that God is deeply and passionately involved in his world; he is no absentee landlord, but is indwelling and incarnate (Col. 1.17). In Christ, God will bring the whole of the universe back to himself, making peace (*shalom* – wholeness) through the cross, both on earth and in heaven (Col. 1.20). This radical transformation has already begun through the presence of the Holy Spirit (Rom. 8.19–23). We have a picture of a sacramental universe: all creation is in God; God is in all creation; celebrated in bread and wine.

Again we see that in their theological reflection, in the light of their experience of Christ, God is declared as creator, transcendent and immanent, in covenant with people as the trinitarian God. The risk of freedom is seen in the cross, but the hope of the redemption of creation is seen in the power of the resurrection and the transforming presence of the Holy Spirit. This is all celebrated in worship, through bread and wine (1 Cor. 11.23–26), as a foretaste of the worship of heaven and of a new creation (Rev. 4.21–22).

### God's transcendence and immanence

In the light of the views of modern cosmology and the life sciences any doctrine of creation has to consider the concept of the beginning (origin) of the universe, and the apparent unfolding of the anthropic principle, even though scientists express differing points of view.

The biblical witness is that God alone is eternal; the first and last. This excluded a dualistic view of matter and spirit, and also pantheism, whereby God might be seen as the force throughout the material world. The Creator is Lord, who brings about creation through the Word. Genesis 1 shows the act of creation as the Word of the transcendent creative will. We can suggest that creation is both dependent and chosen; it is dependent upon a creator, and is the intention of that creator. From the perspective of the New Testament we understand that God is love (1 John 4.7–10), and is self-emptying in nature (Phil. 2.6–8). For such a God the creation of the universe becomes necessary as the place where these attributes can be expressed.

God is no first cause, but the creator who acts with absolute freedom. The universe comes into being through God's creative word. Moltmann maintains that the beginning is not in time: 'The beginning has no presuppositions at all.' There are no preconditions; it is *ex nihilo*. Created through God's free will, the world is neither created from pre-existent matter nor out of the divine being. Creation is not a demonstration of power but a communication of love.[31]

Science operates on the assumption of an ordered world, but we realize that the world's order is contingent, God could have made it otherwise. Following on from a Big Bang beginning, or within our particular universe, the deterministic laws of science are suggestive of design and order. We might suggest that the fine-tuning of the initial conditions and ordered rationality of the created world derives from the transcendent rationality of the Creator. Yet we look for a universe that is both intelligible and also relational.

Intelligible is not the same as deterministic, for to be intelligible the universe must include purpose and choice. Creativity includes choice, purpose and intrinsic value. If we posit a universe governed by laws we are left to ask why we have the laws. The answer to this question may be an existent being. But, if, as cosmologists are now suggesting, there are many possible universes, we ask why this particular universe. With an almost infinite number of possibilities, the answer might be to suggest that this universe is the choice of an existent being. We can propose that this universe is the choice of a creator, who chooses a contingent universe that expresses God's nature – love, freedom and relationship – and that is able to respond to the Creator.

For Moltmann, an ecological doctrine of creation helps us in a new kind of thinking about God. The centre of this thinking is no longer the distinction between God and the world. The centre is the recognition of the presence of God in the world and the presence of the world in God.[32] The Creator is present in creation as the Spirit. This relationship to creation is, for Moltmann, an intricate web of unilateral, reciprocal and many-sided relationships:

> In this network of relationships, 'making', 'preserving', 'maintaining' and 'perfecting' are certainly the great one-sided relationships; but 'indwelling', 'sympathizing', 'participating', 'accompanying', 'enduring', 'delighting' and 'glorifying' are relationships of mutuality which describe a cosmic community of living between God the Spirit and all his created beings.[33]

God is both transcendent and immanent; this immanence is seen not only in the ecological relationships identified by Moltmann, but also, as we have discussed in earlier chapters, in the model of an evolving universe, and in the evolutionary development of life on planet Earth. However, for Christians it is the incarnation of God in Christ that supremely points to God's dynamic and intimate relationship with creation; this is the fullest expression of God's immanence. We need to hold on to this self-revelation of God, for otherwise we may be left with a deism that emphasizes God's transcendent power, purpose and mind, but which, in so doing, places God outside the world and outside our lives. Such a God is ineffectual once God has set creation in progress. Creation is seen by Christians as an act of free love. But the question we must try to answer is how does God continue to act in love.

We cannot think of God's transcendence without God's immanence. Evolution urges us to consider continuous creation, in which God is present to endure breaches of communication between systems, and to find new ways through suffering to open up communication again when it has broken down. As Moltmann puts it, 'It is not through miraculous interventions that God guides creation to its goal and drives forward evolution; it is through passion, and the opening of new possibilities out of his suffering.'[34] The prophetic theology of God's creative acts in history pushes us to understand this immanent activity as anticipating new acts of creation and the consummation of time. We can conclude that God is guiding an evolutionary process that includes not only law but chance and the emergence of novelty.

## A holistic creation

The unity and coherence of the world is not found in a cosmological principle but in the personal will of Yahweh, the creator. We have to move away from the rational, reductionist approach that is dominated by objects and facts. Science now concurs that we have a better understanding if objects are seen in their relationships and environments, including the human observer. Life means to exist in relationship, communion and environments. Our motive for knowledge ceases to be in order to dominate, but rather becomes perception in order to participate. As Moltmann suggests, we can speak of this as a covenant with nature, or a psychosomatic totality, or a community of creation.[35] This recognition of unity in God is seen in Genesis 2, but more clearly worked out in Genesis 1. This faith developed through the political upheavals of the eighth and seventh centuries BCE. The view of the universe as a unified entity is given its fullest expression in the poetry of Psalm 104, which Eichrodt sees as: 'here Israelite feeling for the natural order found the expression best suited to the absolute claims of belief in Yahweh'.[36] Creation is understood as part of history:

> a history determined on the one hand by the self-willed flight of the creature from that life-relationship with God which is essential to him, and

on the other by God's activity, shaping history in an inexhaustible variety of ways in order to bring back to God those who are lost in alienation from him.[37]

God is the source and not the cause of creation.

Humankind depends on everything else; we see a mutual symbiotic union. Through the experience of the covenant, which is with God and creation, a sense of the oneness of the universe is apprehended. The unity is in a common, graduated sharing in God. Pedro Trigo suggests that the image of 'struggle' in the evolution of life is a projection of human society, and that faith in the oneness of creation will not allow us to see a polarized world.[38] Ecology hints to us that meaning is found in relationships – the significance of one thing is found in its connection to other things. We begin to presume meaning and significance even when we have not yet found it. There may be some chemical in a plant that will have great medical importance. Nothing is insignificant because everything is linked. Howard Snyder observes that 'something about the ecology of our own lives and minds tells us these intricate patterns of interrelationship constitute some deep meaning'.[39] Ecology presents a picture of wholeness and distinction, with meaning arising from the relationship between the parts.

Believing that the patterns and linkages of the universe disclose, or at least signal, fundamental meaning is more plausible and more consistent with the nature of human mind and experience; however, even this is not convincing to everyone.[40] Connectedness does not prove meaning. Only within our own lives is this meaning understood – it is my life that tells me what is the significance of ecology. Yet full meaning comes from the perception of a transcendent reality; it comes through faith in a personal God.

It may be helpful to consider the whole of the universe as sacramental, a place where God encounters us with his grace. In the view of the Reformers a sacrament depends entirely on a word of promise given by God. The Genesis accounts of creation certainly fulfil this criterion. The bread, wine and water of the sacraments lend themselves as instruments of God's grace because God made them, and they are part of creation. Donald Baillie believes that when Christianity took these as sacraments it was because this universe is a sacramental kind of place. However, he contends that there needs to be a relation with the historic divine revelation to make a real sacrament, and that therefore 'the sacrament speaks only to faith'.[41] We can, as Baillie does, make reference to Calvin's view of the rainbow in Genesis 9. Calvin writes:

If any dabbler in philosophy, in order to deride the simplicity of our faith, contends that such a variety of colours is the natural result of the refraction of the solar rays on an opposite cloud, we must immediately acknowledge it; but at the same time we will deride his stupidity in not acknowledging God as Lord and Governor of Nature, who uses all the elements according to His will for the promotion of His own glory. And if He had impressed similar characters on the sun, on the stars, on the earth, and on stones, they would all have been sacraments to us . . . Shall not God be able to mark His creatures with His Word, that they may become sacraments, though before they were mere elements.[42]

Nature can, in this way, express God's mercy and faithfulness. Jesus presents us with just such a picture, when he speaks of the 'lilies of the field' (Matt. 6.28–30). Jesus saw God's creative love and care in the flowers of the field, and to faith, like the rainbow, these flowers are sacramental. Baillie concludes 'It is only when God speaks and awakens human faith that the natural object becomes sacramental. But this can happen to material things only because this is a sacramental universe, because God created all things visible and invisible.'[43]

The incarnation speaks of God's deepest possible involvement with creation; the resurrection is the hope of a destiny for all creation; the ascension is the possibility of being caught up in eternity with God; and Pentecost marks out God's continuing involvement with the world now, with the possibility of new creation. The Spirit works through the whole of creation – it is the whole of creation that groans.

## God's covenant and grace

We have seen that God is both transcendent to and immanent in creation, but we also need to discuss how God relates to creation. In questioning the relationship of God with creation, Ruth Page observes that the interventionist God is a powerful onlooker; the God of liberation theology is a suffering onlooker, while process theology holds out nothing more than the God who shares the experiences of creation. If love is the fundamental character of God, it is relevant to ask how love acts. In freedom and love we might expect God to form and maintain relationships with all creatures as they live and develop. This is expressed in both God's letting-be, and in God's accompanying of creation. Page is right to state that from such a presence all kinds of possibilities arise, particularly possibilities of relationship in creaturely freedom and love.[44]

The exemplar of the true nature of the relationship with God is Jesus. Jesus is free to act and speak, he takes risks, and he feels the pain of rejection. He does not present divine power removed from the experience of human life; the Kingdom is among them. The cross shows the cost of maintaining relationship in the face of opposition. We can agree with Page:

From that perspective the resurrection is not the happy ending to a sad story, but the demonstration that God was there through it all and that the darkness of the cross has not put out the light of love. To see this and be changed by it is to find salvation. The concurrence of Jesus with God is for Christians the demonstration of 'what God does'.[45]

Creation and salvation are not separate; God has always been there in freedom and love. In Jesus, the possibility and presence of God with us becomes visible and effective; and Jesus invites others to share in this relationship – the Kingdom of God. From a Christian perspective we see creation together with its future, in which it will be perfected, as the Kingdom of glory. This takes place here on earth through God's Spirit, where human beings are in true relationship with God, who indwells creation. It is here that a community of creation comes into being.

In the Old Testament, Yahweh is not part of the world process. The powerful God of the covenant is the single will behind creation. As covenant God, the Creator is seen from the start to have the characteristics of personal and spiritual activity, together with moral purpose. The Sabbath of creation shows that the world was orientated towards redemption from the beginning. Moltmann helpfully observes that 'when people celebrate the sabbath they perceive the world as God's creation, for in the sabbath quiet it is God's creation that they are permitting the world to be'.[46] For Israel the Sabbath principle is extended through the Sabbath year, when human relationships with creation are further defined – the land is given rest (Lev. 25.1–7); and then through the Year of Jubilee, when slaves are freed, debts cancelled and the land returned to its original tribal designations (Lev. 25.8–55; cf. Luke 4.18). For the Christian Church, it is through Christ's death and resurrection that the first day of the week is celebrated as the first day of the new creation.

We draw on the whole of Scripture, Old and New Testaments, in recognizing that God is revealed as the creator, preserver and saviour of the world and all life. The Bible is fairly clear that God wills human freedom to exist, in order to allow the existence of human responsibility for choosing righteousness or sin.

At the heart of this view of the world is the immanent suffering of God, feeling pain in God's relationship with creation, which is in the mixed condition of progress and decline. That God suffers is undeniable, and that God is fulfilled (in some way) through creation must also be true, but this does not imply that God is changed in God's inner being by creation. We recognize that God's relationship with creation is expressed in covenant love, which includes creaturely freedom and divine risk-taking, creaturely rebellion and divine redemption.

## A redeemed creation

The Christological centre of the Christian faith was foreshadowed in our discussion of creation, where the transcendent–immanent relation between God and all life is already to be found. The Spirit is seen moving over the waters of chaos (Gen. 1.2), and the apostle Paul can speak of creation groaning as it awaits the fruit of the Spirit in human beings (Rom. 8.18–25). So we see that Christians have a contribution to make. God created the earth, entrusted it to human beings, and will redeem the whole of creation. Part of redemption lies in human repentance of extravagance, pollution and wanton destruction of the environment. There needs to be a response to Jesus' call to bring good news to the poor, which means action.

The understanding of human responsibility as stewardship still has a place, as we discussed in Chapter 6. The harmonious relationship between humans and nature is being given a prominent place by the UN conferences on the environment and climate change but, despite statements of principle from a body such as the United Nations, many of the attitudes towards the earth do not address the problems fully. We have responsibility for all living things – there are interdependences of all living systems.

There is a need to address global injustice, and in this the role of consumers can have far-reaching effects. Robin Attfield notes:

> in the limited area over which individuals have some measure of control, decisions affecting the life or death of distant people, of future generations and of entire living species are liable to be made; and once again the values elicited by environmental ethics and environmentally sensitive decision-making will continue to be potentially vital.[47]

The future is in our hands; as John Houghton concludes: 'We are not short of statements of ideals. What tend to be lacking are the capability and resolve to carry them out.'[48] Stewardship is difficult, but we are not on our own, we act in partnership with God, through the presence of the Holy Spirit.

## A worshipping creation

In her worship Israel celebrated in song its deepest faith in God as her creator, sustainer and redeemer. Yahweh was the God of the covenant, related to Israel as God's people and to the world as God's creation. Israel gave praise to God who was active in the world and who, through mighty deeds, had redeemed them from slavery and who continued to walk with them in good times and bad. In the psalms, the theme of praising God as creator is almost as common as praising God as saviour. In Psalm 148 the whole of creation is called to praise God; and in Psalms 65 and 104 the faithfulness of God in creation is expressed in worship. Creation itself gives testimony to the goodness and power of its creator (Ps. 19.1–2), as does the unique place given to human beings (Ps. 8).

The Fathers of the Church, such as Justin Martyr, Theophilus of Antioch and Tatian, developed a theology of creation, often elaborated in opposition to the prevailing Gnostic dualism. They affirmed the goodness of creation, created by God *ex nihilo*, but did not separate natural theology from Christology. McDonagh notes the sensitivity of the Greek Church to the created world in a prayer attributed to Basil the Great (*c.* 330–79):

> O God, enlarge within us the sense of fellowship with all living things, our brothers, the animals, to whom thou gavest the earth as their home in common with us.
>
> We remember with shame that in the past we have exercised the high dominion of man with ruthless cruelty, so that the voice of the earth, which should have gone up to thee in song, has been a groan of travail.
>
> May we realize that they live not for us alone but for themselves and for thee and that they love the sweetness of life.[49]

Celtic spirituality was much aware of the presence of the divine in the world of nature. It is clear that Celtic spirituality drew upon the pre-Christian traditions associated with the sun, with harvest, springs, rivers and holy wells; and Celtic saints are often associated with animals. Such experience of God, and God's closeness and involvement in the ordinary everyday life of people, was and remains a feature of Celtic religion and of the revived Celtic Christianity.

Abbess Hildegard of Bingen (1098–1178), poet, musician, painter, visionary, botanist and herbalist, wrote poetry reminiscent of the pre-Christian Celtic religion. She celebrates the feminine, fertility dimension of creation, and saw a sensuous dimension to the love of Creator for creation. For her, nature evokes joy, wonder, praise, awe and especially love.[50]

In similar manner, Francis of Assisi (1182–1226) did not see the natural world from a utilitarian perspective, as providing food, clothing and shelter for human beings. His writings reflect a sense of joy, wonder, praise and gratitude for the gift of all life. He saw God's presence reflected in all creatures.

Modern scientists speak of a rational beauty in the universe; the universe appears to be marvellously, rationally transparent. The patterns of the physical world are intriguing; there is an order that is both beautiful and exciting, and scientists are often heard to use words like 'wonder' and 'awe' when considering their researches and results. Mathematical equations that explain aspects of cosmology are described as 'beautiful'. One of the greatest surprises that these patterns and results are showing is that the present state of the universe depends on a 'fine-tuning' of the initial conditions that brought it into existence. Such reactions do not necessarily lead to faith, as may be seen in the views of Albert Einstein. God, for Einstein, was manifested in the laws of nature: impersonal, sublime, beautiful, indifferent to human beings, but still important to them. Einstein affirmed the religious sense of wonder and mystery when looking at creation, but could not accept the idea of a personal God. God was the great unknown and unknowable; human beings were part of the mystery. He said, 'The most incomprehensible thing about the universe is that it is comprehensible.'[51]

## A conclusion

There is much that science has yet to discover. While at one level we can describe a rational, mathematical universe, we know that this is not the complete picture. There is something that is more than mathematical about emotions, judgements, music and art. We cannot have a mathematical theory of everything because some things would be therefore excluded on the grounds that they were not scientific. Equations may offer solutions to various quantum worlds and to the development of stars and galaxies, but we cannot find equations to explain the complexities of human personality, nor the mind as an expression of the physical brain.

Science has not eclipsed theology. The Christian can say that consciousness exists and that human agents know, envisage, choose, enjoy, and have ideals, values and purposes. Any account of reality must include these as fundamental aspects of existence. Therefore, ultimate reality cannot be simply unconscious and indifferent. The aspects of consciousness and value have to be included in any account of ultimate reality, for which Christians might reasonably posit God.

So we have to ask: what kind of universe can be the context for the evolution of beings such as us? Yet these scientific arguments have the same fundamental problems as the philosophical arguments of Anselm and Aquinas. They can be pointers to, but not proofs of, the existence of God.

Paul Davies is

> convinced that human understanding of nature through science, rational reasoning and mathematics points to a much deeper connection between life, mind and cosmos than emerges from the crude lottery of multiverse cosmology combined with the weak anthropic principle . . . Somehow, the universe has engineered its own self-awareness.[52]

Davies believes that life and mind are etched deeply into the fabric of the cosmos, 'perhaps through a shadowy, half-glimpsed life principle', and furthermore he concedes that this is a form of religious conviction.

Added to Davies' perception of the universe, Christians will want to affirm that human beings are *imago Dei*, created in the image of God, and beneficiaries of God's revelation.

An optimistic anthropology sees humans as co-creators and agents of evolution. A pessimistic anthropology sees human sinfulness usurping God's place as creator. With Deane-Drummond we may conclude that Wisdom, as presented in the Bible, on the one hand, affirms the special dignity of the human race, but the idea of Wisdom as agent of creation of the world (as presented in the Prologue to John's Gospel, John 1.1–18) shows that it is also cosmic in scope. Wisdom would, however, encourage caution on the part of humans rather than impulsive action.[53] The biblical personification of Wisdom is helpful in that it does not deny reason or science its place, but it puts them in a wider context of revelation, caring concern and purpose, in addition to social justice, restoration, redemption and renewal.

This I believe is the basis for the dialogue between Christianity and science, whether a recognition of the boundary questions, the mystery that confronts science at the limits of its search for meaning, or the recognition that consciousness is the place where a scientific exploration of the brain must end. Whether it is in the ethical problems facing genetic engineering, where much is possible but may not be morally right, or the random, irrational suffering that meets all of us in our lives. It can be argued that if God is love and created all things in love, then it is more helpful to think of creation carried out by the Word of God (Wisdom), who became incarnate in human form (John 1.1–14). God assumes human form in space and time. Our true humanity is to be located in Christ, and when we locate ourselves outside Christ we find ourselves in disharmony with God's purpose for the well-being of creation.

In the Bible the Creator is revealed as the Covenant God and Redeemer God, who became incarnate in Jesus Christ. In union with Christ, Christians are invited into fellowship and partnership in God's mission in and for the world. It is in this role that Christians may become co-creators and co-redeemers with God. It is not that human beings are able to create or to redeem, but in co-operation with God, the Holy Spirit works through human beings to reveal understanding and to make sense of the world.

## Key texts

Paul Fiddes, 1989, *The Creative Suffering of God*, Oxford: Clarendon Press.
——1989, *Past Event and Present Salvation: The Christian Idea of Atonement*, London: Darton, Longman & Todd.
Nancey Murphy, 1997, *Reconciling Theology and Science: A Radical Reformation Perspective*, Kitchener: Pandora Press/Scottdale: Herald Press.

**Further reading**

Richard Dawkins, 2007, *The God Delusion*, London: Black Swan/Random House.
John Hick, 1979, *Evil and the God of Love*, Glasgow: Collins.
Jürgen Moltmann, 1985, *God in Creation: An Ecological Doctrine of Creation. The Gifford Lectures 1984–1985*, London: SCM Press.
W. H. Vanstone, 1977, *Love's Endeavour, Love's Expense*, London: Darton, Longman & Todd.
Keith Ward, 2008, *Big Questions in Science and Religion*, Pennsylvania: Templeton Foundation Press.

**Notes**

1 Steven Weinberg, 1979, *The First Three Minutes*, London: André Deutsch, p. 149.

2 Jacques Monod, 1972, *Chance and Necessity*, London: Collins, p. 67.

3 Richard Dawkins, 2007, *The God Delusion*, London: Black Swan/Random House, pp. 190–1.

4 Paul Davies, 1992, *The Mind of God*, New York and London: Simon & Schuster, p. 232.

5 Jerry A. Coyne, 2009, *Why Evolution is True*, Oxford: Oxford University Press, pp. 250–1.

6 See, for example, Job 38; Isaiah 40.18–28; 42.5; John 5.17.

7 John Barrow, 1990, *Theories of Everything*, Oxford: Oxford University Press, pp. 23–9.

8 See the discussion in Charles Taliaferro, 1998, *Contemporary Philosophy of Religion*, Oxford: Blackwell, pp. 299–349. Here, Taliaferro rehearses the arguments for a good God in the face of the existence of evil. The pervasiveness of evil is recognized as the most widely held objection to theism. The counter arguments of free will and afterlife (where perfect goodness exists) are explored, together with the great(er) good theodicy, which suggests God allowing some evil for the sake of greater goods. To be able to demonstrate altruism and loving care human beings must have a choice, and therefore the possibility of choosing to do harm. For further discussion, see R. L. Sturch, 'Theodicy', in David Atkinson and David Field (eds), 1995, *New Dictionary of Christian Ethics and Pastoral Theology*, Leicester: InterVarsity Press, p. 844.

9 Nigel Wright, 1989, *The Fair Face of Evil: Putting the Power of Darkness in its Place*, London: Marshall Pickering, pp. 73–97.

10 Ronaldo Munoz, 1991, *The God of Christians*, Liberation and Theology 11, Tunbridge Wells: Burns & Oates, p. 91.

11 Paul Fiddes, 1988, *The Creative Suffering of God*, Oxford: Clarendon Press, pp. 32–3.

12 Fiddes, *The Creative Suffering*, p. 31.

13 W. H. Vanstone, 1977, *Love's Endeavour, Love's Expense*, London: Darton, Longman & Todd, p. 65.

14 Vanstone, *Love's Endeavour*, p. 59.

15 Paul Fiddes, 1989, *Past Event and Present Salvation: The Christian Idea of Atonement*, London: Darton, Longman & Todd, p. 207.

16 Fiddes, *Past Event*, p. 208.

17 Fiddes, *Past Event*, p. 209.

18 Jon Sobrino, 1994, *The Principle of Mercy: Taking the Crucified People from the Cross*, Maryknoll NY: Orbis Books.

19 Sobrino, *The Principle of Mercy*, p. 29.

20 Sobrino, *The Principle of Mercy*, p. 30.

21 Sobrino, *The Principle of Mercy*, p. 46.

22 David Atkinson, 1991, *The Message of Job: The Bible Speaks Today*, Leicester: InterVarsity Press, pp. 14–15.

23 Atkinson, *The Message of Job*, p. 16.

24 John Hick, 1979, *Evil and the God of Love*, Glasgow: Collins, p. 317.

25 Fiddes, *The Creative Suffering*, p. 45.

26 Fiddes, *The Creative Suffering*, pp. 210f.

27 Eberhard Jüngel, 1976, *The Doctrine of the Trinity: God's Being is in Becoming*, trans. H. Harris, Edinburgh: Scottish Academic Press, p. 108, quoted in Fiddes, *The Creative Suffering*, p. 263.

28 Fiddes, *The Creative Suffering*, pp. 105f.

29 Exodus 14.

30 Nancey Murphy, 1997, *Reconciling Theology and Science: A Radical Reformation Perspective*, Kitchener: Pandora Press/Scottdale: Herald Press, p. 82.

31 Jürgen Moltmann, 1985, *God in Creation: An Ecological Doctrine of Creation. The Gifford Lectures 1984–1985*, London: SCM Press, pp. 74–6.

32 Moltmann, *God in Creation*, p. 13.

33 Moltmann, *God in Creation*, p. 14.

34 Moltmann, *God in Creation*, p. 211.

35 Moltmann, *God in Creation*, pp. 3–4.

36 Walter Eichrodt, 1967, *The Theology of the Old Testament, Volume Two*, London: SCM Press, p. 113.

37 Eichrodt, *The Theology of the Old Testament*, p. 101.

38 Pedro Trigo, 1992, *Creation and History*, Tunbridge Wells: Burns & Oates, p. 106.

39 Howard A. Snyder, 1995, *Earth Currents: The Struggle for the World's Soul*, Nashville TN: Abingdon Press, p. 243.

40 Snyder, *Earth Currents*, p. 245.

41 Donald Baillie, 1957, *The Theology of the Sacraments*, London: Faber & Faber, p. 44.

42 John Calvin, *Institutes*, IV, xiv, 18, quoted in Baillie, *The Theology of the Sacraments*, p. 45.

43 Baillie, *The Theology of the Sacraments*, p. 47.

44 Ruth Page, 1996, *God and the Web of Creation*, London: SCM Press, pp. 53–8.

45 Page, *God and the Web*, p. 61.

46 Moltmann, *God in Creation*, p. 6.

47 Robin Attfield, 1994, *Environmental Philosophy: Principles and Prospects*, Aldershot: Avebury, p. 241.

48 John Houghton, 1994, *Global Warming*, Oxford: Lion, p. 125.

49 Noted by Sean McDonagh, 1990, *The Greening of the Church*, London: Geoffrey Chapman, p. 167.

50 McDonagh, *The Greening of the Church*, p. 174.

51 Einstein is quoted by Angela Tilby, 1992, *Science and the Soul*, London: SPCK, p. 72, and by Davies, *The Mind of God*, p. 148.

52 Paul Davies, 2007, *The Goldilocks Enigma: Why is the Universe Just Right for Life?* London: Penguin Books, pp. 261–3.

53 Celia E. Deane-Drummond, 2001, *Biology and Theology Today. Exploring the Boundaries*, London: SCM Press, p. 117.

# Index